DECOLONIZING NATIVE HISTORIES

NARRATING NATIVE HISTORIES

Series editors
K. Tsianina Lomawaima
Florencia E. Mallon
Alcida Rita Ramos
Joanne Rappaport

Editorial Advisory Board
Denise Y. Arnold
Charles R. Hale
Roberta Hill
Noenoe K. Silva
David Wilkins
Juan de Dios Yapita

DECOLONIZING NATIVE HISTORIES

Collaboration, Knowledge,

and Language in the Americas

Edited by Florencia E. Mallon

Selected essays translated by Gladys McCormick

DUKE UNIVERSITY PRESS   DURHAM & LONDON   2012

© 2012 Duke University Press
All rights reserved
Designed by Amy Ruth Buchanan
Typeset in Minion and Officina Sans by Tseng Information Systems, Inc. Library of Congress Cataloging-in- Publication Data appear on the last printed page of this book.

CONTENTS

About the Series vii

FLORENCIA E. MALLON 1
Introduction. Decolonizing Knowledge,
Language, and Narrative

PART ONE
Land, Sovereignty, and Self-Determination 21

J. KEHAULANI KAUANUI 27
Hawaiian Nationhood, Self-Determination,
and International Law

RIET DELSING 54
Issues of Land and Sovereignty: The Uneasy
Relationship between Chile and Rapa Nui

PART TWO
Indigenous Writing and Experiences with Collaboration 79

FERNANDO GARCÉS V. 85
Quechua Knowledge, Orality, and Writings:
The Newspaper *Conosur Ñawpagman*

JOANNE RAPPAPORT AND ABELARDO RAMOS PACHO 122
Collaboration and Historical Writing:
Challenges for the Indigenous–Academic Dialogue

JAN RUS AND DIANE L. RUS 144
The Taller Tzotzil of Chiapas, Mexico:
A Native Language Publishing Project, 1985–2002

PART THREE

Generations of Indigenous Activism and Internal Debates............ 175

    BRIAN KLOPOTEK 179
    Dangerous Decolonizing: Indians
    and Blacks and the Legacy of Jim Crow

    EDGAR ESQUIT 196
    Nationalist Contradictions: Pan-Mayanism,
    Representations of the Past, and the
    Reproduction of Inequalities in Guatemala

Conclusion 219

References 221
Contributors 243
Index 247

synergy between intellectual vision and debate, on the one hand, and concrete projects and methodologies on the other, have already found a home there. In both the conference and the series, moreover, we were and are committed to troubling relations between North and South and between the Americas and the Pacific region. At the conference our method was to discuss, with the help of simultaneous language interpretation, common issues across differences of culture, region, and history. We began by asking ourselves questions around five themes.

First, building from the perception that traditional academic narratives about indigenous peoples are still embedded in a colonial framework, both epistemologically and politically, we wondered what it would mean to shift ethnography and other forms of research and narrative away from more traditional and vertical forms of engagement toward more symmetrical, horizontal approaches or counternarratives. How would we nurture collaborative relationships that respect the rights of Native people and their cultural experts to make decisions about the use to which their knowledge is put as well as their right to be recognized as coauthors or participants in the production of knowledge? Who gets to talk about what, and in which language?

Second, we wished to consider the relationship of language to power and also to empowerment. In addition to recognizing the urgent nature of projects to recover and strengthen indigenous languages—projects on which a number of the conference participants have worked and are working—we discussed the inescapable interactions between language, the legitimation of voice, and the power relations embedded in all research contexts. How do social, political, economic, and cultural factors shape the research we do and the stories we tell? As researchers and writers committed to the cultures about which we write, what can we do to further the process of recognition of Native intellectuals, cultural interpreters, and alternative knowledge producers within the broader academic and intellectual worlds?

Third, as a matter related to issues of language and power, we talked about some of the ways in which colonialism had marked orality as inferior to textuality, and thus had considered societies with different record systems as "primitive" or "prehistorical." If language, the law, and the archive have historically served as instruments of colonialism, we wondered, how could these same instruments be used in the construction of autonomy? As researchers, what is our role in the process of recovery, preservation, and extension of Native literary and narrative traditions? What is the relationship between orality and textuality in this process? Is it possible to decolonize language, law, and history so that they become tools in the construction of horizontal relations between peoples?

Fourth, we considered the importance of storytelling traditions. Among many indigenous peoples storytelling has served as a form of cultural preservation and protection, memory and empowerment, legitimacy and autonomy. Is it possible to productively work through the tensions between these broader intellectual narratives within Native cultures and the requirements of evidence in the academy? How can academic researchers weave distinct, divergent, and sometimes conflictual strands into their stories without betraying their own principles or those of their interlocutors?

Finally, we recognized the many challenges associated with making autonomy a viable option in today's world. As indigenous movements throughout the world have demanded respect for cultural, political, and territorial autonomy, questions concerning citizenship, political coalitions, policy options, and the legal ramifications of autonomy have become increasingly complex. How can we establish a useful dialogue among the extremely diverse experiences with and practices of autonomy and sovereignty that exist in the Americas and the Pacific region? How can researchers profitably involve themselves in these debates in a way that is useful to Native societies?

Beginning with these five themes, we threaded them through particular topics, including indigenous sovereignty; collaboration and truth telling in research methodologies; intercultural conversations on translation, inscription, and the boundaries between inside and outside; and the nature of intellectual and cultural authority. Part of what we found along the way was exhilarating, in the sense that there were points of commonality and solidarity across otherwise seemingly unbridgeable distances—geographical, cultural, and linguistic. People who could communicate only through simultaneous interpretation nevertheless found that they could recognize their common struggles to recover Native languages and, through them, a distinct voice. Or they shared perspectives in which the lines between academic and activist, inside and outside, oral and written could be and had been questioned, leading to a mutual, deep cross-fertilization between theory and practice, analysis and experience. And all of us, whether Native or non-Native, recognized a certain commonality in our intellectual work as translators, as people who inhabit frontiers between worlds, or as *bisagras* (hinges) who serve as connections between disparate knowledges, cultures, and places.

Part of what we discovered was sobering, for the challenges before us seemed daunting and at times overwhelming. We noted deep differences between North and South, both in the historical experience of indigenous peoples with colonialism and in the place of indigenous intellectuals in societies and academies. We saw distinctions among indigenous experiences within both North and South, within indigenous groups themselves, and between the Americas and the Pacific world. We perceived internal hierarchies along lines of race, region, language, and gender.

One of the most challenging themes we discussed during the conference, one which emerges in this book generally, was the relationship between academic and activist forms of narration and collaboration. This was an especially vibrant theme in the presentations about Latin America. Six of the nine papers presented on Latin America analyzed experiences of collaboration in which scholar-activists participated in projects intended to put new technologies and tools—writing, social science or linguistic theory, video—at the service of indigenous peoples who wished to use them for their own purposes. In the three essays about this topic that are included here—those on the Tzotzil Maya of Chiapas, the Nasa of Colombia, and the Quechua of Bolivia—non-Native collaborators involved themselves in ongoing negotiation with indigenous leaders who envisioned the use of these tools in political and intellectual projects of their own making. While these collaborators were all educated in the university, not all had established themselves within the academy. And the projects in which they were participating demanded that Native agendas be given priority at all times.

The three papers presented at the conference that dealt with Native peoples in Hawai'i and the continental United States were all by Native academics and, while diverse in theme and scope, shared two goals. First, they aimed to bring indigenous political and historical questions into the heart of academic discussion and to highlight how the presence of Native scholars in the academy changed the nature of intellectual conversation. Second, the three papers were interested in using the tools of academic analysis to foster debate within Native societies that would lead to greater empowerment. The two that appear here, by J. Kehaulani Kauanui on Native Hawaiian options for autonomy and Brian Klopotek on notions of race among Louisiana Choctaws, are the work of committed indigenous academics who wish to use the analytical tools at their disposal to move debates on sovereignty and autonomy forward.

While overall the papers read at our conference cannot be taken as representative, they do suggest distinct histories of articulation of academic and intellectual knowledge to indigenous activism between North and South.

In the United States, indigenous scholars and intellectuals, facing immense obstacles, have been making inroads into the academy and into public debate. While such participation is not a panacea, it does open up new venues of academic and political debate that were not present before. In Latin America, while indigenous political and intellectual revivals are also beginning to open public space for Native perspectives—for example, among the Aymara in Bolivia, the Mapuche in Chile and Argentina, the Maya in Guatemala, the Miskito along Nicaragua's Atlantic Coast, and the Maya, Zapotec, and other groups in Mexico—in general it has been less possible historically for Native intellectuals in the South to claim real space in the academy. In providing examples of the experiences and struggles of indigenous peoples in concrete historical contexts and in relation to particular constellations of political and economic power, we hope to deepen our comparative conversations in ways that will be useful to indigenous peoples and their movements.

Perhaps the most important unifying theme of the conference, and thus of the book, was the need to collaborate in the process of decolonization or, as Roberta Hill put it during her conference comments, to "get colonialism off our backs." All the chapters address the issue of decolonizing methodologies in one way or another, and the theme of decolonization serves as a kind of backbone of the book.[3] As Klopotek explains in his essay, the double meaning of the phrase is productive, in the sense that we aim both to decolonize the methodologies used in research and writing and to elaborate methodologies that decolonize the relationship between researchers and subjects. At the same time, however, the authors represented in the book develop varying takes on what this means.

In the first part of the book, the essays by J. Kehaulani Kauanui and Riet Delsing (whose essay is the only one in the book that did not originate in a conference presentation) solidify the dialogue between the Americas and the Pacific that is an important part of our project. Although the historical differences between the two cases are quite large, we find surprising similarities and parallels. One of these is the timing of the forced incorporation of the territories into distant nation-states, separated by only a decade (1888 for Rapa Nui or Easter Island's annexation to Chile, 1898 for Hawai'i's annexation to the United States). This is not surprising, since the last decades of the nineteenth century were, across the world, a time of intensification of colonialism and of global relations of trade, two reasons the Pacific islands were attractive to economically and militarily expansive nation-states. In this regard it is equally telling that, at the respective moments of forcible annexation, both Chile and the United States had just emerged victorious from expansionist wars and territorial conquest, Chile from the War of the Pacific (1879–84) and the conquest of Mapuche autonomous territory in 1883, the United States from the Spanish-American War (1898).

Despite the vast geographical distance separating Rapa Nui from Hawai'i, taken together they remind us that the process of colonialism is at the very heart of the history of indigenous peoples. One example of that centrality is how territory, including both land and other resources, is expropriated through illegal means. In both Rapa Nui and Hawai'i, as Delsing and Kauanui make clear, concessions that were understood by Native peoples to involve use rights were fraudulently and forcibly transformed into property rights. Even though the political status of the two regions differed greatly—Rapa Nui was a rural, kinship-based society at the time of annexation, while Hawai'i was an independent kingdom and had been recognized as such by European powers and the United States for nearly a century—colonial violence can prove to be a strong leveling force. At the same time, the distinct historical experiences of Rapa Nui and Hawai'i dramatically differentiate their present-day options from those of other indigenous peoples who inhabit the continental United States and mainland Chile.

Through a detailed analysis of Hawai'i's sovereign history in conversation with present-day international debates about the status of indigenous peoples, Kauanui changes the terms of the discussion about indigenous autonomy. Given the earlier history of the Kingdom of Hawai'i, there is, in international law, a historical basis for making a claim to independent status. A part of the movement for autonomy in Hawai'i thus supports the notion of total independence based on international law. There is, however, a sizable sector in Hawai'i whose vision for self-determination would pass through U.S. law; this group prefers to make claims within the U.S. system of federal recognition that has evolved in relation to the indigenous nations on continental soil. Kauanui makes clear that achieving federal recognition for Native Hawaiians would indeed foreclose both the decolonization and the deoccupation models for achieving autonomy, since it would define Kanaka Maoli, or indigenous Hawaiians, as a "domestic dependent" nation with no recourse to independent status.

Delsing demonstrates in her discussion of struggles over sovereignty in Rapa Nui that the perspectives of the Rapanui and the history of their struggle cannot be folded neatly either into Chilean history or into the indigenous histories connected to the Chilean mainland. Originally a Polynesian people, the Rapanui continue to be linked to the Pacific region. And while today the Rapanui are internally divided over the most appropriate strategies to follow in their ongoing confrontation with Chilean assimilationist policies, a significant minority movement has formed around the idea of pursuing political independence in dialogue with other Pacific peoples.

Part 2 of the book discusses the interrelated themes of cross-cultural collaboration, translation, and writing. Joanne Rappaport and Abelardo Ramos Pacho, who have formed part of a collaborative research team led by Nasa intellectuals in Colombia for many years, address the question of collaboration most systematically. Ramos conceptualizes intellectual and theoretical collaboration as a *minga*, a project of collective work for collective benefit, which provides us with the opportunity to think through the connections between physical and intellectual labor and the tensions between academic analysis and political usefulness. Inevitably, he writes, collaboration produces tensions; but these become productive through work. For Rappaport, this work involves a dialogue among ways of knowing—a *diálogo de saberes*—in which indigenous epistemology is primary but not exclusive. Interculturalism, she suggests, must be a grass-roots practice that goes far beyond multiculturalism as an encounter within a context already hegemonized from one side. Building such horizontal relationships is a work in progress, and its success will be found in the political articulation of indigenous and nonindigenous cultural registers.

Rappaport and Ramos also explore the concept of translation and its relationship to writing or inscription. Translation, in this context, is inseparable from indigenous theorizing, for it is a project of appropriation, rethinking, and reconfiguration of language and concepts from indigenous perspectives. This means the improvement and transformation of reality, not only its analysis or representation in a different language. Cultural as well as linguistic translation, therefore, opens up new potentials and possibilities and gives access to an intercultural space where new strategies of negotiation and new ways of living can potentially be suggested. Ramos concludes, along these lines, by suggesting that one goal may be an indigenously grounded objectivity in which the line between academic rigor and political necessities and desires can be more effectively troubled.

Jan Rus and Diane L. Rus discuss how they built on their long-term presence in the highlands of Chiapas among the Chamulas to contribute to the Taller Tzotzil, an already existing Tzotzil-language publishing project, beginning in the 1980s. The Ruses' legitimacy within the Tzotzil community—

they had been given Tzotzil names, which appear at the back of the volumes produced by the Taller—served as a crucial entry point into the project of translation and inscription in which they collaborated. Their long presence in the region also helped them understand more fully issues of alphabet and orthography, which called to mind the presence of Bible translators as well as Protestant missionaries and questions of dialect and the diversity of voices present within the narratives. Indeed, the Ruses' project revealed how deep the negotiations and knowledges involved in a successful project of translation and inscription are, a matter discussed by other authors and summarized by one of our panel commentators, Frank Salomon, when he suggested that indigenous language accounts become text through a collaboration that involves decontextualization and then recontextualization and hence multiple translations.

But even more important, the Ruses' work on the Tzotzil publishing project is an especially dramatic example of an option taken by many principled intellectuals and professionals in Latin America in the 1960s and 1970s—that of the committed, *engagé* collaborator. Rappaport, who has nearly three decades of experience with the Nasa and Cumbal peoples of Colombia, is another example of someone who took this option, though in her case she has claimed a place within the academy in the United States, something the Ruses have eschewed. In part activist anthropology in the mold of Alcida Rita Ramos and Terrence Turner, who also presented papers at our conference, this practice of engagé collaboration had its origins in the radical mobilizations of the 1960s and, by the early 1970s, was inspired as well by liberation theology and the radical pedagogy of Paulo Freire, mentioned by the Ruses.

These forms of activist collaboration, which existed in many parts of the so-called Third World in the 1970s and 1980s, took on a particularly intense quality in Latin America. Part of the reason for this had to do with the specific history of revolutionary movements in the region, movements that often placed at their very center the collaboration between urban intellectuals on the Left and the rural poor, a significant proportion of whom were of indigenous descent. At the same time, the very nature of Latin America's political and economic crises ate away at earlier coalitions between indigenous people and the Left, so that in a number of areas relationships of collaboration that had rested on these earlier coalitions either fell apart entirely or had to be renegotiated. This has been the case with the Chilean Mapuche, whose intellectuals have increasingly taken center stage in defining research and activist agendas, and it has also happened in other areas of Latin America, such as Guatemala and Nicaragua's Atlantic coast.

As Ramos and Rappaport and the Ruses demonstrate, collaborative relationships tend to endure when they involve ongoing negotiations. In reflecting on their long-standing collaboration through the Consejo Regional Indígena del Cauca (CRIC), Ramos and Rappaport demonstrate that it is precisely the moment of friction, of discomfort, in collaboration that is the most productive. Ramos suggests that it becomes so through work: in other words, through concrete tasks and discussions that help deepen a common commitment to a joint project. The Ruses, for their part, built on their long-lasting relationship with Tzotzil Maya communities in the Chiapas highlands, especially in Chamula, to configure a unique indigenous language publishing project that has spanned two decades, adapting its goals according to the changing nature of conditions in the region as well as in response to feedback from the participants themselves. If their project began with the purpose of recovering pieces of community indigenous history and making them more broadly available across the Chiapas region, it was transformed in the 1990s and beyond, not only by the Zapatista uprising of 1994, but also by the deepening economic crisis that reconstructed the spatial locations of Tzotzil Maya people, forcing many to migrate to the local capital city of San Cristóbal de las Casas and then increasingly across the U.S.-Mexican border into southern California.

Similar multifaceted moves are at the center of the project described by Fernando Garcés V. in his essay. As a nonindigenous linguist originally from Ecuador who has been working on a Quechua-language newspaper in Bolivia, Garcés considers his positioning to be a crucial part of his project. A political process at its very core, the production of the newspaper, *Conosur Ñawpagman*, combines its distribution at political events and peasant gatherings in Cochabamba with the recording of new interviews and testimonials for the next round of articles. At the heart of the newspaper's project, Garcés argues, is what he calls the intertextual play between orality and writing. Inscribing orality in text is not only the reproduction of speech in writing, but a new act of communication that involves political mediation. Intertextuality, in such a context, includes orality in a process in which both the reception and construction of texts are crucial. Moving beyond a purist or academically grounded notion of the preservation of classical Quechua in text, Garcés argues for the interaction between Quechua and the Spanish written word in order to create new usages and to strengthen the Quechua language. As he suggested in his oral remarks at the conference, the point is not to preserve Quechua either by limiting it to academic use or putting it in a museum (*museoficar*), but to revitalize the social strength of the language by supporting its life-giving and lively usages in daily practice.

Garcés's participation in the publication of a Quechua newspaper has been framed, as in the case of Rappaport and Ramos and of the Ruses, within a broader history of collaboration with indigenous peasant organizations. For him, therefore, intellectual goals must of necessity be interlaced with issues of empowerment and social justice. While his knowledge as a linguist helps him conceptualize the value of a grass-roots newspaper in terms of the larger project of Quechua language revitalization, his experience as an activist provides him with the tools through which he can value a real-life process of language recuperation in which everyday usage, when inscribed in text, allows for new practices that creatively extend the relevance of the language.

The emphasis on the revitalization of indigenous languages through dynamic and creative forms of translation and inscription and through the honoring of indigenous practices and epistemologies that includes all levels of society is a powerful theme in the chapters by Garcés, Ramos and Rappaport, and the Ruses. These notions reverberate strongly with the call made by Edgar Esquit to extend and deepen our understanding of the multiplicity of Maya histories and knowledges. Among some educated pan-Maya intellectuals in Guatemala, he suggests, the uncovering of a unified Maya history can present a past heretofore hidden by official Guatemalan versions of history. While this is an important task, when the members of a particular professional sector among the Maya elaborate it, in dialogue with other knowledges outside of and unknown to Maya oral traditions, they can create their own official history that positions them as "civilized" in relation to their Maya brothers and sisters.

It is precisely these kinds of internal tensions and divisions, and how they might unexpectedly help to reproduce existing relationships of discrimination and inequality, that form the core of Klopotek's and Esquit's explorations in part 3. In his work with the Louisiana Choctaws, Klopotek examines the ways in which racial classification systems specific to the U.S. South, themselves the result of colonial relationships of racial power, are reflected in the definitions of indigeneity used by southern Indian communities. He suggests that a fuller critique of the racial hierarchies embedded in the general system of white privilege, of how the "one-drop rule" as applied to people of

African descent has led to anti-Black sensibilities among Native Americans as a mechanism of self-defense, might in the long run be a positive move for indigenous people.

Esquit, for his part, questions current uses of the notion of internal colonialism by pan-Maya intellectuals.[4] When the concept is used to explain political relations between Maya and ladinos as separate yet homogeneous groups, he suggests, it may hide as much as it reveals.[5] To what extent, he asks, might such a usage result in an understanding of a people's rights and culture as separate from economics? Would it not be more productive to think of political relations as organized, in a more complex way, along many lines of difference and hierarchy that exist between and inside both Maya and ladino groups? In this context Esquit suggests that we consider instead the colonial shape of power relations, which allows us to connect class to notions of race and ethnicity, thus opening the way for a deeper recognition of the multiplicity of experiences, perspectives, and history among the Maya.[6]

Both Klopotek and Esquit, as young indigenous intellectuals, are raising questions about the political and intellectual practices of a previous generation of leaders. Their locations within very different societies—Klopotek is a Choctaw academic in the United States, Esquit a Maya anthropologist in Guatemala—configure their options as they negotiate between activism and intellectual work. Yet at the same time, they share a desire to expand definitions of indigenous identity and belonging so that broader coalitions of people who identify as indigenous, including those traditionally excluded from leadership, can work more effectively to define common goals.

The desire to open up indigenous politics to wider coalitions involves as well the question of gender, as Esquit explains in his paper and as also emerges in the Tzotzil publishing project. As the Ruses explain, Diane Rus's collaboration with Maruch Komes on Komes's life history initiated a broader discussion of a Maya women's weaving and embroidering cooperative as an economic response to crisis. Yet even as this generated new resources for the cooperative it created deep debates about women's economic autonomy. Internal tensions over gendered power relations have also emerged in other contexts of indigenous mobilization, as is divulged in the recent autobiography by the feminist Mapuche leader Isolde Reuque, who was present at the conference.[7]

Taken together, then, the presentations at the conference and the essays in this book explore a myriad of themes relating to the challenges of decolonization—intellectual, academic, and political. Noenoe Silva and Stéfano

Varese, given the perhaps impossible task of summing up the papers and our discussions as a prelude to a last general plenary session, represented in their comments some of this complexity of solidarity and difference. Silva, a Native Hawaiian political scientist whose work has demonstrated how the recovery of Hawaiian language sources changes the history of U.S. annexation and our understanding of Hawaiian intellectual life (Silva 2004, 2007), emphasized the importance of stories and language to the empowerment of peoples, illustrating her points throughout with narratives from her own experiences and those of her people. She also spoke of the importance and the difficulty of fostering Native scholars. She underlined both the possibilities and the dangers connected to this task, but in the end she suggested that only by having Native voices and presence in the academy can we aspire to a truly intercultural education in which indigenous epistemologies and languages have a powerful voice and standing for all.

Stéfano Varese, on the other hand, an activist anthropologist educated in Peru but who has worked on indigenous activism and sovereignty throughout the Americas, focused on the power of political mobilization. He stressed the danger inherent in the academy's absorption of projects aimed at sovereignty, the recuperation of language and territory, and the rewriting of history, suggesting that indigenous intellectuals need to be organic in the Gramscian sense. He emphasized the political dimensions of the projects of recovery and reclaiming, whether these involved language or landscape, history, memory, or sovereignty. Ultimately, he warned against overly academic projects that, even in the hands of indigenous intellectuals, might recolonize indigenous knowledge. The differences of emphasis and vision in the general comments of Silva and Varese can help frame a last set of reflections that emerged from and were prompted by our discussions at the conference. As the subsequent conversations, both formally at the plenary and along the edges in more informal one-on-one exchanges, made clear, these differences arose precisely from the diversity of experience and historical context that exists today among indigenous peoples in the Americas and the Pacific. But they can also be seen in the context of our common project of decolonization, which must involve an understanding of how a respect for and understanding of variation can lead to new forms of creativity.

In her discussion of the power of language and stories, Silva was drawing on a deep tradition of struggle to honor the truths and epistemological perspectives contained in Native oral traditions. As several of the essays in this book argue, the development of more horizontal and respectful forms of research and analysis must necessarily pass through a rethinking of and re-encounter with the forms of knowledge contained in and passed on through oral tradition. At the confluence of several intellectual debates, discussions about oral history and alternative forms of knowledge and narrative have become increasingly wide ranging in recent years. Whether in the form of *testimonio*, oral history, or subaltern studies, these conversations and confrontations have spanned the globe. While not all the discussions have concerned indigenous issues, many of them have, and Native and non-Native scholars of indigenous cultures have played prominent roles in them. While even a representative sample of these conversations is too large to cite here, often the main issues at stake concern the assessment of claims to truth according to established rules of evidence.[8] Given the distinct nature of oral tradition and oral history as a performative medium based on imparting knowledge and wisdom gained through direct personal experience or connection, the rules of evidence associated with the scientific method are less relevant or applicable. For some, this makes oral tradition a lesser form of evidence, precisely because it is not verifiable.[9]

Two complementary answers to this challenge have taken shape. One takes on the academic project of verifiable research results and demonstrates how alternative forms of knowledge production and transmission, especially oral tradition, contribute new, important, and distinct perspectives to our quest for knowledge. They do so precisely because they are not data but systems of thought that provide, as Julie Cruikshank writes in her work on Yukon communities, "a window on the ways the past is culturally constituted and discussed. In other words," she continues, "stories were not merely about the past, they also provided guidelines for understanding change" (Cruikshank 2002, 13). Similar claims are made in a very different context by the oral historian Alessandro Portelli, who argues that the performative and apparently subjective form of oral history is its greatest strength, precisely because it allows us to dig beyond fact to meaning (Portelli 1991, 1997). And it is precisely in this access to meaning and interpretation that we can find a practical answer to the challenge set forth by Chakrabarty (2000) when he calls on us to resist the positivist closure of narrative that keeps us from understanding alternative versions of history that do not start from and end in Europe.[10] A second way to confront the objectivist critique has been to question the assumption of superiority on which it is based. Some scholars, including Linda Tuhiwai Smith (1999), have used postcolonial and other forms of critical theory in dialogue with indigenous knowledge to evaluate the intellectual basis upon which dominant theories and methodologies have been built. Others, such as Devon Mihesuah and Angela Cavender Wilson (1998, 2004), have addressed specific historiographies and their minimization or erasure of Native sources.

It was precisely this rich tradition that Silva referred to when she discussed the power of stories. She also was making reference to her own work on Hawaiian language sources, and how the highlighting of new versions, whether oral or written, can and should turn our interpretations of both the past and the present on their heads. And for Silva, doing so within the academy, through the increasing presence of Native scholars within its gates, is an absolutely crucial priority. This is also the most important point put forward in the recent anthology *Indigenizing the Academy* (Mihesuah and Wilson, 2004), not in the sense merely of inclusion but also of transformation. As Silva noted in her comments, several of the authors represented in that book, including Mihesuah and Taiaiake Alfred, demonstrate that bringing indigenous perspectives into the academy makes sense if and when a critical mass of indigenous scholars can begin to change the way in which academic knowledge itself is organized, produced, and taught.[11] This means not only claiming a space within academic circles for indigenous points of view, but envisioning a time when indigenous languages, histories, and epistemologies are part of the knowledge that everyone seeks out.

On this point, Silva and Varese brought the most distinct perspectives to the table. Historical differences between North and South—how Native-state relations have been negotiated, the role of academic learning in society, the nature of indigenous social and political movements and their relationship to other forms of resistance—help explain in part the diverse visions of indigenous participation in the academy. If today a second generation of indigenous scholars, on the basis of much struggle and sacrifice, is establishing a beachhead in university systems in the United States, Canada, and New Zealand, such is not yet the case, with few exceptions, in Latin America.[12] The always-present danger of the academy colonizing the indigenous scholar, rather than the other way around, is a serious threat in the South. But perhaps even more stark is the variation in the depth and degree of participation by indigenous activists in class-based movements for social change.

Indeed, as Armando Muyolema argued in his presentation at the conference, one of the central distinguishing characteristics of indigenous movements in Latin America historically has been their close interaction and interrelation with popular class-based movements. In Latin America the lack of treaty or nation-to-nation negotiations led to an early fragmentation of Native territories into small communities and to direct negotiation between national states and these small, land-based political units. As a result, the indigenous question was deeply embedded in the broader land question, and in the majority of cases the most promising line of struggle lay in a class alliance with other landless or rural poor. This alliance was buttressed by the generally dependent status of Latin American countries, which increased the pressure for a common coalition in favor of national development, especially in the heady years of reform between the Second World War and the end of the Vietnam War.

During these three decades national-popular states based on coalitions of leftist intellectuals and political parties, trade-union organizations, and some peasant groups held out promises of egalitarian reform as they confronted entrenched oligarchies and landowning elites, while at the same time promoting relations of so-called internal colonialism in which some of the poor ended up being more deserving than others. Still, at a moment in history when change seemed possible, many found it more important to maintain the unity of all popular forces than to take exception to the ongoing forms of inequality within the reformist alliance. The greater strength of class-based social and political movements in Latin America, moreover, increased the attraction, among laboring indigenous peoples in city and countryside, of a class-based coalition. One major exception to these tendencies could be found among lowland indigenous peoples, particularly in the Amazonian regions of Venezuela, Colombia, Peru, Bolivia, and especially Brazil, where Native peoples had little permanent interaction with emerging nation-states except through violent extractive industries and the spread of epidemic diseases (Ramos 1995, 1998; Turner 1995, 2002; Varese 1970).

It was only with the generalized failure of national-democratic and socialist attempts at reform and national liberation, therefore — most notably in the 1970s and early 1980s — that the class-alliance strategy was finally brought to crisis for many indigenous peoples in Latin America. Yet, as Charles R. Hale and Rosamel Millamán have recently argued (2006), the evolution of culture-based demands for indigenous peoples has led to a new kind of trap for activists interested in autonomy, since neoliberal states in process of transition toward democratic rule have articulated a rights-based discourse that provides limited new privileges for indigenous peoples within the context of the new political order. This has given rise, in their estimation, to the emergence of (borrowing a term from the Aymara historian and activist Silvia Rivera Cusicanqui) the *indio permitido*, or "permissible Indian," a new figure who, in return for limited new cultural and political rights, is colonized into the existing system. So in the end, it seems that for a host of historical reasons many Native intellectuals in the South have perhaps a deeper, more enduring suspicion of and hostility toward institutions, both political and academic. This was, in part, the perspective reflected in Varese's concluding comments.

And yet we must not overdraw the contrasts between North and South but use them—as we use other differences and tensions—as entry points for deeper reflection. In our final plenary session, Leilani Basham, a Native Hawaiian scholar, addressed the nonindigenous people in our midst, reminding us that respect for difference and for the integrity of cultures must lie at the heart of all forms of collaboration. The minute we start to feel proprietary, she implied, it's time to let go, to establish a respectful distance. Jennifer Denetdale added to this observation that, as Wilson has noted, not only colonialism but decolonization as well engenders violence. "When we speak and we speak honestly and we speak across cultures," Denetdale said, "one of the things that will happen is that there will be tension, it will be uncomfortable. Don't be afraid, stay there, see what it feels like, see what it tastes like."[13] Denetdale's comments echoed Ramos's earlier suggestion that collaboration inevitably leads to tension, but that tension and contradiction can be productive through work. They also raised, once again, the painful or uncomfortable quality of the frontier, that place where, as Gloria Anzaldúa wrote, "the Third World grates against the first and bleeds" (Anzaldúa 1987, 3).

As intellectuals, scholars, researchers, and writers who inhabit a variety of frontiers, we face these contradictions daily. Attempting to build nonviolent knowledge must, perhaps, inevitably be done along the frontier—between worlds, between cultures and languages, between histories and territories. What tools do we have? Many, including the law, history, the archive, the academy, and writing itself, have also been the tools of colonialism. And given the history of our world, could it be any other way? To build nonviolent knowledge with tools steeped in violence may be the core of our project. And we need to build such knowledge globally, since the forces that oppose it are global, too. As Ramos suggested during the discussions, it is indeed a challenge to use the same tools the colonizers have used. But, he insisted, it is a challenge we can take on creatively and ambitiously, with the purpose of transforming both their use and their meaning. We offer this book in that spirit.

Notes

1. Colleagues at Wisconsin who participated in the early intellectual planning stages for the conference are Ned Blackhawk, Ada Deer, Roberta Hill, Patricia Loew, Larry Nesper, Frank Salomon, and Theresa Schenck. Ned Blackhawk in particular was most helpful in identifying potential participants working on Hawai'i, the United States, and Canada. Our conference was held in conjunction with the graduate student conference of the CIC American Indian Studies Consortium, organized that year in Madison by Ned Blackhawk. Some of the participants made important contributions to our plenary discussions. For logistical and organizational support, I owe thanks to the Institute for Research in the Humanities and especially to Loretta Freiling; and to the American Indian Studies Program, especially to Denise Wyaka. Financial support for the conference was provided by the Burdick Vary Fund of the Institute for Research in the Humanities; the Anonymous Fund and the University Lectures Committee of the University of Wisconsin; and the NAVE Fund of the Latin American, Caribbean, and Iberian Studies Program. The following programs, offices, and divisions of the University of Wisconsin contributed to the purchase, housing, and maintenance of the simultaneous interpretation equipment used at the conference, which is now available on campus for use by other interpreters: the Language Institute; the Global Studies Program; the Office of Human Resource Development; the Division of International Studies; the Department of History; the Office of Facilities, Planning and Management; the Division of University Housing; the Medical School; the Wisconsin Union; and Learning and Support Services. Simultaneous interpretation was provided by Gladys McCormick, Adan Palau, Yesenia Pumarada Cruz, and Donna Vukelich. I'm grateful to Roberto Galo Arroyo for permission to use his art on the cover of the paperback book. At Duke University Press I'm grateful, as always, to Valerie Millholland, Mark Mastromarino, and Miriam Angress. Carol Roberts did her usual excellent work on the index.

2. The literature on these issues is too extensive to cite here. Among the pioneers in the application of colonial and postcolonial theory to a study of indigenous issues is Linda Tuhiwai Smith (1999). Other starting points for postcolonial theory might include Said 1978; Chatterjee 1986; Guha and Spivak 1988; Prakash 1995; Dirlik, Bahl, and Gran 2000; Loomba, Kaul, Bunzl, Burton, and Esty 2005.

3. The phrase "decolonizing methodologies" comes from the title of Smith 1999.

4. Originally formulated as a concept by Pablo González Casanova (1965) and Rodolfo Stavenhagen (1965), "internal colonialism" has been taken up, and its mean-

ing transformed, by indigenous intellectuals in Guatemala and Bolivia. See Cojtí Cuxil 1996; Rivera Cusicanqui and Barragán 1997; Qayum 2002.

5. In modern Guatemala, the word *ladino* is used to designate a Hispanicized person, usually of mixed European and indigenous descent; in many other parts of Latin America that person would be termed *mestizo*.

6. This call for more consciously inclusive forms of indigenous politics is echoed as well by Víctor Montejo (2005).

7. Indigenous women, Reuque suggested at the conference, can be doubly marginalized or doubly invisible; and yet, as her experience with her book has demonstrated, indigenous women are also a source of great cultural and political dynamism. See Reuque Paillalef 2002a, b.

8. Some examples are Cruikshank 2002; Howe 2002; James 2000; Mallon 2001, 2002, 2005; Montejo 1987, 1999; Portelli 1991, 1997; Wilson 1998.

9. An example of these debates can be found in *Hispanic American Historical Review* (1999).

10. I engage in a dialogue with Chakrabarty on these issues in Mallon 2005.

11. See especially Mihesuah's essay "American Indian History as a Field of Study" and Alfred's essay "Warrior Scholarship," both in Mihesuah and Wilson 2004.

12. One might argue that within Latin America indigenous intellectuals have made limited progress in entering academic circles in Bolivia, Guatemala, Colombia, Chile, and on Nicaragua's Atlantic coast, but all gains are partial and very hard to maintain, given the financial difficulties of universities in general. The tendency is for indigenous intellectuals to develop their own institutions, which are financially fragile as well. An especially trenchant example of these problems is represented in Chile by the publication of Marimán, Caniuqueo, Millalén, and Levil 2006, a book of essays by four young Mapuche historians, of whom only one, Marimán, has so far had access to a Ph.D. program.

13. Jennifer Denetdale, General Comment, Plenary Session, Conference on Narrating Native Histories, University of Wisconsin, Madison, 10 April 2005, transcription from recording of the session.

PART ONE   *Land, Sovereignty, and Self-Determination*

SINCE THE 1970S the internationalization of indigenous mobilization and the formation of globalized coalitions of Native peoples have changed the face of indigenous cultural politics and of indigenous claims to autonomy. One of the venues through which Native activism has been most dramatically felt has been the United Nations, where indigenous peoples have successfully pressured for the passage of broad-ranging resolutions supporting Native rights to self-determination, autonomy, and territorial and cultural integrity. Both the International Labor Organization's (ILO) Convention 169, adopted in June 1989 and put in force in September 1991, and the United Nations Declaration on the Rights of Indigenous Peoples, ratified in September 2007, have broken new ground in the area of international recognition of indigenous rights.

During the 1990s, as Native peoples pressured existing nation-states to ratify and observe the principles of ILO Convention 169 in their dealings with indigenous peoples within their borders, it became clear that UN resolutions can serve as powerful weapons for mobilization. Additionally, the intensification and deepening of international debate on indigenous issues, buttressed by back-to-back Decades of Indigenous Peoples declared by the United Nations (1990–2000, 2000–2010), have increased consciousness on the question of Native peoples and their rights, not only among political elites but also in intellectual and academic communities worldwide. And this new awareness has doubled back into Native societies, encouraging new forms of activism.

The two essays in part 1 situate the struggles of two indigenous peoples, the Kanaka Maoli of Hawai'i and the Rapanui of Rapa Nui, or so-called Easter Island, squarely within this evolving story of international indigenous mobilization. Informed by literatures in international politics, international human rights, and debates over indigenous self-determination, these essays take a broad view of the interactions between indigenous peoples and the states that colonized them. The focus is not on local forms of cultural practice or historical memory, but on the historically changing alternatives available to indigenous peoples as a whole in their struggle to retain land, culture, and resources and to achieve sovereignty and self-determination.

Kehaulani Kauanui places the historical struggle of Kanaka Maoli both in the context of U.S. federal government debates and within discussions in international law. As she makes clear, the case of Hawai'i is in some ways unique because, during the nineteenth century, the Kingdom of Hawai'i received international treaty recognition as a sovereign state. Subsequently, however, the U.S.-backed overthrow of the kingdom in 1893, the illegal annexation of Hawai'i as a U.S. territory in 1898, and the irregular vote that led to statehood in 1959 have all added layers of complexity and colonialism, making questions of national sovereignty, deoccupation, and indigenous rights deeply conflictual among the islands' inhabitants. Indeed, as Kauanui explores in her essay, none of the alternatives existing today—whether indigenous self-determination under U.S. federal law or under international law, decolonization under international law, or deoccupation based on the kingdom's previous existence as an independent state—attend simultaneously and effectively to the needs of all those involved.

Consciously developing a different kind of anthropological perspective, Riet Delsing traces the revitalization and recovery of identity and memory in Rapa Nui both as a story embedded in the narrative of the Chilean nation-state and as an international practice framed by the last generation of globalized indigenous mobilization. Delsing shows how the history of Chilean expropriation and colonization of the Rapanui is both embedded in the evolution of the Chilean nation-state and is a chapter in the broader story of Chilean Pacific imperialism and territorial expansion. At the same time, she traces the links between the evolution of a new Rapanui consciousness and the development of a Pacific-based indigenous consciousness. In the end, she suggests that the recent turn to militancy by a sector of Rapanui activists is articulated to the expansion of international indigenous activism and to the Rapanui's recognition of themselves as a Polynesian, rather than an American, people.

Taken together, the two essays assume three important tasks of the collection as a whole. First, they show how, in two specific historical cases, the international indigenous movement and UN debates on indigenous rights have changed the struggles for autonomy and self-determination over the last two generations. The richness of historical context provided is extremely important, because some analysts have tended to assume that, rather than coming to fruition in the context of the UN debates, indigenous struggles actually originated in them. These essays demonstrate, to the contrary, that the changing international context has afforded new venues and languages within which to place already existing and ongoing struggles over cultural recognition, resources, and self-determination.

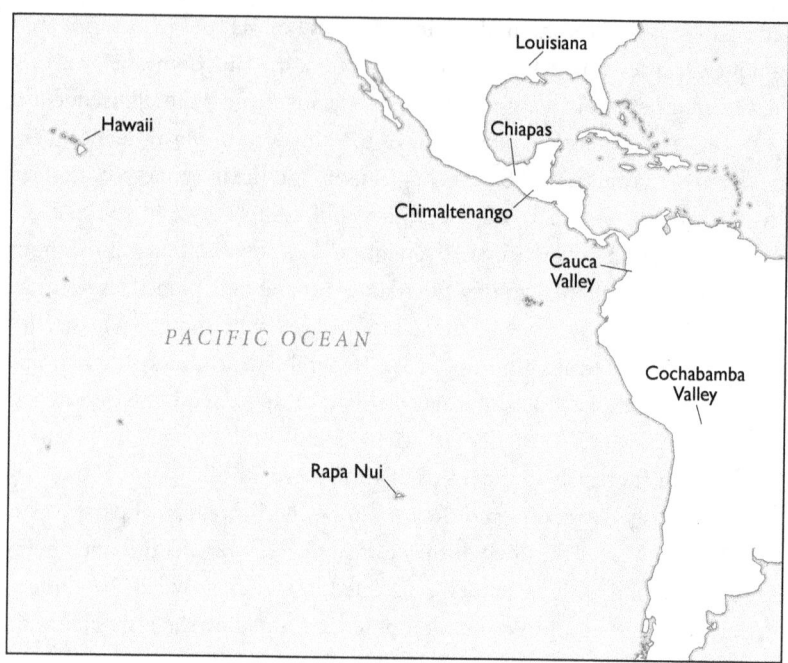

Map of regions discussed in the book.
Credit: Cartographic Laboratory, University of Wisconsin, Madison.

The second task the essays take on is to decenter the focus of the volume from the Americas. By concentrating on the Pacific region, and specifically on two Polynesian peoples, the authors remind us to look outside our national, or even continental, boundaries in considering the relationship between indigenous peoples and colonialism. Despite the dramatic differences in the history of Hawai'i and Rapa Nui, certain similarities in historical periodization and even in linguistic terminology (for example, the use of the word *canaca* in Rapa Nui and *kanaka* in Hawai'i to denote indigenous people) stand out. This process of decentering can perhaps be best appreciated visually by looking at the accompanying map. As the reader will see, in order to show Hawai'i it was necessary to cut off a portion of eastern South America, giving the image a certain counterintuitive feel.

The third task these essays perform is to raise the question of methodology in the writing of indigenous history and Native narrative. We tend to assume that Native history, because it is about indigenous communities, is best written from an ethnographic perspective that seeks to get inside the cultures about which we write. Certainly a close understanding of cultural categories and practices, of people's narratives and memories, must stand at the center of how Native history is rendered. Yet at the same time, as we reflect in this book on notions of decolonization, we must also take to heart the fact that broad national and international narratives and analysis are equally important as Native peoples continue to engage nation-states, intellectuals, political organizations, and academic practitioners. Perhaps, in this sense, decolonization can also begin at home, as we think through the multiple ways and registers in which to render indigenous narratives, history, and experience in the ever more globalized world.

J. KEHAULANI KAUANUI

Hawaiian Nationhood, Self-Determination, and International Law

This measure does not preclude Native Hawaiians from seeking alternatives in the international arena. This measure focuses solely on self-determination within the framework of federal law and seeks to establish equality in the federal policies extended towards American Indians, Alaska Natives and Native Hawaiians.
—U.S. Senator Daniel Kahikina Akaka (2001a)

Let me be clear—It is not my intention, nor the intention of the delegation, to preclude efforts of Native Hawaiians at the international level. The scope of this bill is limited to federal law.
—U.S. Senator Daniel Kahikina Akaka (2001b)

U.S. Senator Daniel Kahikina Akaka's assurances, made in 2001, were in regard to a legislative initiative to recognize a Native Hawaiian nation within the confines of U.S. federal policy on Tribal Nations that still remains before the U.S. Congress. Beginning in the 106th U.S. Congress in 2000 and continuing at least through the 111th Congress in 2011, Akaka, a Native Hawaiian Democrat from the State of Hawai'i, introduced this federal legislation in order to secure the recognition of Native Hawaiians as an indigenous people who have a "special relationship" with the United States and thus a right to internal self-determination. Passage of the bill would lay the foundation for a nation-within-a-nation model of self-governance defined by U.S. federal law as "domestic dependent nations" to exercise the right to self-government. The U.S. government has included Kanaka Maoli (indigenous Hawaiians) in over 160 legislative acts relating to Native Americans.[1] However, it has not included Kanaka Maoli in its policy on Native self-determination. Akaka's assertions that passage of the bill would not preclude Kanaka Maoli from seeking "alternatives in the international arena" have been his standard response to challenges posed to him by individuals and organizations opposed to the legislation because they favor Hawaiian independence from the United States—that is, the restoration of a Hawaiian state under international law. These groups include Hui Pu as well as those who are part of the Hawaiian Independence Action Alliance: the Pro-Kanaka Maoli Independence Working Group, Ka Pakaukau, Komike Tribunal, HONI (Hui o Na Ike), Ka Lei Maile Aliʻi Hawaiian Civic Club, Koani Foundation, ʻOhana Koa, NFIP—Hawaiʻi, Spiritual Nation of Kū—Hui Ea Council of Sovereigns, Living Nation, Settlers for Hawaiian Independence, MANA (Movement for Aloha No Ka ʻAina), as well as the Hawaiʻi Institute for Human Rights.

Akaka's response, however, echoed repeatedly by Hawaiʻi's state and federal officials over the past decade, speaks only to the rights of indigenous peoples under international law (Namuo 2004). But because his mention of "alternatives in the international arena" here and elsewhere is ill-defined, he has led many to infer that Kanaka Maoli could pursue full independence in a postfederal recognition political scenario, if they so desire. What proponents of the Akaka bill refuse to acknowledge is that this strategy differs from the prevalent Hawaiian independence position from the outset. While many proponents of U.S. federal recognition presume that activists in the Kanaka Maoli independence movement merely want continued access to the United Nations as indigenous peoples, the vast majority of proindependence Kanaka Maoli support two entirely different legal strategies under international law, decolonization and deoccupation, neither of which is based on indigeneity. Decolonization is specific to colonized peoples in non-self-governing territories, while deoccupation pertains to occupied states.

The history of the Kingdom of Hawaiʻi, which was recognized as a state by all major global powers throughout the nineteenth century, provides Kanaka Maoli and others with a rare legal claim that shows the current state-driven push for federal recognition to be problematic for outstanding sovereignty claims.[2] This essay critically analyzes the limits of both Akaka's federal proposal for internal self-determination and the rights of indigenous peoples under international law to argue that passage of the Native Hawaiian Government Reorganization Act would indeed threaten the independence claims of the Hawaiian nation, which are not necessarily protected by the Declaration on the Rights of Indigenous Peoples. In other words, I show how the independence claim for the sovereignty of the Hawaiian kingdom exceeds the current rights accorded to indigenous peoples at the United

Nations because the monarchy was recognized as a state prior to the U.S.-backed overthrow in 1893.

The case of Hawai'i illuminates the limitations of international law as a remedy for the politically fraught history of the kingdom and of Kanaka Maoli as an indigenous people. First, I offer some historical background in order to delineate the diplomatic relations of the Hawaiian kingdom and the United States, the U.S.-backed overthrow of the kingdom, and unilaterally imposed U.S. annexation and contested statehood for Hawai'i as the fiftieth state of the American Union. Next, I critically examine the prospect for internal self-determination under U.S. domestic policy as proposed in the Native Hawaiian Government Reorganization Act of 2009, also known as the Akaka bill, in order to assess the limits of that model of governance as it is detailed in the legislation. I also explore the ways in which the bill, if passed, could work to preempt and preclude the Hawaiian sovereignty claim under international law.

The next section delineates the terrain of indigenous peoples' rights under international law as distinct from the rights of states. I suggest that although indigenous peoples' rights are expanding, they still pose limits for the Hawaiian sovereignty claim—given the legal genealogy of the Hawaiian kingdom, an independent state—as it currently exists because of the way that international law continues to privilege the rights of states over the rights of peoples. Independence proponents who advocate restoration of the kingdom reject both indigenous self-determination under U.S. policy as well as indigenous self-determination under international law as legal strategies for recuperating Hawaiian sovereignty. Most also reject decolonization under the United Nations Charter, for reasons discussed below, and instead advocate for deoccupation. However, that legal strategy also has shortcomings vis-à-vis the plight of Kanaka Maoli, which I address.

The history of occupation and colonialism has generated a variety of options, but none of them seem sufficient in their current scope since each has serious limitations and demands an alternative approach to begin to address this complicated historical legacy in a way that promotes restorative justice.

From Kingdom to U.S.-Occupied Colony

Official diplomatic relations between the Kingdom of Hawai'i and the United States transpired over five decades. The treaties negotiated between the two were made after the U.S. government and other nations had already recognized the kingdom as an independent state. In 1842 King Kamehameha III dispatched a delegation to the United States and later to Europe that was endowed with the power to secure the recognition of Hawaiian independence by the major world powers of the time. On 19 December 1842 the delegation secured the assurance of President John Tyler of the United States of American recognition of the independence of the Kingdom of Hawai'i, and subsequently it secured formal recognition by Great Britain and France.

The treaties between the Kingdom of Hawai'i and the United States were not concerned with land or governance; they specified only relations of peace and friendship, commerce, and navigation. The first, signed at Washington on 20 December 1849, delineated protocols for perpetual peace and amity between the countries. It provided for reciprocal commerce and navigation, including the regulation of duties and imports at favored foreign nation rates and permission for U.S. whaling ships to dock at selected Hawaiian ports. The second treaty was negotiated in 1870 and concerned an arrangement between the postal services of the kingdom and the United States. The third treaty, known as the Reciprocity Treaty, was signed in 1875. This agreement for commercial reciprocity meant no export duty was imposed on Hawai'i or the United States and allowed for tax-free goods exchanged between the two nations to enter and leave Hawaiian and U.S. ports. In 1884 the two nations negotiated a convention to renew and supplement the treaty of 1875. This allowed the United States privileged access, over other nations, to use Pearl Harbor. The convention specified that the U.S. government had exclusive right to enter the harbor and to establish and maintain there a coaling and repair station for the use of U.S. vessels. Contrary to popular opinion, this supplement to the treaty ceded nothing to the United States in the way of territory. Last, in 1882 the two nations negotiated a convention between the Post Office Department of the United States and the Post Office Department of the Kingdom of Hawai'i concerning the exchange of money orders.

Although neither lands nor sovereignty were ceded in any of these treaties by either party, the number of elite foreigners residing in Hawai'i eventually grew to the point where they threatened the autonomy of the kingdom. White Americans had migrated to the Hawaiian Islands from the time of the first Christian mission in 1820 sponsored by the American Board of Commission for Foreign Missions. As Lilikala Kame'eleihiwa (1992) has documented, white Americans and European merchants constituted the foreign population in Hawai'i by the 1840s, when the missionaries' descendants pressured King Kamehameha III to privatize communal landholdings. The

Mahele land division of 1848 increased the wealth of these foreigners, who managed to secure vast extensions of land (Kameʻeleihiwa 1992). In turn, white settlers' presence and power increased on the islands throughout the nineteenth century (Silva 2004; Osorio 2002; Kameʻeleihiwa 1992). Anglo-American legal impositions transformed Hawaiian society throughout that period and made for a distinct form of colonialism accompanied by global movements of capitalism and Christianity that affected the everyday lives of Hawaiians with regard to work, family, marriage, and even sexuality (Merry 2000).

Eventually, the foreign elites formed their own militia, the Honolulu Rifles, associated with the U.S. military (Silva 2004, 122; Osorio 2002, 239–40). In 1887 the Honolulu Rifles seized strategic points in the city, and mounted armed patrols forced the ruling monarch, King Kalakaua, to sign what became known as the Bayonet Constitution, a document that stripped him of his most important executive powers and diminished the Kanaka Maoli voice in government. The king was no longer able to appoint members to the House of Nobles. The Bayonet Constitution created an oligarchy of the *haole* planters and businessmen by primarily empowering white Americans and Europeans. The new constitution gave U.S. citizens the right to vote in Hawaiian elections, while a large sector of the Kanaka Maoli electorate was excluded through rigorous property qualifications and Asians were entirely disenfranchised as aliens (Osorio 2002, 243–45, 251–54; Kent 1993, 55). Every decision would have to have the approval of the cabinet, now made up of foreigners. In addition, the new order prevented the king from dismissing the cabinet himself since the power was given to the legislature, which could dismiss any cabinet with a simple majority vote (Silva 2004, 122–26; Osorio 2002, 194–97).

Although the House of Nobles never properly ratified the Bayonet Constitution, Queen Liliʻuokalani's attempt to promulgate a new constitution to replace it (once she succeeded to the throne after her brother Kalakaua's death) prompted the unlawful overthrow of the kingdom. In 1893 U.S. Minister of Foreign Affairs John L. Stevens, with the support of a dozen white settlers, organized to overthrow Queen Liliʻuokalani. The queen yielded her authority under protest because she was confident that President Benjamin Harrison would endeavor to undo the actions led by one of his ministers. However, this was not the case, and those who overthrew the kingdom established the provisional government. Eventually, after sending an investigator on the matter, the next president, Grover Cleveland, declared the action under Stevens an act of war and acknowledged that the coup, backed by U.S. Marines, was unlawful (Cleveland 1893). But he never moved to restore formal recognition to the queen.

As this struggle for control was taking place, the provisional government established the Republic of Hawai'i on 4 July 1894, with Sanford Ballard Dole as president (Trask 1993; Silva 2004). Besides asserting jurisdiction over the entire island archipelago, this group seized roughly 1.8 million acres of land—Kingdom Government and Crown Lands—and declared them free and clear of any trust or claim. This de facto government ceded these same lands to the United States when it illegally annexed Hawai'i in 1898. This is the land base at stake in the political struggle today, one sorely contested through contemporary legal challenges.

The United States did not annex the Hawaiian Islands by treaty. Rather, it purportedly annexed the archipelago through its own internal domestic law, the Newlands Resolution. This legislation passed in 1898 despite massive indigenous opposition, as documented by Noenoe Silva (1998, 2004). Kanaka Maoli organized into two key nationalist groups, Hui Aloha 'Aina and Hui Kalai 'Aina, each of which submitted petitions representing the vast majority of the indigenous people; the combined signatures amounted to over thirty-eight thousand. Because only one of the two petitions has been recovered, it is unclear how many individuals signed both petitions. However, only forty thousand Kanaka Maoli resided in Hawai'i at the time (Silva 1998, 2004). In the two petitions, Kanaka Maoli clearly stated their opposition to becoming part of the United States "in any shape or form."

In 1897 the U.S. Senate accepted these petitions, and in the face of such resistance found it impossible to secure the two-thirds majority vote needed for a treaty. Regardless, under President William McKinley, proannexationists proposed a joint-senate resolution, even though admitting Hawai'i in this way, that is, as a new territory and not a state, violated the U.S. Constitution. A joint-senate resolution could pass with only a simple majority in both houses of Congress. The Newlands Resolution passed in 1898 when the U.S. government "annexed" Hawai'i. The resolution also mandated that the republic cede absolute title to the public lands formerly belonging to the Hawaiian Kingdom and Crown. The U.S. government incorporated Hawai'i as a colonial territory through the Organic Act of 1900, which created specific laws to administer the allegedly public lands. These laws again stated that the lands were part of a special trust under the federal government's oversight (Resolution No. 55, 2nd Session, 55th Congress, July 7, 1898; 30 Sta.

at L. 750; 2 Supp. R. S. 895). These lands remain the centerpiece in the struggle to restore Hawaiian independence because even though they amount to only slightly less than one-third of the lands throughout the archipelago, they have never fallen into private hands.

From Non-Self-Governing Territory to Fiftieth State of the United States of America

In 1946 the United Nations compiled a list of non-self-governing territories on which the U.S. government included Hawai'i (Trask 1994). Although Hawai'i was on the list and was therefore entitled to a process of self-determination to decolonize, the U.S. government predetermined statehood as the status for Hawai'i by treating its political status as an internal domestic issue. The ballot used in 1959 when the people of Hawai'i voted to become a state of the Union included only two options: integration and remaining a U.S. colonial territory (Trask 1994, 68–87). Among those allowed to take part in the vote, settlers as well as military personnel outnumbered Hawaiians. Citing the internal territorial vote, the U.S. State Department then misinformed the United Nations, which in turn considered the people of Hawai'i to have freely exercised their self-determination and chosen to incorporate themselves as part of the United States (Trask 1994).[3]

By UN criteria established in 1960, but already in debate the previous year and thus known to the United States at the time of the earlier vote, the ballot should have included independence and free association as choices. On 14 December 1960, the United Nations General Assembly issued a Declaration on the Granting of Independence to Colonial Countries and Peoples—Resolution 1514 (XV).[4] Also in 1960, the assembly approved Resolution 1541 (XV), which defined free association with an independent state, integration into an independent state, or independence as the three legitimate options of full self-government.[5] United Nations General Assembly Resolution 1541 refers to territories that are "geographically separate and distinct ethnically and/or culturally" without specifying what "geographically separate" must entail (Barsh 1986, 373). Nonetheless, this chapter of the resolution has been accepted as applicable mainly to overseas colonization, while relegating indigenous peoples to a condition of "internal colonization" (Barsh 1986, 373). At stake is prohibiting the indigenous claim to the same self-determination granted to "blue water" colonies by Resolution 1514, "which can logically lead to independence" (Griswold 1996, 101n14). Hence the phrase "all peoples

Hawaiian Nationhood 33

have the right of self-determination" has been mainly applied to inhabitants of territories destined for decolonization rather than to indigenous peoples (Griswold 1996, 93).

Since 1960 only peoples recognized as colonized have had the right to freely determine their political status. For example, in the case of East Timor in 1999, the East Timorese finally had the opportunity to vote on their political status through a UN-sponsored plebiscite, and they voted to fully decolonize from Indonesia. Although the East Timorese are an indigenous people, it was the status of East Timor as a colony of Indonesia since 1975 (and before that of Portugal since the mid-sixteenth century) that qualified them for the right to full self-determination, not their status as an indigenous people per se. It seems reasonable to infer that the right of the East Timorese to full self-determination is due to the blue water doctrine under international law, which defines colonial territories plainly as those far from the colonial metropoles asserting rule over them.

At the same time, the United Nations recognized Hawai'i as a non-self-governing territory from 1946 to 1959, during which time Kanaka Maoli and others were eligible for full decolonization. Some argue, therefore, that the most straightforward legal argument in support of independence is the decolonization model. The Pro-Kanaka Maoli Independence Working Group, Ka Pakaukau, and the Komike Tribunal have consistently worked to educate the Hawaiian community about the aborted option under the decolonization model and have advocated that contemporary Kanaka Maoli should be entitled to a plebiscite to exercise their right to self-determination and determine what model of governance they prefer. However, many sovereignty activists who advocate for kingdom restoration reject this strategy of reinscription on the list of non-self-governing territories. They make a distinction between a colonial territory (e.g., Guam, a U.S. territory) and an occupied state such as the Hawaiian kingdom. As an alternative, those organized to restore the Hawaiian kingdom government advocate for de-occupation rather than decolonization and rely on the international laws of occupation by drawing on regulations created during The Hague Convention IV of 1907, specifically Article 43 (Sai 2001).[6] Accordingly, those who identify as subjects of the kingdom are demanding that the recovery process as well as all charges against the United States, be guided by The Hague Regulations, not by the UN Charter providing for self-determination (Sai 2001). In other words, they avoid an analysis of colonialism because they assume that to talk about colonialism in Hawai'i is to legitimate Hawai'i as a former U.S. colony rather than an occupied state. Because the kingdom had already secured recognition of its independence in 1842, deoccupation supporters declare their status as kingdom nationals of a nation that has already achieved self-determination. Since the U.S. Congress unilaterally annexed Hawaiʻi through its own domestic law, supporters of deoccupation argue that the kingdom was never really annexed and therefore its territory continues to be merely occupied by the United States. Unfortunately, this political discourse of achievement has been framed in a way that is demeaning to indigenous peoples who have not formed states and reveals a reluctance to emphasize oppression specific to Kanaka Maoli living under U.S. domination. Many proponents of kingdom restoration, much like the neoconservatives opposed to the Akaka bill, have dismissed indigenous self-government as race-based government, and they have done so by casting the kingdom as a "colorblind" government because non–Kanaka Maoli were included as kingdom subjects.[7]

To complicate matters further, there is no acknowledgment that American colonialism arguably began long before the formal takeover of Hawaiʻi by the United States, let alone that the assimilationist policies imposed on Kanaka Maoli throughout the twentieth century are colonial in nature. Any discussions of decolonization—including those in the cultural arena not dependent on UN protocols, such as indigenous language revitalization in response to years of indigenous language suppression, to cite just one example—are too quickly dismissed in legal terms. The problem then takes the form of a battle over international law rather than focusing on the white supremacist practices and policies that are part and parcel of the colonial subordination of Kanaka Maoli, whether one considers Hawaiʻi a former U.S. colony or not. The myriad of oppressions faced by the vast majority of Kanaka Maoli include high infant mortality and low life expectancy; disproportionate rates of diabetes, hypertension, heart disease, cancer, depression, and suicide; intergenerational trauma; criminalization and high rates of incarceration; as well as other social ills linked to indigenous land dispossession and poverty induced by colonial status.

The formation of Hawaiʻi as the fiftieth state of the Union has been used to silence the possibility of decolonization from the United States. Here, it seems that the blue water doctrine holds no effective meaning, even though Hawaiʻi is over two thousand miles from California and nearly five thousand miles from Washington, D.C. Therein lies the paradox. While Hawaiʻi was a distant U.S. colony during the first half of the twentieth century, it was an independent state before the U.S. takeover, which complicates conventional and legal notions of self-determination in discussions of most indigenous peoples. And yet, it is clear that Kanaka Maoli are also an indigenous people.

Internal Self-Determination: The Akaka Bill Proposal

One of the main rationales offered by Akaka for his legislative proposal for federally organizing a Native Hawaiian governing entity is the U.S. congressional Apology Resolution of 1993 (Public Law 103–150), in which the U.S. government apologized to the Hawaiian people for the U.S. military's role in the overthrow. This joint-senate resolution, signed by President William J. Clinton came about as a result of efforts by Akaka, who worked to have the resolution passed during the one-hundred-year anniversary of the overthrow. Although the apology includes a disclaimer at the end, stating that nothing it contains can be used to settle a case against the United States, it still is a finding of fact. The apology maintains that "the indigenous Hawaiian people never directly relinquished their claims to their inherent sovereignty as a people or over their national lands to the United States, either through their monarchy or through a plebiscite or referendum" (U.S. Public Law 103–150, 103d Congress Joint Resolution 19).[8] The apology also calls for some form of reconciliation and self-governance for Native Hawaiians. It specifically states that Congress "expresses its commitment to acknowledge the ramifications of the overthrow of the Kingdom of Hawaii, in order to provide a proper foundation for reconciliation between the United States and the Native Hawaiian people; and ... urges the President of the United States to also acknowledge the ramifications of the overthrow of the Kingdom of Hawaii and to support reconciliation efforts between the United States and the Native Hawaiian people" (U.S. Public Law 103–150, 103d Congress Joint Resolution 19). Akaka has framed his legislative proposal, the Native Hawaiian Government Reorganization Act of 2009, as the step toward reconciliation supported in the Apology Resolution. But it was also prompted by the case of *Rice v. Cayetano*, in which the U.S. Supreme Court ruled Hawaiian-only voting conducted by the state Office of Hawaiian Affairs for trustee elections unconstitutional.[9] Shortly after the ruling, Akaka set up a Task Force on Native Hawaiian Issues and then proposed legislation to federally recognize a Native Hawaiian governing entity as a domestic dependent nation with the aim of creating an internal government that would be immune to legal challenges to the 14th and 15th constitutional amendments. As a result, many

Native Hawaiians staffing state agencies such as the Office of Hawaiian Affairs and the Department of Hawaiian Home Lands, which are dependent on state and federal funding for specifically indigenous projects like Papa Ola Lokahi (Native Hawaiian Healthcare) and Nā Pua No'eau (Center for Gifted and Talented Native Hawaiian Children), and the vast majority of Hawaiian civic clubs support the legislation.

The Akaka bill sets up the process for the formation of a governing entity to be approved by the U.S. government. The entity would be formed by a commission of nine members appointed by the secretary of the interior, whose duty first and foremost would be to report to the secretary.[10] The legislation allows for the recognition only of a Native Hawaiian governing entity and not of the rights of that entity, which would be subject to later negotiation between the U.S. federal government, the Native Hawaiian entity, and the Hawai'i state government.

The bill was first introduced in 2000 in the 106th Congress, where it did not survive committee, and during each subsequent Congress it has been defeated by Republican opposition (Kauanui 2005b). Conservatives' refusal to support the measure became more pronounced when the administration of George W. Bush took a position against the legislation, opposition which lasted throughout that administration. Although throughout that period the legislation gained committee approval in both the House and the Senate, it remained stalled when it came to a floor debate. Despite multiple revisions and reintroductions of new drafts aimed at satisfying the concerns of the Department of the Interior and appeasing Republican critics, who called the proposal a plan for "race-based government," the legislation never progressed to a vote.[11]

Under the new leadership of President Barack Obama there is widespread support for the bill. Since the start of the 111th Congress on 3 January 2009 three sets of proposals have been made, all titled the Native Hawaiian Government Reorganization Act of 2009: S. 381 and H.R. 862, introduced on 4 February 2009; S. 708 and H.R. 1711, introduced on 25 March 2009; and S. 1011 and H.R. 2314, introduced on 7 May 2009. S. 1011 was given a hearing before the U.S. Senate Committee on Indian Affairs on 6 August 2009 and H.R. 2314 was given a hearing before the U.S. House Committee on Natural Resources. At the time of this writing both await a floor debate and vote.[12]

Those who support independence oppose federal recognition because at the very most it would allow for no more than a domestic dependent entity under the full and exclusive plenary power of Congress. Most immediately, federal recognition would set up a process for extinguishing most claims to land title—except for whatever the state of Hawai'i and the federal government may be willing to relinquish in exchange for that recognition—and even then the U.S. federal government would hold it in trust. What is at stake here is the 1.8 million acres of former Kingdom Crown and Government Lands and the obliteration of the Hawaiian nation's title to them. As the U.S. Supreme Court case of 2009 regarding these lands shows, there is absolutely no guarantee that any future Native Hawaiian governing entity would hold any of these lands.[13]

Counter to Akaka's assurances, there is also the likelihood that passage of the bill could foreclose the sovereignty claim for Hawaiian independence under international law. The legislation appears to be a preemptive attempt to squash outstanding sovereignty claims unsuccessfully extinguished by Hawai'i's being admitted as the fiftieth state of the American Union. If the bill passes, the will of the people will seem to have been expressed—as a form of self-determination in support of federal recognition—in a way that would make international intervention much more far-fetched, given the likelihood that the world community would see the Hawaiian question as even more of a U.S. domestic issue than it does today. In any case, it would certainly entrench the Hawaiian sovereignty claim further within the U.S. government since the Native Hawaiian governing entity, as proposed in the Akaka bill, would be subordinate to both the Hawai'i state government and the U.S. federal government.

Alternatively, supporters of federal recognition insist that nothing in the Akaka bill would compromise Hawai'i's national claims under international law. But they do not attend to the ways in which the United States asserts its plenary power to keep indigenous sovereigns both domestic and dependent. In this context it is important that a provision included in S. 708 was swiftly removed from the later version, S. 1011. Section 11 of S. 708. was titled "Disclaimer" and stated, "Nothing in this Act is intended to serve as a settlement of any claims against the United States, or to affect the rights of the Native Hawaiian people under international law." Despite this change, neoconservative opponents to the bill have sought to spread misinformation about the legislation. This had led Akaka to provide further assurances in direct contradiction to those he once provided to supporters of Hawaiian independence. In a hearing before the U.S. Senate Committee on Indian Affairs, he repeatedly asserted that the bill does not allow Hawai'i to secede from the United States (Akaka 2009).

This legislation limits Hawaiian self-determination because of its fundamental legal distinction between Indian tribes and foreign nations under the U.S. Constitution and federal law with specific regard to the unextinguished sovereignty of the Hawaiian kingdom. The name alone represents what is problematic for Hawaiian sovereignty and nationhood under international law. Embedded in its title, the "Native Hawaiian Government Reorganization Act of 2009," is a fundamental historical lie: there can be no attempt to *re*organize a Native Hawaiian government because the Kingdom of Hawai'i was an internationally recognized state that in the nineteenth century afforded citizenship status to more than just indigenous Hawaiian people. This name misconstrues the nature of the government-to-government relationship the United States had with the kingdom. The bill should be named more accurately as the "Native Hawaiian Government Organization Act."

The bill asserts that "the Constitution vests Congress with the authority to address the conditions of the indigenous, native people of the United States," drawing on Article I, Section 8, Clause 3 of the U.S. Constitution, which reads as follows: "The Congress shall have power . . . to regulate commerce with foreign nations, and among the several states, and with the Indian tribes." The U.S. Supreme Court has ruled time and time again that this clause, known as the Commerce Clause, means the U.S. federal government has total and complete power over tribal nations (Wilkins 1997). Section (3) of the bill also states that "the United States has a special political and legal relationship to promote the welfare of the native people of the United States, including Native Hawaiians." In other words, the U.S. government calls it "special" because it regards tribal nations as internal nations that are both domestic and dependent because they are forced to exist within the broader legal boundary asserted by the U.S. government. Yet the U.S. government never legally regarded the Hawaiian kingdom as domestic or dependent. Under the U.S. Constitution, the Kingdom of Hawai'i was regarded as a foreign nation, an independent sovereign state.

The U.S. Congress has repeatedly delegated its authority to the executive branch of the U.S. government. With regard to Indian tribes, it delegates its authority specifically to the U.S. Department of the Interior. This matters for the purposes of the bill since the legislation proposes to create and empower the U.S. Office for Native Hawaiian Relations, within the U.S. Department of the Interior, to coordinate the "special political and legal relationship between the United States and that Native Hawaiian governing entity." Foreign nations do not have any relationship to the U.S. Department of the Interior precisely because that department is concerned with areas considered by the U.S. government to be internal to the United States, areas such as Indians tribes, U.S. Island Territories, and National Parks. Foreign nations relate to the U.S. Department of State.

Section 4, which details the purpose of the bill, claims that it will "provide a process for the reorganization of the single Native Hawaiian governing entity and the reaffirmation of the special political and legal relationship between the United States and that Native Hawaiian governing entity for purposes of continuing a government-to-government relationship." At the same time, it makes it clear how the legislation limits the scope of self-determination: "Native Hawaiians have—(A) an inherent right to autonomy in their internal affairs; (B) an inherent right of self-determination and self-governance; (C) the right to reorganize a Native Hawaiian governing entity; and (D) the right to become economically self-sufficient" (Section 4, part 5).

Sections 5 and 6 of the bill give the U.S. Department of Defense free rein. Whereas Section 5 requires the proposed U.S. Office of Native Hawaiian Relations to consult with the Native Hawaiian Governing Entity "before taking any actions that may have the potential to significantly affect Native Hawaiian resources, rights, or lands," it makes an exception for anything having to do with the needs, wants, and desires of the U.S. Department of Defense: "This section shall have no applicability to the Department of Defense or to any agency or component of the Department of Defense." This means that U.S. militarism in and from Hawaiian waters and lands can continue without end and that neither the Office nor the Native Hawaiian Governing Entity could do anything to stop it according to U.S. law. Similarly, Section 6, after outlining the composition and duties of the Interagency Coordinating Group set up to coordinate federal programs that address the conditions of Native Hawaiians and are administered by federal agencies other than the Department of the Interior, reiterates that "this section shall have no applicability to the Department of Defense or to any agency or component of the Department of Defense."

Section 8 reaffirms the delegation of U.S. government authority to the State of Hawai'i in order to address the condition of Native Hawaiians under the Hawai'i state admissions act. With regard to negotiations, this section specifies that after the Native Hawaiian governing entity is created, *both* the United States and the State of Hawai'i may enter into negotiations with the Native Hawaiian governing entity. This sets the bill apart from other forms of federal recognition of Native nations, which do not typically give state governments any part in the negotiations, with the exception of matters related to Indian gaming. This bill allows the State of Hawai'i to sit at the table to negotiate matters including the transfer of lands, natural resources, and other assets and the protection of existing rights related to such lands or resources; the exercise of governmental authority over any transferred lands, natural resources, and other assets, including land use; the exercise of civil and criminal jurisdiction; the delegation of governmental powers and authorities to the Native Hawaiian governing entity by the United States and the State of Hawai'i; any residual responsibilities of the United States and the State of Hawai'i; and grievances regarding assertions of historical wrongs committed against Native Hawaiians by the United States or by the State of Hawai'i. None of these things are guaranteed in the bill — not land, not jurisdiction, not assets, not governmental power. They are all open to negotiation once representatives of a Native Hawaiian governing entity sit down with federal and state agents. There is no equal footing here; all negotiations must take place within the framework of U.S. federal law and policy with regard to Indian tribes and under U.S. plenary power, where the U.S. government asserts total and complete power, and in this case the State of Hawai'i will have an equal role.[14]

Notably, Section (e) of the bill states, "Nothing in this Act alters the civil or criminal jurisdiction of the United States or the State of Hawai'i over lands and persons within the State of Hawai'i." It further states, "The status quo of Federal and State jurisdiction can change only as a result of further legislation, if any, enacted after the conclusion, in relevant part, of the negotiation process established in section 8(b)." In other words, when the representatives of the Native Hawaiian governing entity sit at the table to negotiate with federal and state agents, they cannot negotiate for civil or criminal jurisdiction over any land. In order for them to do so, more legislation would need to be passed.

This section of the bill also includes a disclaimer: nothing in the act can create a cause of action against the United States or any other entity or person, or alter "existing law, including existing case law, regarding obligations on the part of the United States or the State of Hawai'i with regard to Native Hawaiians or any Native Hawaiian entity." It further states that nothing in the bill can create any new obligation to Native Hawaiians under federal law, and it specifically outlines and protects the federal government through sovereign immunity against lawsuits for breach of trust, land claims, resource-protection or resource-management claims, or similar types of claims brought by or on behalf of Native Hawaiians or the Native Hawaiian governing entity. And it asserts that the State of Hawai'i "retains its sovereign immunity, unless waived in accord with State law, to any claim, established under any source of law, regarding Native Hawaiians, that existed prior to the enactment of this Act."

This last section, among others, especially raised concerns within the Native Hawaiian Bar Association (NHBA). On 11 June 2009, the NHBA submitted testimony to the House Committee on Natural Resources regarding the House version of the Akaka bill (H.R. 2314). Although the NHBA expressed its support for the bill, its testimony outlined some major concerns. The first is the role of the U.S. Department of Defense as it relates to the Office of Native Hawaiian Relations and the Native Hawaiian Interagency. The second is the role of the U.S. Department of Justice (DOJ) because, unlike earlier versions of the bill, the current legislation does not include a provision authorizing the designation of a DOJ representative to assist in the implementation and protection of the rights of Native Hawaiians and their political, legal, and trust relationship with the United States. The third concern was the section of the bill relating to "claims and sovereignty immunity." The NHBA notes,

> We believe it is unnecessary and premature to include provisions on claims and sovereign immunity prior to federal recognition of a Native Hawaiian Government and recommend that these provisions under section 8(c) be taken out of the bill. Such provisions could be contemplated during implementation legislation after federal recognition is conferred and negotiations between the Native Hawaiian Governing Entity and the State of Hawai'i and Federal Government are completed. The bill's provisions on claims and federal sovereign immunity appear to be overly broad and may prohibit lawsuits by individual Native Hawaiians for claims that could be pursued by any other member of the general population.

In response, Rep. Neil Abercrombie of Hawai'i suggested the legislation be revisited to assess whether another revision was needed.[15]

Although the U.S. Senate Committee on Indian Affairs proceeded to hold a hearing for the companion bill to H.R. 2314, S. 1011, the intervention by the NHBA may serve to slow down the process to allow more critical analysis of the proposal overall, at least among those in the Kanaka Maoli communities both within the islands and throughout the U.S. continent. However, should the Akaka bill pass, Kanaka Maoli would be shut out of the decolonization model, which would technically leave open the venue for redress offered by the United Nations Declaration on the Rights of Indigenous Peoples. But, as we shall see below, for a variety of reasons this is an unsatisfactory alternative.

Self-Determination and the Rights of Indigenous Peoples

On 13 September 2007, the United Nations General Assembly adopted the Declaration on the Rights of Indigenous Peoples. The result of nearly three decades of activism, it is the most comprehensive international human rights document addressing the rights of indigenous peoples all over the world. Indigenous peoples worldwide have worked for decades to ensure that their *preexisting* human rights are recognized and upheld by global nation-states, especially since the domestic laws in most settler states have not protected their ability to assert their self-determination. Key issues of struggle include the right of ownership and control of territory and resources, protection of sacred sites and lands, self-governance, and decision-making authority vis-à-vis the dominant population. Central to all of these is the question of indigenous peoples' right to self-determination under international law. Because the basic criteria defining colonies under international law include foreign domination and geographical separation from the colonizer, indigenous peoples up until now have been at a disadvantage in terms of the application of decolonization protocols, an issue heatedly debated throughout the world community because indigenous peoples are often considered to be subject to internal colonization.

This limitation reflects the long-term battle over whether indigenous peoples should be considered peoples in the context of Chapter XI of the United Nations Charter of 1945, which includes the Declaration Regarding Non-Self-Governing Peoples in Article 73 and within United Nations General Assembly Resolution 1514, which reads, "All peoples have the right to self-determination; by virtue of that right, they freely determine their political status and freely pursue their economic, social, and cultural development."[16] Regarding the question of self-determination for indigenous peoples, the still-cited report by José Martinez Cobo, commissioned by the United Nations, states, "Self-determination constitutes the exercise of free choice by indigenous peoples, who must, to a large extent, create the specific content of this principle, in both its internal and external expressions, which do not necessarily include the right to secede from the State in which they may live and to set themselves up as sovereign entities. *This right may in fact be expressed in various forms of autonomy within the State*" (emphasis added).

There is no consensus on whether indigenous peoples have the right to full self-determination—an option that would allow for the development of nation-states that are independent of their former colonizers, like the postcolonial Third World—or whether that right is limited to internal self-determination within the existing nation-states in which they are included. The use of the term *peoples*, which signifies legal rights under international law over and above the term *people*, has been the most contentious part of this debate. This form of discrimination can be traced to the Law of Nations, which institutionalized the international legal discrimination against indigenous peoples (Newcomb 2008).

The establishment in 1982 of the Working Group on Indigenous Populations (WGIP), under the United Nations Economic and Social Council, led the effort to draft a specific instrument under international law that would protect indigenous peoples worldwide. The WGIP was informed by early organizations, such as the International Indian Treaty Council, formed in 1977, which was the first organization of indigenous peoples to be reorganized as a Non-Governmental Organization (NGO) with Consultative Status to the United Nations Economic and Social Council. Another example is the American Indian Law Alliance, founded in 1989, which also has special consultative status with the Economic and Social Council of the United Nations.

Initially, the WGIP submitted a first draft of a declaration on the rights of indigenous peoples to the Sub-Commission on the Prevention of Discrimination and Protection of Minorities, which was eventually approved in 1994.[17] The draft was sent to the United Nations Commission on Human Rights for further discussion. The declaration was stalled for many years because of concerns by states with regard to some of its core statements, namely, the right to self-determination of indigenous peoples and the control over natural resources existing on indigenous peoples' traditional lands. By 1995 an open-ended intersessional working group was formed with the understanding that some version of the declaration would be adopted by the General Assembly within the International Decade of the World's Indigenous Peoples (1995–2004). The United Nations Commission on Human Rights extended the mandate of the WGIP into the Second International Decade of the World's Indigenous Peoples (2005–2015) and also urged it to present for UN adoption a final draft declaration on the rights of indigenous people.

The Human Rights Council of the United Nations was the first to adopt the Declaration on the Rights of Indigenous Peoples, in June 2006, and offered a recommendation that it be adopted by the General Assembly.[18] In the vote of the General Assembly, the declaration was passed with a vote of 143 in favor, 4 against, and 11 abstentions. Notably, the 4 votes against the adoption came from white settler states, all with a strong indigenous presence in terms of political resistance to First World domination: Australia, Canada, New Zealand, and the United States. Many attribute the opposition of these states to governmental fears that indigenous peoples would secede and seek independence, acts which potentially threaten to disrupt the contiguous land mass of the settler nation-states that encompass them.

Regarding the issue of self-determination, however, the newly adopted Declaration on the Rights of Indigenous Peoples is ambiguous. On the one hand, Article 3 states, "Indigenous peoples have the right of self-determination. By virtue of that right they freely determine their political status and freely pursue their economic, social, and cultural development." But on the other hand, the last article, Article 46, states, "Nothing in this Declaration may be . . . construed as authorizing or encouraging any action which would dismember or impair, totally or in part, the territorial integrity or political unity of sovereign and independent States." For example, the U.S. government would surely be threatened if the Navajo Nation were to seek independence, given that the asserted boundaries of the states of New Mexico, Colorado, Utah, and Arizona fall within the Diné's traditional territory. Given these two seemingly contradictory articles, how are we to understand what the right to self-determination means and to what extent that right can be realized by indigenous peoples?

Article 26 states the following with regard to traditional lands:

1. Indigenous peoples have the right to the lands, territories and resources which they have traditionally owned, occupied or otherwise used or acquired.
2. Indigenous peoples have the right to own, use, develop and control the lands, territories and resources that they possess by reason of traditional ownership or other traditional occupation or use, as well as those which they have otherwise acquired.
3. States shall give legal recognition and protection to these lands, ter-

ritories and resources. Such recognition shall be conducted with due respect to the customs, traditions and land tenure systems of the indigenous peoples concerned.

Parts 1 and 2 here are explicit in terms of the right to land. They could certainly be cited in support of the Hawaiian sovereignty proponents in the reclamation of the Hawaiian Kingdom Crown and Government Lands controlled by the state government of Hawai'i under the United States, as well as other lands in the archipelago heretofore unalienated under the kingdom during the Mahele land division of 1848, which privatized traditional communal lands. The question remains how the claim to traditional lands by indigenous peoples can be asserted in light of the article meant to protect the territorial integrity of states.

Since Kanaka Maoli (among the vast majority of kingdom heirs) live in a historically occupied state, the question of territorial integrity could be evoked by those supporting an independent Hawaiian state, not simply the settler state of the United States.[19] The principle of territorial integrity is usually operative vis-à-vis other states: that is, one state is prohibited from invading and accessing another state's territory, although this happens nonetheless. Article 46 can be used as political leverage to advocate for the territorial integrity of the Kingdom of Hawai'i as a state. The U.S. government violated the Hawaiian state's territorial integrity when it supported an illegal overthrow and unilaterally annexed Hawai'i in contravention to U.S. federal law, its treaties with the kingdom, and international law operative at the time. Hence, deoccupation supporters demand that the U.S. government withdraw from Hawai'i. Still, the U.S. government casts independence claims as attempts at secession, a complete misnomer.

Prior to the passage of the declaration many governmental officials assumed that the right of indigenous groups to self-determination would lead to secession, and this assumption was used to deny indigenous peoples this right (Lâm 1992). Even members of the WGIP and the UN special rapporteurs have shared this assumption of states (Lâm 1992). Maivân Clech Lâm suggests that it is possible for indigenous peoples to exercise self-determination without threatening the territorial integrity and sovereignty of the surrounding state, especially since most have visions of becoming autonomous without becoming nation-states. In fact, most seek mutually negotiated free association (Lâm 1992; Griswold 1996, 98). Situations differ depending on the state in question and its location. For example, most indigenous movements throughout North and South America continue to fight for an expansion of cultural, political, and territorial autonomy within the respective settler states that encompass them. Within these debates is the continuous contestation over the concepts of sovereignty, self-determination, self-government, and autonomy, which differ in meaning and intention within different contexts.

In the context of the United States, even if indigenous peoples have no vision of becoming nation-states, the most basic components of fuller autonomy would likely disrupt the territorial integrity of the surrounding state. For example, if the U.S. government were to honor and abide by all of the treaties it signed with indigenous nations; return most of the National Parks to the indigenous peoples from whom they were taken; federally recognize all tribal nations and entities who seek this U.S. domestic model of acknowledgment (which includes over two hundred tribal entities that have submitted their petitions and remain on the Bureau of Indian Affairs' waiting list); and restore all previously terminated tribes with federal acknowledgment, one can certainly imagine a major reordering of society in a way that would affect the existing state and the territory the U.S. government currently claims as its own. None of these four actions need be tied to the goal of indigenous nations becoming nation-states; however, the likelihood that the federal government would act on any of these matters at this moment in time seems quite far-fetched. Indeed, indigenous possession is a contradiction inherent in the U.S. nation-state and its very foundations.

Today, international lawyers who favor nation-states argue that indigenous peoples do not have an unqualified right to self-determination under international law, while those who favor indigenous peoples argue that they do (Lâm 1992). There is no consensus regarding this model, which is why so many indigenous activists have devoted much time and effort to advocating that the United Nations and the Organization of American States (OAS) adopt the Declaration on the Rights of Indigenous Peoples affirming that indigenous peoples have an *unqualified* right to self-determination.

The Indigenous Caucus at both the United Nations and the OAS had consistently taken the position that indigenous peoples are colonized and therefore fall under the decolonization model. UN documents and international practice demonstrate that self-determination is a right available to all peoples. But there was widespread controversy over when a group of persons constitute a people who are entitled to self-determination under international law. When the U.S. National Security Council took a position on indigenous peoples before the United Nations Commission on Human Rights and its Working Group on the Draft Declaration on Indigenous Rights, along with a similar OAS draft declaration, the council stated that the United States urged the use of the term *internal self-determination* for indigenous peoples. In other words, the U.S. position was that using the term *self-determination* was advisable only if it was defined in a way that meant that the right to self-determination signified indigenous peoples' right to negotiate their respective political statuses within the framework of the existing nation-state. The debate over indigenous peoples' demand for the use of the term *peoples* was crucial to activist demands under international law. The U.S. government has continuously opposed the use of the term *peoples*, which marks distinction to peoplehood and attendant collective rights to sovereignty. However, with the adoption by the United Nations of the Declaration on the Rights of Indigenous Peoples, such opposition may potentially change—especially if the declaration becomes a convention with the full force of international law.

Conclusions

The complex history of Hawai'i and its multiple transitions from sovereign kingdom to occupied colonial territory to fiftieth U.S. state presents a unique challenge as we think through the options for decolonization that are available to Kanaka Maoli and other heirs of the kingdom. Given the layers of history and foreign intervention, there is no clear or easy way to resolve this problem, especially so long as the U.S. government continues to dominate nations across the globe with its political and military power. The history of both American colonialism and U.S. occupation has generated a variety of options—but none of them seem sufficient in their current scope since each has serious limitations.

As we saw in the discussion of the Akaka bill, the status of domestic dependent nation that would be granted Native Hawaiians through a process of federal recognition neither recognizes the kingdom's history of sovereign existence nor takes into account the unjust occupation and overthrow of the monarch by the U.S. government. At the same time, relying on presently existing international law regarding indigenous peoples also has the limitation that, in its present state, it still gives priority to existing nation-states and puts the preexisting rights of indigenous peoples as nations on the back burner. While this may change, for the moment neither of these options gives Kanaka Maoli or other heirs of the kingdom the satisfaction of recognizing their previously independent status.

Yet, as we also saw briefly, the deoccupation model, while taking account of such independent status, also denies the internal colonialism in terms of culture, language, and territory to which the Kanaka Maoli have been specifically subjected. It seems as though recognition of the previous sovereignty of the kingdom currently rests on the denial of internal forms of domination. In the end, therefore, there does not seem to be one alternative that both recognizes the kingdom's history of sovereignty and provides Kanaka Maoli with the cultural and territorial restitution to which they aspire. Furthermore, although Kanaka Maoli constituted the majority of the kingdom's subjects prior to the overthrow in 1893, Kanaka Maoli and other heirs of the kingdom together are a demographic minority in Hawai'i's current population. This begs the question as to how the kingdom government would be restored if independence became a feasible political goal, since within the contemporary world community minority-led governments are viewed as unacceptable. In response to this problematic, the normative solution under international law that would have all citizens equally enfranchised without any differential status for Kanaka Maoli and other heirs raises the possibility that Kanaka Maoli would once again be a vulnerable indigenous minority under an independent Hawaiian government and thus have to rely on the indigenous rights provided under current international law, as it is now in any case.

In an "Urgent Open Letter to U.S. President Barack Obama" dated 13 April 2009, a self-selected group of Kanaka Maoli, *kupuna* (elders), *kumu* (educators), and representatives wrote on behalf of the Kanaka Maoli people as well as of other heirs of the Kingdom of Hawai'i. Signatories also included a number of our *kako'o* (supporters) who were invited to add their names.[20] The letter's primary purpose was to inform the president of the signatories' categorical opposition to the proposed legislation. It also proposed an alternative bilateral approach to begin to address the complex legacy detailed in this essay in a way that promotes restorative justice. The letter read in part as follows:

> The Bill arrogantly attempts to unilaterally characterize the historical transgressions of the United States against our people and kingdom, and to unilaterally specify their remedy. We insist otherwise. U.S. crimes against our Kanaka Maoli people and other Kingdom heirs from 1893 on require, for their redress, that a mechanism composed of U.S. agents and wholly independent representatives of Kanaka Maoli and Kingdom heirs

be bilaterally set up by your Administration and us to make findings of fact and conclusions of international law that could serve as a road-map for the resolution of the political and legal issues now outstanding between our two parties.

As this essay has made clear, the complex histories of colonialism, occupation, and discrimination to which Native peoples have been subject across the globe have no single solution, precisely because each case has its own particular characteristics. Given the especially fraught history of the Hawaiian case, the combination of international law and honest bilateral dialogue might be the only venue open for redress. But it is also my hope that, if brought to fruition, such dialogue might provide an example of what could be possible for indigenous nations in other parts of the world.

Notes

This essay began as a presentation delivered at the Native American Studies Symposium "Narrating Native American History in the Americas," University of Wisconsin, Madison, 7–10 April 2005. I would like to thank Florencia Mallon and Ned Blackhawk for inviting me to present my work there, as well as the following individuals and institutions that created opportunities for me to present various working versions of this piece: Jessica Cattelino and Miranda Johnson for inviting me to present at the Comparative Colonialisms workshop hosted by the Anthropology Department of the University of Chicago; Aileen Moreton-Robinson for inviting me to present an earlier version for the inaugural lecture for the Indigenous Studies Research Network, Queensland University of Technology in Brisbane, Australia; and Alyssa Mt. Pleasant for inviting me to present at the American Studies colloquium at Yale University.

1. Congress has enacted numerous special provisions of law for the benefit of Native Hawaiians in the areas of health, education, labor, and housing. Along with American Indians and Alaska Natives, Native Hawaiians have been included in over 160 federal acts for Native Americans since 1903. To some degree, then, the U.S. Congress has recognized that a special relationship exists between the United States and the Native Hawaiian people when it extended some of the same rights and privileges accorded to American Indian, Alaska Native, Inuit, and Aleut communities. Relevant legislation includes the Native American Programs Act of 1974 (42 USC 2991 et seq.), the American Indian Religious Freedom Act (42 USC 1996), the National Museum of the American Indian Act (20 USC 80q et seq.), the Native American Graves Protection and Repatriation Act (25 USC 3001 et seq.), the National Historic Preservation Act (16 USC 470 et seq.), and the Native American Languages Act (25 USC 2901

et seq.). Also, under Title VIII of the Native American Programs Act of 1975, Native Pacific Islanders are defined as Native Americans. There are also several Hawaiian-specific federal acts, comparable to those providing for American Indians and Alaskan Natives, such as the Native Hawaiian Health Care Act and the Native Hawaiian Education Act. In all of these acts Hawaiians are defined by the most inclusive definition: "Any individual who is a descendent of the aboriginal people who, prior to 1778, occupied and exercised sovereignty in the area that now constitutes the State of Hawaii."

2. The United States and members of the international community also recognized the Kingdom of Hawai'i's independence through treaty relations with the major powers of the world, including not only the United States (1849, 1870, 1875, 1883, and 1884), but also Austria-Hungary (1875), Belgium (1862), Denmark (1846), France (1846 and 1857), Germany (1879), Great Britain (1836, 1846, and 1851), Italy (1863), Japan (1871 and 1886), the Netherlands (1862), Portugal (1882), Russia (1869), Samoa (1887), Spain (1863), the Swiss Confederation (1864), and Sweden and Norway (1852).

3. The fiftieth anniversary of U.S. statehood for Hawai'i, in 2009, marked an opportunity for scholars to investigate the details of the vote issued by the colonial administration in the Hawaiian Islands at the time. Some of the issues that need research attention include the executive decisions that allowed both U.S. military and other non-Hawaiian residents to vote (regardless of whether or not they were descendants of the Kanaka Maoli and non-Hawaiians residing in the Islands prior to the unlawful U.S. annexation), and a careful study of the reports issued by the U.S. representative to the United Nations, who reported that Hawaiians had already exercised self-determination in the vote of 1959 and therefore should be removed from the UN list of non-self-governing territories.

4. See www.un.org/Depts./dpi/decolonization/declaration.htm.

5. In 1962 the General Assembly established a special committee, now known as the Special Committee of 24 on Decolonization, to examine the application of the declaration and to make recommendations on its implementation. http://www.un.org/Depts/dpi/decolonization/declaration.htm.

6. See also http://www.hawaiiankingdom.org/.

7. Here, too, the proponents of kingdom restoration engaging in this problematic critique do not acknowledge that indigenous governing systems by and large have always managed to incorporate outsiders too, even if they do not do so under the auspices of a state government. Moreover, there seems to be little understanding that contemporary tribes that have been granted U.S. federal recognition, for example, may limit their citizenry to those of who are their specific indigeneity, but this may also be because the U.S. government maintains that its trust obligation is limited to those who have ancestry from any given Native Nation and not non-Natives.

8. Unfortunately, as discussed below, in the U.S. Supreme Court ruling in *State*

of Hawaii v. Office of Hawaiian Affairs, et al., the court ruled that the apology was merely symbolic and had no legal effect when it comes to the question of land title.

9. For a critical account of this legal case, see Kauanui (2002).

10. This process of appointments already set the proposal apart from the Indian Reorganization Act of 1934.

11. For a critical analysis of the neoconservative forces on the Islands that organized against the legislation because they regarded it as a proposal for race-based government, see Kauanui (2008).

12. For information on S. 1011 and H.R. 2314 and their predecessors, see http://thomas.loc.gov/cgi-bin (accessed 11 August 2009).

13. On 31 March 2009 the U.S. Supreme Court issued its ruling in *State of Hawaii v. Office of Hawaiian Affairs, et al.* The State of Hawai'i asked the high court whether or not the state has the authority to sell, exchange, or transfer 1.2 million acres of land formerly held by the Hawaiian monarchy as Crown and Government Lands. Prior to the state's appeal to the U.S. Supreme Court, the Hawai'i Supreme Court unanimously ruled that the state should keep the land trust intact until Kanaka Maoli's claims to these lands are settled and prohibited the state from selling or otherwise disposing of the properties to private parties; it did so based on an Apology Resolution of 1993 issued by Congress to the Hawaiian people. The U.S. Supreme Court reversed the judgment of the Hawai'i Supreme Court and remanded the case for further proceedings with the stipulation that the outcome not be inconsistent with the U.S. Supreme Court's opinion. The contested land base constitutes 29 percent of the total land area of what is now known as the State of Hawai'i and almost all the land claimed by the state as public lands. These lands were unilaterally claimed by the U.S. federal government when it unilaterally annexed the Hawaiian Islands through a joint resolution by the U.S. Congress in 1898, after they had been "ceded" by the Republic of Hawai'i, which had established itself a year after the armed and unlawful overthrow of the Hawaiian monarchy under Queen Lili'uokalani in 1893. The Court insists that the apology does not change the legal landscape or restructure the rights and obligations of the state. The ruling states that the apology would "raise grave constitutional concerns if it purported to 'cloud' Hawai'i's title to its sovereign lands more than three decades after the State's admission to the union." The Court further opined that "Congress cannot, after statehood, reserve or convey submerged lands that have already been bestowed upon a State." But if the Apology Resolution has no teeth in the court of the conqueror, how is it that the Newlands Resolution that unilaterally annexed Hawai'i does?

14. This part of the legislation should worry Native Nations across Indian Country since it gives state governments a central role alongside the Native governing entity and the federal government. Although Akaka, ever since his proposal was first introduced in 2000, has continuously asserted that his measure seeks to establish equality in the federal policies extended toward American Indians, Alaska Natives, and Native

Hawaiians, the most recent version of the legislation makes it clear that that is not at all the case. Section 9, titled "Applicability of Certain Federal Laws," actually spells out the inapplicability of certain federal laws—those pertaining to federally recognized Indian tribes that would not apply to the Native Hawaiian governing entity. All of these laws that exclude the Native Hawaiian governing entity happen to be laws that greatly benefit tribal nations. The Native Hawaiian governing entity would not be allowed to claim rights under the Indian Gaming Regulatory Act. The Native Hawaiian governing entity would not be allowed to have the secretary of the interior take land into trust on behalf of the Native Hawaiian governing entity. This is important because only land held in trust by the federal government on behalf of Native Nations is allowed to be used by Indian tribes as part of their sovereign land base where they can assert jurisdiction. The Native Hawaiian governing entity would not be allowed to rely on the Indian Trade and Intercourse Act to challenge how the State of Hawai'i acquired the Kingdom of Hawai'i Crown and Government Lands. No other Native Hawaiian group would be eligible for recognition under the Federal Acknowledgment Process. The Native Hawaiian governing entity would not be eligible for Indian Programs and Services.

15. Some within the Native Hawaiian community in Hawai'i have speculated that Abercrombie's responsiveness to the NHBA's concerns may be appropriately linked to his campaign for election as Hawai'i's state governor in 2010.

16. www.un.org/aboutun/charter.

17. www.un.org/esa.

18. www.ohchr.org.

19. Thanks to Andrea Carmen, executive director of the International Indian Treaty Council (the first organization of indigenous peoples to be reorganized as a nongovernmental organization), who, in an interview for my radio show, "Indigenous Politics: From Native New England and Beyond," explained that Article 46 can be interpreted for the benefit of Hawaiian independence from the United States. Carmen also noted that the article became a catchall for states and that it was inserted after 2004 when countries that supported the declaration, including Mexico, Guatemala, Peru, and others, prompted such a move. It was adopted by the Human Rights Council in 2006. For more information, listen to the interview, which aired on 13 January 2009 and is archived online: http://indigenouspolitics.mypodcast.com.

Also featured on a different program of my show was Tonya Gonnella Frichner, founder and president of the American Indian Law Alliance. This program includes a comprehensive account of the activist history that led to the passage of the declaration as well as a critical analysis of the politics of careful negotiations that led to the compromises over these seemingly contradictory articles of the declaration.

See http://indigenouspolitics.mypodcast.com.

20. For a list of the signatories, see the letter as it appeared in *Counterpunch*: http://www.counterpunch.org/blaisde1104152009.html.

RIET DELSING

Issues of Land and Sovereignty

The Uneasy Relationship between Chile and Rapa Nui

On New Year's Eve 1999 a large crowd gathered at the ceremonial site of Tahai on Rapa Nui to celebrate the advent of the new millennium.¹ Rapa Nui, the small island in the South Pacific also known as Easter Island, was annexed by Chile in 1888. That same morning some Rapanui youths had damaged the Chilean National Television (TVN) equipment set up on the site to cover the celebrations. They were protesting against the violation of a sacred, ceremonial place and also demanding access to the considerable sum paid by TVN to the municipality of Rapa Nui for the rights to film the event, which was to be broadcast live, worldwide, via the BBC network. Minutes before midnight the best-known Chilean television hosts, flown in from the mainland for the occasion, distributed flower garlands among the islanders and the tourists participating in the event, so that the world could enjoy the exotic character of this most unique millennium celebration.

When fireworks lit up the spectacular site, with its famous stone statues (*moai*), and the crowd was cheering, some of us noticed that this was not the only manifestation of "Rapanuiness." A few steps away, in the dark night, a small group of Rapanui wearing traditional *mahute* (bark cloth) capes and carrying torches stood silently against the starred sky, next to a lonely moai and a Chilean flag which was blowing in the stiff breeze. The flag was purposely put beneath a Rapanui flag as a challenge to Chilean sovereignty over the island. This incident illustrates some of the political and cultural tensions in Rapa Nui. The events surrounding the millennium celebration show not only the Rapanui's insistence on asserting their collective cultural identity, but also their entanglement with the Chilean nation-state and tourism. Since the 1990s there had been a growing awareness among Rapanui of their specific cultural identity, expressed in practices and discourses around the issues of land, language, and cultural performances, along with a striking increase in cultural exchanges with other Polynesians.

More than a century has passed since the annexation, and the Chilean nation-state has created not an environment leading to cooperation with the Rapanui people but one of resistance. In this essay I explore some of the issues at stake in this enduring conflict. After a review of the early years of Chilean colonization I show how successive Chilean laws have attempted to integrate Rapa Nui into the nation-state, and how they are an obstacle to traditional Rapanui relations with their land and territory. I conclude with an examination of the changing forms of political relationship between Chile and Rapa Nui.

My work is based on several years of anthropological research and life experience in Rapa Nui. Starting in 1996 I have conducted fieldwork on the island on various occasions ranging from a couple of weeks to ten months. Since then, my life has become intertwined with the people of Rapa Nui, with their joys and their struggles. Over the past decade I have explored Rapanui gender relations, issues of globalization, and, in the context of my dissertation research, cultural politics, Rapanui relationships with the Chilean nation-state, and their thrust toward self-determination. In these inquiries I have adopted a multisited approach (Marcus 1995; Marcus and Fischer 1986) since my main premise is that the movement of people, ideas, institutions, communication systems, and capital across the Pacific Ocean is central to the articulation of a modern Rapanui cultural identity. My voice is that of an anthropologist, inquisitive and curious about cultural processes—the subject of our trade—but also that of somebody with a personal investment in social and political change in Rapa Nui and elsewhere.

A Brief History

The annexation of Rapa Nui did not take place in a historical vacuum. It was the result of the Chilean Republic's imperialist aspirations in the late nineteenth century. After gaining independence from Spain in 1818, Chile was still consolidating its territory in the 1880s when it made two major conquests that increased its territory by a third. To the south, it militarily defeated the Mapuche people, who had struggled for three hundred years, first, against Spanish and, later, Chilean colonizers. To the north, Chile defeated Bolivia and Peru in the War of the Pacific (1879–83), and Chile annexed substantial parts of their territories that were inhabited by the indigenous Aymara, Quechua, and Colla peoples. The major objective of this war was to gain control of the mineral riches, nitrate in particular, of the Atacama desert, part of which was located in Bolivian and Peruvian territories (Silva Galdames 1995).

But Chile's expansionist drive did not limit itself to the American continent. A growing number of foreign merchants, mainly British, used the Chilean port of Valparaíso as a way station for trade with the Pacific coast before the opening of the Panama Canal in 1914. Valparaíso became the most important port on that coast, which allowed Chilean merchants to create their own trade routes across the Pacific, in India and East Asia, in search of new markets for Chile's copper and nitrates (Bushnell and Macaulay 1988, 109). Before the end of the century Chilean consulates had been opened in Shanghai, Canton, Manila, Calcutta, Sydney, and Brunei. Chilean sailors and merchants became familiar with Polynesian geography, and this led to dreams of western expansion into the Pacific (Porteous 1981). In the late 1800s several European and American nations annexed islands and archipelagos in the Pacific. In this context of imperialist fervor Chile annexed Rapa Nui.

A captain of the Chilean navy by the name of Policarpo Toro Hurtado visited Rapa Nui in 1875 and again in 1886. After his second visit he submitted a proposal for annexation to his superiors in the navy. President José Manuel Balmaceda of Chile approved of the idea, and Toro went to Tahiti in 1887 with the intention of buying the Rapanui's lands and animals, which had been seized by European-Tahitian businessmen and the Tahitian Catholic Church (*Revista de Marina* 1983, 316, 317). Toro then annexed the island in September 1888 by signing the "Agreement of Wills" (*Acuerdo de Voluntades*) with the Rapanui chiefs.

The official Spanish text of the agreement consists of two parts: the "Cession," in which the chiefs grant sovereignty to Chile, and the "Proclamation," in which Toro accepts the cession of sovereignty in the name of the Republic of Chile (Vergara 1939, appendices XII and XIII). In 2001 the Rapanui-language version of these documents started to circulate on the island. A translation of this version back into Spanish reveals that the Rapanui did not hand over sovereignty to the Chileans in the sense in which the concept is understood in current international law.[2] This disparity coincides with oral tradition, according to which *ariki* Atamu Tekena gave a bunch of grass to Toro but put a handful of soil in his own pocket, a gesture meant to express that he was allowing the Chileans to make use of land and crops but that he was not handing over Rapanui territory.[3] This enactment is performed for me over and over again whenever I ask Rapanui about their political relationship with Chile.

The Early Years of Chilean Colonization

Misunderstandings about the separateness of land and territory were present from the very beginning of Chilean colonization. After the annexation in 1888, Toro's brother, Pedro Pablo, stayed in Rapa Nui for four years as an "agent of colonization" (Toro 1892) and wrote an interesting report about his experiences. Besides his observations about Chilean versus Rapanui political authority, Chilean "civilization" versus Rapanui Polynesian culture, and the Chilean legal system versus Rapanui customary law, he made the first assessment of Rapanui landownership seen through the eyes of a Chilean who had firsthand knowledge of the situation. "Private and permanent ownership does not really exist in the countryside," he said. "Each individual cultivates and sows a plot of land, which he abandons after the harvest to take another one later on" (Toro 1892, 205). Toro had no understanding of the Polynesian system of land tenure, which allowed for collective use of clan lands, and he may not have been aware of the existing clan system.

Most interesting are his recommendations to the Chilean government, which give a striking vision of how the island and its people should become integrated into the Chilean nation-state. His suggestions are a stunning example of capitalist discourse on the advantages of private property. First, he suggested that the island be submitted to Chilean jurisdiction by creating a subdelegation annexed to the Department of Valparaíso. Second, he proposed to constitute indigenous private property rights by equally dividing the land in plots, "sufficient to satisfy the necessities of each family" to maintain itself independently. The *canacas* (natives) should be obliged to fence off their respective properties. The creation of private property would stimulate work, production, and exchange. It would create healthy competition since each *indígena* (indigenous person) would see himself as exclusive owner of his property and "more or less rich," according to his own efforts, economic ability, and dedication. Toro supposed that in the beginning the canacas would resist these innovations concerning the private property of land, but that such resistance would never be serious, and the canacas would slowly but surely become convinced of the advantages of the new system (Toro

1892, 212). Toro also thought it would not be difficult to substitute the legal authority of the whites for the traditional authority of the indigenous chiefs, among whom the subdelegate could assign his subordinates. It is remarkable how prescient Toro's vision would prove to be, as today the Western concept of individual private property has invaded, slowly but surely, Rapanui customary forms of communal land tenure and the notion of *kainga*,[4] or ancestral lands, is losing ground among many Rapanui.

After the initial years of colonization Chile lost interest in the island, possibly because of the country's bloody civil war in 1891 and the realization that it was not the tropical paradise Toro had imagined it to be.[5] The Chilean government first rented out the island to a French-Chilean businessman based in Valparaíso who in 1903 passed on the lease to Williamson Balfour and Company, a Scottish trading company with headquarters for South and North America in Valparaíso. The *Compañía* (as it is still referred to today) converted most of the island into a sheep farm for the export of wool, and its representatives became the virtual rulers of the island for the next fifty years, until 1953. The Chilean government was present in the form of its navy, which sent a ship once yearly and stayed in contact with the representative of the Compañía. However, during this long period the Rapanui were not treated as Chilean citizens. Chile's legal system was put into practice by the navy only in the most rudimentary way, while its administrative and institutional structures were virtually absent.

At the end of the nineteenth century some Rapanui were beginning to lose their intimate contact with and deep connection to the kainga, where they had been living according to tribal affiliations and customary practices in which the land was intrinsically inalienable. Legend says that the island was partitioned into two territorial confederacies, the *Ko Tu'u Aro Kote Mata Nui*, the major clans which occupied the northern and western part of the island, and the *Ko Tu'u Hotu Iti Mata Iti*, the minor clans which lived in the southeastern part (Routledge 1919; Métraux 1940; McCall 1976). Each confederation was divided into patrilineal clans, or *mata*. The six western mata wielded religious and political power and emphasized fishing, while the four eastern mata were mainly agriculturalists. These specific economic activities made them dependent on one another.

At least two factors were involved in the process of alienation that took place in the late nineteenth century. Owing to slave raids and the introduction of previously unknown diseases only slightly more than one hundred Rapanui had survived by the time of the Chilean takeover, out of a population of two thousand in the early 1860s. This suggests that some of the original clan lands must already have been depopulated toward the end of the century. A second factor is that the Church and the early Chilean colonizers gathered the Rapanui in a single settlement, Hanga Roa, for purposes of evangelization and colonial control. The early colonizers also prohibited the islanders from using their original clan lands for planting and raising animals.

Early documents presented by Rapanui to the Chilean government show that several islanders complained about the fact that their lands and animals were taken away. These lists of protests started the process of alienation from tribal lands. The very act of listing in itself brought about a distancing from earlier ways of relating to the land as name, age, and property were recorded.[6] Certain lands were claimed by several individuals, sometimes people with different surnames, suggesting that the land had belonged to specific clans. In those years this new way of asserting a relationship with the land may have gone unnoticed, but in hindsight the individualization on paper seems to be a first step toward privatization. Although the listing of land and animals shows Rapanui resistance against abuses of the Compañía, it also introduced the idea of individual property.

The Chilean Republic Consolidates Its Hold on the Island

A few years after the annexation it became standard practice that island disputes were arbitrated by naval officers during their yearly visits (Porteous 1981, 50). While the Compañía was mainly interested in the profits of the wool business, the navy's objective was to carry out the project of the Chilean nation-state. Territorial rights and landownership remained the major issues. Beginning in 1917 the navy started to distribute plots to be used for agricultural purposes (Vergara 1939, 81). The Rapanui had to convince navy personnel that they needed land for specific purposes. In a publication of 1926 entitled *Memorias, Balances, Inventarios y Registro de Propiedades*, the navy lists all the plots assigned to Rapanui up to that year. Afterward it became standard practice to give five hectares to young married couples. These cessions would be confirmed by the commanders of the navy ships during their visits to the island. Each land title was accompanied by a drawing indicating the size and location of the plot. The navy compiled another document in 1962, the *Libro de registros de propiedades llevado por la Armada de Chile, Isla de Pascua*. Like all navy records, these publications are no longer available on the island but copies were made, and recently the Ministerio de Bienes

Nacionales got hold of one.[7] If it had not been for copies made by individuals, this historical information would be lost, as was the case with the treaty documents. The tone and content of the land titles indicate that the navy acted as a colonial agent, applying strict military rules that had to be observed by the islanders. The reiteration of the navy's deeds in successive registers shows that it was quite keen on keeping things in order. By the 1960s, 525 provisional land titles had been extended (Andueza Guzmán 2005), and the area of Hanga Roa, where the Rapanui live in family groups according to traditional clan distributions, grew over the years from one thousand to three thousand hectares.

The Chilean government's position was that these provisional titles allowed the beneficiaries to use the plots of land for agricultural purposes, but the Chilean state reserved ownership to the land. This is ironic, to say the least, if one considers that this interpretation is a reversal of what the Rapanui offered to Chile at the moment of annexation. At that time ariki Atamu Tekena assigned the usufruct of Rapanui lands to the Chilean state but by putting a handful of soil in his pocket explicitly expressed the wish to remain in charge of the kainga. Interestingly, the Rapanui considered the provisional titles as property titles, an interpretation the state did not object to in future legal determinations about land use in Rapa Nui.[8] This is an excellent example of how the Rapanui have been able to circumvent Chilean legal decisions and interpret them according to their cultural needs.

The Inscription of 1933

In the 1930s Rapa Nui was still a British sheep farm, run as if it were a ship by its administrators and the Chilean navy authorities. By then the foreign authorities had replaced Rapanui traditional leaders, stripped them of their lands, and turned them into farmhands.[9] However, an important change was made in 1933. Tired of the cat-and-mouse game being played over Rapanui lands by the Compañía and the Chilean state, the government took action. A high-level government commission headed by a Chilean bishop determined that private landownership did not exist on the island according to Chilean law, and in November 1933 the government registered the entire island as Chilean public land (*tierra fiscal*). It declared itself "owner of Easter Island, also called Rapa Nui," with an area of 15,796 hectares. The document says that Chile acquired the island through occupation by virtue of article 590 of the Civil Code (Vergara 1939, appendix XLI). This article states that "all the land situated within the territorial limits that lacks another owner is state property" (Vergara 1939, appendix XLIV). The commission's arguments were correct in that the early transactions and sales to the Compañía had not been registered in the proper government office (Rochna-Ramírez 1996, 40), and when the government renewed the lease with the Compañía for another twenty years in 1936, it referred to the whole island except for the land occupied by "the natives, the lepers and the naval authority."[10]

In the inscription of 1933 the Chilean state ignored once again the very existence of the Rapanui as a people with ancestral rights to their land and territory. This time Chile stated that it had acquired the island through occupation, not, as it had asserted in 1888, through cession. This claim was not mentioned again in later discussions about the Chilean state's political relationship with the island, possibly because it would have put Chile in a bad light on the international legal stage.[11] The Rapanui were not informed about the inscription of their entire territory as public land and became aware of this act more than thirty years later.[12]

In hindsight, the inscription has benefited the Rapanui because neither foreigners nor non-Rapanui Chileans are allowed to own land on the island. This unintended consequence has become a major tool in the hands of contemporary Rapanui to make a case for collective private landownership. Contrary to what has happened in other Polynesian island states, such as Hawai'i, where non–Hawaiian Americans and foreigners can own land, the blunder by the Chilean state in 1933 allowed Rapanui to secure their lands, albeit under the tutelage of that very state.

Chilean Integrationist Policies and the Privatization of Rapanui Lands

The Easter Law (Ley Pascua) and the Pinochet Law (Ley Pinochet)

Several decades passed before two Chilean laws dealing with Rapanui landholding were enacted. In Law number 16.441, the so-called Ley Pascua of 1966, the Rapanui were recognized for the first time as full-fledged Chilean citizens. It authorized the president of the Republic to grant individual property titles (*títulos de dominio*) to Chilean nationals in urban territories belonging to the state (*territorios fiscales urbanos*), and stipulated that most rural lands belonging to the state (*tierras fiscales rurales*) could be given in concession to Chilean government institutions. The Ley Pascua is significant in that it represents the first time private landownership in Rapa

Nui was introduced through a Chilean law. In the name of equality, this right was extended not only to Rapanui, but also to non-Rapanui Chilean citizens. However, these dispositions did not have a major effect on the island. The titles to individual ownership referred only to the urban area of Hanga Roa, where virtually all Rapanui lived. The vast majority did not bother to get land titles for places where they and their families had been living for several decades. No titles were given to Chileans living on the island on the basis of the Ley Pascua (Barrientos 1998, 6). For several years to come, remarkably, Rapanui islanders continued living their lives in their Hanga Roa homesteads without significant changes as far as land tenure was concerned.

A much bigger step toward individual private landownership was taken in 1979, when the Chilean military dictator Augusto Pinochet issued a decree with the force of law (DL-2885) that became known as the Ley Pinochet.[13] General Pinochet showed a special interest in Rapa Nui, in accordance with his geopolitical views and nationalist goals for Chile, which included the homogenization and integration of the Chilean population into the nation-state. Consequently, the Rapanui were not referred to as a people. The decree gave the president the authority to extend free titles in urban and rural public areas (*terrenos fiscales*) to Chileans born on the island whose father or mother also had been born there. These titles could also be given to Chileans not born on the island if one of their parents had been born there, had lived there for at least five years, and exercised a profession or permanent activity on the island. In practice this meant that Pinochet was giving land titles to Rapanui, although in theory non-Rapanui who were born on the island could own Rapanui land. Once again, no reference was made to the fact that the law was applicable only to the roughly three thousand hectares (out of a total of sixteen thousand) comprising Hanga Roa and its vicinities, to which the Rapanui had been reduced in the late 1800s. This law decree had a much more invasive effect than the Ley Pascua since its intention was to oblige the Rapanui to take land titles. The law was reinforced by an offer of subsidized government housing, which could be obtained only if land titles were accepted and inscribed.

The Ley Pinochet met with massive resistance from the Rapanui, who felt that individual land distribution was being forced upon them. Their reaction was to form, in 1980, a Consejo de Ancianos (Council of Elders).[14] The council's opposition to the Ley Pinochet was based mainly on the argument that the Chilean state did not have the authority to give titles to Rapanui land. As one Rapanui clearly put it, "Why do we have to accept a title of something that is already mine? It is as if somebody wants to give me the shirt I am wearing" (*Revista Análisis*, February 1988). Nevertheless, Rapanui started to inscribe their properties and acquire private property titles during the 1980s; by 1990 the number who had done so totaled 359 (Gómez 2004). The law decree stipulated that if people could prove they had been living on or using a piece of land for more than ten years, they would have the right to a land title. The validation of land occupancy (*poseedor regular*) became a very popular way for the Rapanui to accept land titles. The recognition of a relationship between land and people appealed to Rapanui cultural idiosyncrasy (see Andueza 2005). Living on or using a plot of land for agricultural purposes (or both) for a considerable amount of time reinforced these connections. Thus some Rapanui responded to Chilean laws, although not altogether for the reasons intended by the legislator, whose purpose was to instill the concept of individual private property in Rapanui cultural practice and turn them into regular Chileans for whom private ownership is a basic cultural paradigm.

The Indigenous Law (Ley Indígena)

The situation changed again after Chile's return to democracy in 1990. The indigenous cause was high on the agenda of Patricio Aylwin, the first democratically elected president after the dictatorship. In 1993 a special law was issued, the so-called Ley Indígena (No. 19,253), which established norms of protection, promotion, and development of Chile's indigenous population. In contrast to the Ley Pinochet, which aimed at absorbing indigenous people into the Chilean population, this law recognized the existence of indigenous people and their differences. The Ley Indígena recognized that land was the lifeblood of indigenous cultures. Some Rapanui suggested that rather than include Rapa Nui in the Ley Indígena, the Ley Pascua of 1966, which was specific to the Rapanui, be amended to reflect the new situation, but this initiative went nowhere. These Rapanui argued that the differences between Rapa Nui's Polynesian population and American indigenous peoples on the mainland are too great to include them both in a single law.[15] The Ley Indígena, like previous laws, maintained the concept of individual private property, although it states explicitly for the first time that only people of Rapanui descent can own land in Rapa Nui and that the land cannot be transferred to non-Rapanui. The National Corporation for Indigenous Development (CONADI) was formed to implement the Ley Indígena in each of the places where indigenous people live.

In hindsight, it can be suggested that the Ley Indígena, although designed to benefit the Rapanui as a people, has had several negative consequences in Rapa Nui. First, it divided the Rapanui community, a division that still exists today. The Council of Elders split on the issue of land distribution. The council's leader and some other council members who had been fervently opposed to the Ley Pinochet became strong supporters of the Ley Indígena. Members of the dissident group, who opposed private land titles, maintained that it was not the right of the Chilean government to impose land distribution in Rapa Nui.

This situation was mainly caused by a complicated interaction between Rapanui leaders and Chilean party politics. In general, Rapanui identify with neither Chilean party politics nor the political and ideological paradigms on which they are based, since they have no historical and cultural relevance in Rapa Nui. Nevertheless, leaders of the Council of Elders had strongly supported Aylwin, the candidate of the Center-Left government coalition, and felt committed to the Ley Indígena. The result was that the dissident group of the council lined up with the opposition to the newly elected Democratic government, which consists of an ideological, extreme Right—erstwhile defenders of the dictatorship—and a more moderate neoliberal, big business–oriented central Right.

The Ley Indígena also created, solely for Rapa Nui, a Development Commission (CODEIPA), whose membership would be made up partly of Rapanui and partly of mainlanders. It consists of the Rapanui governor, the Rapanui mayor, the head of the Council of Elders, five members elected by the Rapanui community, and six representatives of various Chilean ministries that operate on the island, five of whom are continental Chileans. This composition guarantees a Rapanui majority in the CODEIPA. It was to be in charge of, among other things, land distribution through one of the Chilean ministries (Bienes Nacionales). The split in the Council of Elders created a problem because the ultimate leader of the council would be one of the commission's members. With two individuals claiming the leadership of the Council of Elders, the Development Commission could not be put into operation until 1998, when elections were held in the Council and the original leader won by a narrow margin.[16]

An even more serious effect of the Ley Indígena was the distribution of fifteen hundred hectares of government-owned land to the Rapanui.[17] The ministry in charge assigned these lands in plots of five hectares rather haphazardly, often not respecting the tribal affiliations of the applicants, which created problems between and discontent among Rapanui. Two hundred fifty-nine individual land titles were handed out in 2001. Today, some twelve hundred Rapanui are waiting for a second redistribution. Many who earlier resisted land titles have now registered. Although most Rapanui still do not agree with the system in their discourse, they submit to it in practice. However, the government is in the process of adjusting the criteria for distribution, as there is not enough land available, so the plots will be smaller this time around. The process has been delayed, and in 2006 the CODEIPA was still revising the records of each applicant, which has created a lot of discontent and mistrust in the community.[18] Also, a new relationship with the Chilean government is in the making (see below), and this may reverse the landholding situation altogether.

Another negative effect of the land delivery is that Rapanui have started to trade their plots of land for motorcycles, used cars, and other material goods of their liking, which has allowed some Rapanui to accumulate land. This has stimulated the development of a real estate market, albeit between Rapanui, in the past couple of years, unheard of before. This circumstance implies a further erosion of the concept of kainga, since it separates the Rapanui further from their traditional clan lands and disintegrates their traditional social organization. The Ley Indígena allows for individual private property but to the detriment of collective private property.

Loopholes in the law have also permitted outsiders to invest in the island, a phenomenon that requires close supervision on part of the Rapanui. An emblematic case, the first of its kind, was the construction and inauguration in early 2008 of a five-star hotel by the exclusive Chilean hotel chain Explora. The Explora hotels belong to the Chilean Pedro Ibañez, a wealthy businessman and entrepreneur. After consulting for several years with various Rapanui families, Explora officials convinced a successful Rapanui businessman, Mike Rapu, to acquire land from his family and obtain a second plot from another Rapanui—a total of 9.6 hectares—to execute this project. With the help of various lawyers the Ley Indígena was bypassed. When I asked Rapu why he went ahead with this project, he repeatedly stressed the trust the owner of the Explora hotels had put in him and the mistrust other Rapanui had inspired (interview Mike Rapu Pate, 2006). It is interesting that personal relations seem to have played a major factor in such a significant financial operation. Explora has set a precedent and opened the door to future foreign investments.

On the other hand, thanks to the Ley Indígena, permission to build a casino in Rapa Nui was denied on legal grounds in September 2006, namely, because that the Chilean casino law and the Ley Indígena are mutually incompatible (*El Mercurio*, 9 September 2006). This decision put an end to a heated yearlong debate in Rapa Nui and on the mainland about the advantages and disadvantages of having a casino on the island. The casino law requires a fifteen-year permit to operate, while according to the Ley Indígena indigenous lands can be rented out for a maximum period of only five years. Even though these five-year periods are renewable in the Ley Indígena, the casino law does not allow for this figure. Both CONADI and CODEIPA were against the casino, as was a large part of the Rapanui community. Rapanui University students residing on the mainland organized various protests during 2006 in Santiago and Valparaíso, protests in which I participated. The Council of Elders and the mayor of Rapa Nui were in favor of the casino. Their argument was that the project would bring cash to the island. The casino project, which involved an investment of fourteen million dollars, was a joint venture of a Chilean investor and a Rapanui businessman.

The Ley Indígena has thus been manipulated and has had unpredictable consequences for the Rapanui community and Chilean lawmakers alike. The Rapanui have certainly not benefited from the rules and regulations imposed by a nation-state that insists on sovereignty over a territory which it has abused historically.

From Colonialism to Self-Determination?

These discrepancies in the interpretation and use of existing law and the interplay between the Chilean state's intentions and Rapanui discourse and practice can also be seen in the various stages of political status the Chilean state has imposed on the Rapanui people and their territory.

Three distinct moments can be distinguished in Chile's political relationship with Rapa Nui. The first is the Annexation of 1888, when Chile asserted sovereignty over the island. As discussed earlier, the Republic of Chile then quickly lost interest in its insular possession, and the island was turned into a sheep farm. Arguably, during those first years of colonization the Rapanui were barely aware of the presence of a nation-state exercising sovereignty over the island. Chile's judicial and administrative systems were imposed in the most rudimentary way. The situation changed somewhat in 1917, when Chile declared Rapa Nui to be a subdelegation (Subdelegación Marítima) of the Naval Department (Gobernación Marítima) of the port of Valparaíso. Navy officials were then officially named as representatives of the Chilean government in Rapa Nui, and the connection with the central government was channeled through its Ministry of Defense. This situation lasted for five decades. During those years the Rapanui endured physical and psychological abuses by representatives of the Compañía and navy officials and had no constitutional rights whatsoever. Nevertheless, their cultural practices, especially their language and social organization, remained largely intact.

La Ley Pascua

This state of affairs changed drastically in 1966 with the passage of the Ley Pascua. A young Rapanui schoolteacher, one of the first Rapanui educated on the mainland, staged a rebellion in 1964.[19] Partly as a result of this revolt the Ley Pascua was approved by the National Congress in 1966. The law put an end to navy rule and created the Department of Easter Island as part of the province of Valparaíso, with its own municipality and public services (Makihara 1999, 101). The most important consequence of the Ley Pascua is that the Rapanui were finally recognized as Chilean citizens and were given the right to vote.

After the law was passed, three hundred newcomers, mostly Chilean functionaries and their families, arrived on the island to set up the new administrative system in representation of Chilean ministries and other institutions. Chilean workers were brought in from the continent for the construction of the airport, as well as some 60 American army personnel who came to set up a base for surveillance of artificial earth satellites in compliance with an agreement between the Chilean and U.S. Air Force. By 1968 the outsiders added up to a total of 665 people, as compared with a Rapanui population of 1,200, with the result that there were more foreign and continental adults than Rapanui adults on the island (Cristino et al., 1984). One can only imagine the impact this arrival of nonislanders had on Rapanui's lifestyle and world. Besides the influx of people, there was an influx of goods and services. Electricity and piped water lines were installed, and roads were built. Trucks and jeeps were imported. The improvement in communications realized by the building of the airport and the subsequent air traffic opened the island up to the world in an unprecedented way. The concentration of services and government buildings in Hanga Roa made it the only inhabited center on the island, a fact which loosened the ties between the Rapanui and their ancestral lands even more. None of this was adequately planned nor anticipated in the Ley Pascua. The Chilean legislators failed to comprehend and predict the impact Chilean laws and institutions would have on the daily life of the Rapanui. On the other hand, the Chileans who were assigned to the island did not have enough cultural sensitivity to perceive these possible alterations of Rapanui culture and social organization. The Ley Pascua fomented westernization in a way the Rapanui are still coping with today, and it did not provide tools to safeguard cultural difference and enhance self-determination.

La Comisión de Verdad Histórica y Nuevo Trato para los Pueblos Indígenas (Commission on Historic Truth and New Relationship with Indigenous Peoples)

Today, almost fifty years after passage of the Ley Pascua, another change in political status for Rapa Nui is in the making. The protests by Rapanui in the 1980s over land and territory strengthened their awareness of cultural difference, while in Chile in those same years the first protests against the military regime led to the recovery of democracy in 1990, after seventeen years of dictatorship. Indigenous rights and demands appeared on the national agenda through the creation of the Ley Indígena in 1993, which informed Chilean civil society about indigenous issues and demands. This process culminated in 2001 in the creation of a government entity known as the Commission on Historic Truth and New Relationship with Indigenous Peoples (La Comisión de Verdad Histórica y Nuevo Trato para los Pueblos Indígenas). Then-president of Chile Ricardo Lagos charged the commission with studying the historic relationship between Chile's indigenous peoples and the Chilean state and suggesting recommendations for new state policies (*una política de estado*).

The truth commission put out its final report in 2003, and its recommendations for Rapa Nui included the ratification of the "Agreement of Wills" of 1888 by the National Congress, the creation of a statute of autonomy, the recognition of the exclusive right of the Rapanui to landownership on the island, and the promotion and financing of development programs in Rapa Nui (*Informe de la Comisión*). These recommendations were formulated by the Rapanui authorities who were recognized as such by the Chilean government: the mayor, the head of the Council of Elders, and the governor, in his capacity as head of the Rapanui Development Commission.

Another set of recommendations had been formulated in workshops that took place on the island in 2002. The organizers of these workshops had been elected and appointed in a meeting with representatives of the Chilean government who visited the island in February 2002 to create the Rapanui chapter of the truth commission. These organizers were later reconfirmed in a meeting with the Rapanui community. Nevertheless, their final report was not taken into consideration and was replaced by a text presented by the authorities recognized by the Chilean government.

El Parlamento Rapanui

Meanwhile, in 2001 a group of Rapanui created the Rapanui Parliament, several of whose members formerly belonged to the second Council of Elders, which virtually dissolved after it lost the elections of 1998. Their main demand was that the Chilean state return Rapanui territory and that land distribution should be based on ancestral principles. They also declared autonomy in their act of constitution and demanded a government of their own (*Constitución Parlamentaria*, 2001). The document does not specify what exactly is meant by *autonomy*, but this was the first time a Rapanui organization had made claims to self-government during the Chilean epoch.

Although the group is not considered to be a serious interlocutor by the Chilean government and represents only a minority of the Rapanui community, it has earned recognition abroad by networking informally in Polynesia and the Pacific. Lately they have also represented Rapa Nui in international organizations in New York and Geneva, such as the United Nations Permanent Forum on Indigenous Issues, the United Nations Working Group for Indigenous Populations, and the Indigenous Peoples Pacific Caucus, where it has revealed its complaints and demands to the Chilean state. In June 2006 some members of the Rapanui Parliament traveled from Rapa Nui to join other Rapanui living in Europe and the United States to participate in a meeting of the nongovernmental International Forum of Indigenous Peoples (FIPAU), held in Pau, France. From there they went to Geneva to participate in UN meetings held parallel to and in conjunction with the important meeting of the recently created United Nations Human Rights Council in July 2006. In both instances Rapanui were participating in international arenas as indigenous people with specific rights to land, territory, and self government, thus circumventing a nation-state they consider to be in violation of their rights as a people.

Special Status for Rapa Nui: A Special Territory with a Special Statute

For several years Rapanui authorities, the mayor in particular, insisted on the need for a *política de estado* of the Chilean government toward Rapa Nui.[20] At the same time the work of the truth commission was proceeding, Rapanui authorities, together with Chilean public personalities, including ex-president Aylwin, started to elaborate a proposal for a Special Statute for the Administration of Easter Island. It took almost three years to formulate and was completed in August 2005. The proposal includes a reform of the Chilean Constitution in order to create Special Territories in Easter Island and the Archipelago of Juan Fernández. These territories would have a certain degree of administrative autonomy but would depend directly on the central government (*Propuesta* 2005, 5–6).

In the meantime, the government solicited suggestions from the Rapanui community as to what should be included in the proposal, which led to passionate discussions on the island. In May 2006, a year before the final approval of the special territory status, the local office of CONADI organized a seminar that lasted several days and gathered some seven hundred Rapanui to discuss a government proposal similar to the one developed by the public personalities that basically maintains the existing administrative structure. The difference between the two proposals was that the governor of Rapa Nui would no longer depend on the Fifth Region (Valparaíso) but directly on the central government through its Ministry of the Interior.

From the seminar held in Rapa Nui several discussion groups resulted, and two main Rapanui proposals emerged by September 2006. One was very similar to the government's proposal and was intended to increase the possibilities of being taken into account by the Chilean government. Nonetheless, this group of Rapanui insisted that there should be a local government at the top consisting of six elected Rapa Nui members, alongside the governor (or high commissioner), appointed by the Chilean president, and a representative of the Council of Elders. The other, more radical proposal insisted on the reinstallation of the Kingdom of Rapa Nui, headed by an ariki and administered by a Council of Elders chosen by the Rapanui families, with the participation of one representative of the Chilean government. In the discussions of these two proposals the importance of the traditional Rapanui social organization based on the thirty-six families was central, as was the issue of land and territory (kainga). Even the more moderate proposal recommended that new property titles not be extended until the previously completed distribution of fifteen hundred hectares had been properly analyzed. Both proposals also insisted that any future land distribution should be carried out according to the territorial divisions of each clan.[21]

To assist the Rapanui in these discussions and in their request, the Chilean government appointed an international consultant, who visited the island in December 2006 and made recommendations for the content of the special statute. He emphasized in his resulting report that Chile's political Constitution determines that the heads of regions and provincial governors have the exclusive trust of the president of the Republic and thus cannot be elected by popular vote (Gómez 2006).[22] Unless structural changes occur in the highly centralized model of the Chilean state, it will be difficult for the Rapanui to get political autonomy. From the perspective of the state, the only thing they can aspire to, for the time being, is administrative autonomy.

Rapanui have complained about the fact that they do not have the appropriate analytical tools to discuss the Chilean proposal for the special statute and that the appointment of a consultant came very late in the process. The discussion groups worked for several months in 2006 on a daily basis without fully grasping the true significance of the centralized character of the Chilean state. They also grappled with the difficult legal language in which the proposal is couched and would sometimes switch from Spanish to Rapanui in order to better understand the meaning of specific parts of the proposal.

Toward the end of 2006, the Chilean government organized some workshops on the special statute. They did so with public functionaries on the island as well as with Rapanui students on the mainland. On both occasions no copies of the government's document were made available to the participants beforehand. When a student in Santiago asked why the group had not received this relevant documentation so they could have studied it before the meeting, the Rapanui governor, Carolina Hotus, who was present at the workshop, answered that she did not want to confuse them (personal information). This lack of proper orientation seems indicative of the relations the Chilean government maintains with the Rapanui.

During a visit by President Michelle Bachelet of Chile to the island in November 2006, on her way back home from the yearly meeting of the Asia-Pacific Economic Cooperation held in Vietnam, she promised more autonomy for Rapa Nui, but she did not differentiate between administrative and political autonomy and thus concealed the important difference between the two. These are just a few examples of how the Chilean government is still not sending clear signals to the Rapanui people concerning issues of such vital importance for their political future. There may be more than one reason for this, but I suggest that mistrust of the Rapanui people's capacity to understand Western ways of thinking is one of them. By the same token, however, Chileans still have to acquire a real understanding of Rapanui cultural ways.

In January 2007 a second seminar between the Rapanui discussion groups and Chilean government officials from the Ministry of the Interior took place. It resulted in a proposal that most Rapanui present at the meeting agreed upon (*Propuesta unificada de Estatuto Especial de Administración de Rapa Nui*). The main points of this proposal are the following: the governor of Rapa Nui, appointed by the Chilean president, would form part of a Council (*Koro Nui*) consisting of six elected members; as far as landholding goes, individual private landownership would be recognized only for those individuals who already have secured property titles to date. In the rest of the island collective landownership would be applied according to "the traditional use and customs that existed on the island before 9 September of 1888"; all public land being used for government purposes would be handed over to a Rapanui corporation.[23] The proposal about collective landownership is an implicit critique of all Chilean legislation to date and a major manifestation of Rapanui cultural resilience against all odds.

After a yearlong process of discussions, one might think that this would have been the final consensus proposal on the part of the Rapanui. But it was not. Mayor Petero Edmunds blocked the proposal by sending a letter to the Ministry of the Interior in February 2007 in which he argued that the signers of the draft proposal were not representative of the Rapanui people and as a matter of fact were opposing the government of *La Concertación*—the ruling government coalition—and that he and the head of the Council of Elders, the Rapanui's legitimate representatives, had not been invited to participate in the discussions.[24] He also stated that the proposal contradicts the Chilean Constitution and the principle of a unitarian state. Further, he expressed opposition to the proposed expropriation of the land for the Hotel Hanga Roa, defended the rights of Chilean inhabitants on the island, and stated that the majority of Rapanui do not wish to be separated from Chile. He also emphasized that all the preparatory work for the special statute had already been done by the Grupo de Personalidades, of which he himself formed part.

In July 2007, Law no. 20.193 reformed the political Constitution of Chile, allowing the category of Special Territory to Rapa Nui and the Archipelago Juan Fernández, whose government and administration has to be determined by a special statute established by a *Ley orgánica constitucional* (constitutional organic law). Not until May of 2008 was a new proposal for a special statute finally presented to Congress, without any further input or approval from the Rapanui community in open meetings. The newly elected representative of CONADI, Rafael (Rinko) Tuki, who participated in the workshops on the topic in 2006 and whose signature appears on the draft proposal of January 2007, does not agree with the content (personal information).

One can distinguish at least three points of view in present-day Rapanui politics in the context of the discussions around Special Territory Status. One group of Rapanui proposes to try to convince the Chilean state to incorporate Rapanui wishes for self-government, especially in relation to collective landownership, but is willing to compromise as to the ultimate political authority over the island. Implicitly, these Rapanui accept de facto Chilean sovereignty over Rapanui territory. A small group, mainly belonging to the Rapanui Parliament, insists that the Agreement of Wills of 1888 was illegal and wants to proceed from that point, in the full knowledge that the Chilean state will not respond to this request. It is not quite clear what the political agenda of the current official leaders of Rapa Nui is. Although they have waged a historical struggle for Rapanui rights, they now insist on the rights of the Chilean nation-state over Rapa Nui.

Conclusion

I have shown here that the relationship between Chile and Rapa Nui is marked by Chile's insistent claim of sovereignty over Rapanui territory. Successive laws and decrees have put a strong emphasis on the privatization of land, in order to replace ideas of collective private landownership. The separation of the Rapanui from their ancestral lands (kainga) and the relentless insistence on the benefits of small-scale private landownership have eroded Rapanui customary law, as was predicted by Pedro Pablo Toro more than a century ago.

Chile's actions on the island are determined by the shifting concerns of successive governments and by the persisting concept of a unitarian state. Since the late 1960s—coinciding with the integration of Rapa Nui into the national administrative system—Chile has gone through various political stages, including the first freely elected Socialist government in Latin America and a brutal dictatorship. Such laws as the Easter Law of 1966, the Pinochet Law Decree of 1979, and the Indigenous Law of 1993 clearly reflect the political philosophy of these respective governments. Nevertheless, Chilean legislators of all political colors have insisted on the importance of individual private landownership, the trademark of Western civilization.

These legal interventions, based on a political system alien to the Rapanui worldview, have caused cultural misunderstandings that are little understood and need to be clarified by both Rapanui and Chileans. I argue that during the twentieth century Chilean lawmakers failed to conceptualize the important differences between individual and collective private landownership, while only the latter makes cultural sense for many Rapanui. I also contend that over the past several years Chilean politicians have been covering up the important difference between administrative and political autonomy, under the circumstance that self-determination is so important if the Rapanui are to achieve their cultural goals.

It can also be suggested that the Chilean state's interventions in Rapa Nui have created divisions between Rapanui during the period under consideration in this essay. Because of Rapa Nui's colonial dependence on Chile, Rapanui leaders are virtually obliged to work within both systems and participate in the intricate institutional and political structure that Chile has imposed on Rapa Nui. Although they are considered by Chilean politicians as their main liaison with Rapa Nui, these leaders are often out of touch with their people. The consequence has been a lack of strong leadership over the past several years, causing disinterest in common cultural goals among a considerable part of the Rapanui community. It has also caused internal power struggles between Rapanui that are difficult to assess and overcome. Cooptation of indigenous leaders is a well-known colonial strategy, and one can see it at work in Rapa Nui.

Chilean legislation has met with Rapanui resistance over the past decades, as we saw in the general rejection of the different laws, all aimed at the privatization of Rapanui land. Several Rapanui now insist on reviving this connection with the land and their traditional social organization, which are so intimately connected. At the same time, some Rapanui have started to articulate their cultural difference as a Polynesian people and to organize accordingly. These Rapanui are pointing out the cultural blunders committed in every single piece of Chilean legislation and are asking for political self-determination, even if within the Chilean nation-state. Only a profound change of the Chilean Constitution would allow this to happen.

Whatever the decisions made by Chilean governments, the Rapanui will continue on the path toward self-determination, supported by other Pacific peoples and the international community. At the same time, Chilean civil society will, one hopes, guide its political leaders in the direction of a participatory democracy, in which cultural difference becomes an asset instead of a threat to sovereignty. These two processes of social and political change, in Rapa Nui as well as in Chile, have a certain degree of urgency.

Notes

1. In accordance with common practice in the literature I use the terms *Rapa Nui* when referring to the island and *Rapanui* when referring to the people, the language, etc.

2. This translation problem can be compared with a similar one surrounding the Treaty of Waitangi, accorded between the Maori of Aotearoa/New Zealand and the British Crown (see Fenton and Moon 2002).

3. In the early days the *ariki-mau* was the head of the *Miru* clan, the paramount chief and undisputed leader of the island. In the later period the island was no longer united, and the leaders of the clans challenged each other in a yearly contest. After the dissemination of the Rapanui population at the end of the nineteenth century and the breakdown of the clan system, there was only one ariki, whom the Rapanui called kin, after the English term *king*. I have heard contemporary Rapanui argue that it is not clear if the term *ariki* means "chief" or "king."

4. The concept of *kainga* has more than one meaning. I use it here as a territorial unit, constituting the estate of a clan or descent group (see Métraux 1971; Kirch 2000, 272)

5. President José Manuel Balmaceda (1886–91) committed suicide in 1891, at the end of the civil war, which lasted for seven months and caused between five and ten thousand Chilean deaths (Loveman 2001, 159; Subercaseaux, 1997, 16). The Chilean cultural historian Bernardo Subercaseaux argues that the war took place at the crossroads of Chile's passage to a "social, economic and political modernity" and that the year 1891 "has been conceived as a kind of metaphor of the modern country" (1997, 34–36). Chile, says Subercaseaux, forged itself as a modern nation-state in the reconstruction period after the war, in which a new political and ideological landscape formed and new social, cultural, and political actors appeared. This difficult process of striving for internal national cohesion may have distracted attention from Chile's adventure in the Pacific.

6. E.g., Daniel María Teave, thirty-six years of age, owner of the lands between

Hotu 'Iti and Hanga Te'e; Timoteo Pate, thirty-six years of age, owner of part of Poike; Simeon Riroroko, twenty-one years of age, owner of Anakena, etc. (*El Consejo* 1988, 297).

7. This information comes from an interview I conducted in 2002 with Naval Governor Patricio Carrasco, who told me that no navy records on the island exist before 1990.

8. On several occasions Chilean governments have preferred not to officially intervene in Rapanui concepts of land tenure, presumably because these did not interfere in Chilean mainland politics. On the other hand, most Rapanui do not readily make the connection between sovereignty and territory. Only very recently have some Rapanui started to openly question the Chilean claim that the island is Chilean territory.

9. Since the annexation the Rapanui had elected ariki in place who were in constant disagreement with the Chilean sheep farmers. The situation had become unsustainable by 1902, when the commander of the yearly navy ship *General Baquedano* named Juan Tepano, a Rapanui, as "chief or *cacique* with the task of vigilance and representative of the islanders for the *subdelegado marítimo* [port captain]" (Document of the Ministry of National Defense). This was a strategic colonial decision, since the navy needed a buffer between the company and the Rapanui. As a youth Tepano had served in the Chilean army during the War of the Pacific and had been acculturated, so to speak. It was the first time the Chileans intervened in Rapanui leadership decisions. The commander also ordained that Tepano was to be subordinate to the company representative and *subdelegado*, and he took five of the resistance leaders to Chile (*Ministerio de Marina. Oficios de la Dirección General de la Armada*, 1902).

10. This information is extracted from a document of 1936 of the Chilean Ministry of Defense. It refers to "13.747 hectares" out of 15.796.

11. Contemporary international law distinguishes four ways of exercising sovereignty over territories, namely, by occupation, prescription, conquest, or cession (Wallace 1997, 92–100). *Occupation* refers to the situation in which a state establishes title to a territory which is *terra nullius*, this is, owned by no one or inhabited by savages. The argument for occupation is difficult to sustain in Rapa Nui because it was a stratified and organized Polynesian society at the time of the Chilean takeover. After all, it was the ariki who signed the treaty with the Chileans. *Prescription* refers to the situation in which sovereignty can be invoked by claimants who discovered and occupied a territory and who want to consolidate their claim. A state can validate an initially doubtful title, provided that the display of authority is public, peaceful, and continuous. Prescription thus involves a de facto exercise of sovereignty (Wallace 1997, 97). This situation is also referred to as occupation *cum animo domini*. The Chilean state argues that it exercised public, peaceful, and continuous authority over the island. However, contemporary international law establishes that "another claimant or a dispossessed sovereign can bar the establishment of title by prescription" (Wallace 1997, 97). This is a possibility to be explored by contemporary Rapanui.

Sovereignty through *conquest* refers to the acquisition of enemy territory by military force in wartime. This is clearly not the case for Rapa Nui. *Cession* is the transfer of sovereignty by one sovereign to another. This is the argument for Chilean sovereignty over Rapa Nui most frequently used today, by Chileans and Rapanui alike. However, the recent translation of the Rapanui version of the cession and proclamation documents unsettles this argument, as it shows that, according to this translation of the Rapanui version of the treaty, the Rapanui chiefs did not cede their territory to the Chilean state. I argue that the only way for Chile to claim sovereignty today is through prescription, but that the Rapanui can object to this by means of diplomatic protests in the appropriate international forums (Wallace 1997, 97).

12. Another act, carried out without the consultation of the Rapanui, was the creation of the Rapanui National Park and its nomination as a National Historic Monument in 1935 (Makihara 1999, 86).

13. This decree corresponded to a more general policy of privatization of agricultural lands, mostly belonging to indigenous people on the mainland, mainly the Mapuche. In 1979 Pinochet issued a decree (DL 2.536) that did away with Mapuche communal landownership. This was followed by another one in 1980 (DL 3.516) allowing for the division of land into small plots of half a hectare, thereby violating Mapuche cultural principles. These decrees formed part of a profound legal transformation carried out between 1978 and 1981 that reformulated all former dispositions about property rights over natural resources. The purpose of these reforms was the implementation of an economic model focused on exportation (Toledo 2005, 5).

14. This council was still headed by its first leader, Alberto Hotus, in 2007 and still exists today. It is composed of representatives of the thirty-six Rapanui families that trace their ancestry to the original tribes. Its purpose is to defend both the Rapanui's right to their land, territory, and culture and other Rapanui interests (see *El Consejo de Jefes de Rapa Nui* . . . , 1988).

15. Personal communication, Alfonso Rapu.

16. The head of the council has created a system of patronage over the years. Alongside his central role in the council, he has held several important government posts and has built a power base on the island and on the mainland that is hard to match and difficult to contest. His consistent support on the mainland can be explained by the fact that he has been loyal to the Center-Left government coalition in power since the return to democracy in 1990. Especially through his role as national advisor of CONADI, he has been able to influence the intricate Rapanui family network by handing out favors in exchange for votes.

17. This gesture corresponded again partly to a Chilean election campaign.

18. This information comes from interviews I conducted in 2001 with Alvaro Durán (lawyer for CONADI) and Alvaro Lafuente and Rodrigo Sepúlveda (functionaries of the Ministerio de Bienes Nacionales), and, in 2006, with Luis Guillermo Alvarez (also a functionary in Bienes Nacionales).

19. A Chilean association by the name of Friends of Easter Island had arranged through the Ministry of Education for eleven scholarships to be awarded to students to study on the mainland, since no secondary education existed on the island. One of the students, Alfonso Rapu Haoa, was only thirteen, the youngest of the group. He returned to the island eight years later with a teaching degree in hand. He says that in Santiago he was "always very concerned about the great poverty and abandonment that my people suffered, my family, my brothers and sisters, and I started to think about how to take them out of that world, get them out of the darkness and put them in the light, so they would be able to walk" (interview, 17 May 2002).

20. The concept of *política de estado* became part of the Chilean political vocabulary at the beginning of the 2000s. The mayor probably adopted the term from Chile.

21. This information was gathered during my visit to the island in August–December 2006, during which I participated regularly in the meetings of one of the discussion groups.

22. In meetings between Gómez and Rapanui that participated in the discussion groups, he said that nation-states have made indigenous peoples invisible, that there is no mutual understanding between the Chilean state and Rapanui as yet, and that it is important to pay attention to the kind of language employed in conversations between the two parties. He also emphasized the power of organizing.

23. The proposal also contains recommendations for a special budget, the creation of a special body for the defense and protection of Rapanui culture and cultural patrimony, and, crucially, for the regulation of immigration to the island. Uncontrolled immigration is one of the main complaints the Rapanui have. Although I firmly agree with the importance of this issue, I do not address it in this essay.

24. By not participating in any of the workshops or other, more general meetings organized with the Rapanui community in 2006, the mayor and the head of the Council of Elders, Alberto Hotus, marginalized themselves.

PART TWO *Indigenous Writing and Experiences with Collaboration*

THE THREE ESSAYS in part 2, bounded on both sides by sections that establish a dialogue between North and South, are about Latin America. Taken together, they tell a particularly Latin American story of more than a generation of activism and cross-cultural collaboration between Native communities and their intellectuals on one side and non-Native radical intellectuals on the other. While the three essays are quite different, a fact I explore below, the similarities among them help us understand an especially salient moment in the history of continental indigenous peoples across the Latin American region.

In contrast to Native peoples based in the continental United States, whose struggles have often revolved around the recognition of treaty-based rights and the achievement of federal recognition—something that Kauanui's essay on Hawai'i in part 1 helps us put in a more complex context—indigenous peoples in Latin America have historically struggled mainly at the individual community level. This is because the process of colonization in most cases reorganized indigenous society from the start, breaking down regional or imperial coalitions and rearticulating local societies and their leaders to an emerging colonial state. By the beginning of the twentieth century, this history had generated two interrelated, though sometimes contradictory, trends in the relationship between Native peoples and national states. While Native struggles for cultural preservation and economic viability were usually organized around the protection of communal political autonomy, often the only way to protect local lands was by demanding that the national state intervene against rapacious regional landowners. As a result, indigenous peoples in twentieth-century Latin America were often caught between ethnocultural imperatives on one side and the need to form part of broader popular, class-based coalitions on the other.

These competing alliances and loyalties were made even more complicated by the emergence of national-popular states. Beginning with the Mexican Revolution of 1910 and spreading through the region in the wake of the Great Depression of the 1930s, coalitions of middle-class politicians and popular sectors instituted welfare-oriented states. While in some cases, such as Mexico and Bolivia, the measures instituted by these states included agrarian reform, everywhere they also aimed to integrate indigenous peoples into the nation through education. As Native peoples confronted the promise of resources in conjunction with the requirement of integration, the emergence of indigenous political identities occurred both from within and against the legacy of the national-popular state. And given the two-pronged nature of indigenous political mobilization, non-Native collaborators have been an important presence throughout the twentieth century.

The three regions treated in part 2 exhibit some important contrasts in this general history. In the state of Chiapas, in southeastern Mexico, political and economic reform has been postponed through much of Mexico's modern history. The Mexican Revolution came late to Chiapas and mainly from outside, and when the indigenous communities were integrated into the emerging postrevolutionary state in the 1930s it was at the cost of accepting the emergence of a new local elite under the hegemony of the official revolutionary party. In the Cauca Valley in Colombia, where the indigenous groups that form part of the CRIC are located, the Nasa and Guambiano peoples have experienced a parallel history of marginalization and postponement. At the same time, given the Colombian state's ongoing difficulties with effective national integration, they were sometimes able to transform their marginalization into a form of cultural preservation. Still, in both the Mexican and Colombian cases, the indigenous peoples featured here have lived on the margins of emerging national states. The Quechua communities of the Cochabamba Valley in Bolivia, on the other hand, have often been considered the showcase of the agrarian reform realized by the Bolivian Revolution of 1952 and have historically had a reputation as combative and central to the populist politics of the Bolivian state. The importance of the valley's peasant unions and the close relationship they have with Quechua communal organizations emerge in large part from this history.

The three essays presented here discuss the past twenty to thirty years, when the role of the nonindigenous collaborator has been transformed as the viability of the national-popular state has unraveled. The three essays explore the implications of this transformation, in distinct contexts and with different results. Not only are the rules and parameters of the collaborations different, but so is the nature of the indigenous society and of the political activity to which the collaborators are connected. Equally important, the collaborators themselves occupy diverse positions within their own societies.

As a nonindigenous Ecuadorian linguist specializing in Quichua, Fernando Garcés V. has chosen to collaborate with *Conosur Ñawpagman*, a Quechua-language newspaper produced and circulated in the southern corner of the Cochabamba Valley. In this politically militant region, which gave birth to now-president Evo Morales's Movimiento Al Socialismo, the newspaper has evolved into an instrument at the service of the peasant union that connects different Quechua communities in their ongoing struggle to preserve their land, culture, language, and local knowledge. Under these conditions, Garcés considers that the editorial team of the newspaper serves as a bridge between the rich metaphorical lexicon of oral Quechua and the conventions of the written word and can be a powerful example of more effective ways to standardize written Quechua on the basis of contemporary practice. At the same time, the language itself must be defended through writing and through the creative inscription of orality in written form, but with the specific purpose of defending the culture and communal resources from colonial appropriation. As a result, then, the newspaper collaborates with Quechua peasant organizations in a sort of "globalization from below."

The dialogue and collaboration featured in the essay by Joanne Rappaport and Abelardo Ramos Pacho, as they point out, has been ongoing for three decades, although the specific project discussed here is a history of an intercultural and bilingual education project formulated by Consejo Regional Indígena del Cauca (CRIC). Articulated with and by the CRIC, this historical research project was successful, the authors explain, precisely because it articulated different cultural registers and, through their mutual interrogation, reimagined them all. The intermediate bridge position also discussed by Garcés is here inhabited by both Native and non-Native intellectuals and researchers, who together struggle to harness their research agenda to the priorities of the CRIC, which are themselves the collective product of a conversation among traditional communal authorities, shamanic specialists, local teachers, and non-Native collaborators. As Ramos explains, one can see research as a *minga*—collective work by and for the benefit of the community. This is an example of indigenous theorizing, which takes shape in a multiethnic and intercultural environment in which translation entails the improvement as well as the reinterpretation of ideas and concepts.

The essay by Jan Rus and Diane Rus takes, in their own words, the form of a diary that traces the emergence of the Taller Tzotzil, an indigenous publishing project, in the context of a dramatically changing world among Tzotzil Maya communities in Chiapas between the 1970s and the present. In contrast to the other essays, which strive to theorize about indigenous knowledge and literacy and to decolonize existing intellectual categories and practices from the perspective of indigenous epistemologies, the Ruses' narrative traces the economic, political, and cultural changes on the ground, so to speak, as Tzotzil Maya communities struggle with the consequences brought on by the insertion of their region into the international globalized economy. In a detailed yet ultimately understated way the Ruses take the reader through their transformation from locally committed ethnographers who were deeply connected in Chamula in the 1970s to scribe-collaborators who helped bring into public view histories and narratives that had previously been considered secret. The process through which this occurred, and the internal as well as broader tensions and conflicts that accompanied it, unfold organically through an account of how the Tzotzil publishing house originated, evolved, and changed over several decades. Among the larger events woven into this account are the increasing migration of community members to the United States and the Zapatista uprising of 1994.

As is clear in all three essays in part 2, Native knowledge, education, and literacy are deeply embedded in indigenous histories, political struggle, and local community life. Non-Native collaborators work within these specific contexts and establish dialogues and, as Ramos would put it, mingas that are appropriate to each case. At the same time, the personal and intellectual trajectories of the collaborators themselves play a role in the relationships established. As a practicing member of the U.S. academy, Joanne Rappaport uses her experience as a collaborator to rethink and retheorize the nature of research and the ways in which intercultural work can change the perspectives we bring and the questions we ask. Garcés uses the experience of the newspaper to question the separation between orality and writing and the nature of intertextuality, while at the same time counterposing the forms of local knowledge contained in Quechua peasant *yachay* to the supposed universality of Western categories. And Jan Rus and Diane Rus, by choice activist anthropologists who have eschewed full participation in the U.S. academic mainstream, strengthen their position as narrators who accompany Tzotzil Maya communities as they make sense of a rapidly changing world.

In the final analysis, these essays help us trace the multiple ways in which indigenous narratives, histories, and political action in Latin America have not only participated in and benefited from intercultural collaboration, but also contributed in powerful ways to the development of grass-roots mobilization more broadly. In Colombia, the Constitution of 1991, written in dialogue with indigenous organizations and political activists, has helped frame in new ways the possibilities of multiethnic nationhood. In Bolivia, the indigenous peasant movement that generated Morales's Movimiento Al Socialismo has made clear that effective globalization must respect and collaborate with local needs and forms of knowledge, and it has helped elect Morales, Bolivia's first indigenous president. And in Chiapas, the Maya communities that helped generate the Ejército Zapatista de Liberación Nacional continue to challenge political transitions that serve only the interests of the political and economic center of the country. These large transformations, too, are part of indigenous history and must be interpreted as such.

FERNANDO GARCÉS V.

Quechua Knowledge, Orality, and Writings

The Newspaper Conosur Ñawpagman

In this essay I reflect on some aspects of Quechua knowledge, orality, and writing found within a concrete case inscribed in writing: the *Conosur Ñawpagman* newspaper.[1] To this end, I offer reflections on this means of communication, focusing on its objectives as well as its linguistic and epistemic usage practices. I concentrate especially on the inscription of oral discourse and thereby offer a pragmatic and epistemic defense of Quechua peasant *yachay*.[2] I begin by offering three clarifications by way of introduction: how and why I use the term *peasant*; what, more concretely, I mean by Quechua *yachay*; and a short reflection on my authority, as an outsider, to represent Quechua voices.

In contemporary social science discourse, scholars are working to move beyond a classist-Marxist vision so as to rightly recognize other forms of exclusion. Among those forms of exclusion, ethnic identity occupies a privileged place. Events of the past decades have contributed to the centrality of interest in culture and identity within social and political analyses of different national and multinational spaces (Garcés 2006). Several scholars have linked this newfound attention to other forms of exclusion to the changes contemporary global capitalism has suffered over the past thirty years (Castro-Gómez 2003; Jameson 1984; Žižek 1993). In the case of Abya Yala, scholars have increasingly emphasized that the colonial restructuring of local societies involved systems of inequality, based on social class, and of exclusion, based on categories like race and gender (Quijano 2000; Santos 2003).[3] Under such conditions, my use of the term *peasant* necessarily calls for a rethinking of the imaginary of class, enriching it with a concern for the processes by which contemporary identities are politicized (Regalsky, 2003).

A second reason for my using the term *peasant* involves the term's historical baggage in the Bolivian context. What can be called the indigenous vein in Bolivia has combined the experiences of organizations with so-called traditional indigenous structures and those of others whose historical experiences have prompted them to organize their interests as Andean communities through the structure of the rural union. An important example of this is the Tiawuanaku manifesto, which Sarela Paz describes as a key milestone in the maturation of the notion of indigenous peoples in the Andean world. Via that manifesto, urban and rural Aymara sectors converged with diverse peasant sectors around *Katarismo*, expressing "the culture's historical horizons and ideological themes." For this author, "The Manifesto gathers peasant Quechua/Aymara voices that revindicate their autochthonous culture and the origin of double oppression: economic in terms of peasants and cultural in terms of excluded peoples" (Paz 2005, 2).

Here we see that the term *peasant* retains a presence as a category of self-denomination among rural Bolivians and within Bolivian social movements, even as in the new context of struggle they have also reformulated their identities as aboriginal or indigenous.[4] In the Department of Cochabamba, where the bilingual newspaper treated in this essay primarily circulates, it is the form most frequently found. None of the above denies the validity of discourses and practices that revindicate the aboriginal and indigenous character of many communities and collectivities in Bolivia. I think that in this case we can gain more from a comprehensive, capacious vision than from a restrictive, exclusive one.

As part of this more capacious vision, it is important to reflect systematically on the term *Quechua yachay*, by which I mean the collective knowledge produced and reproduced orally by Quechua-speaking communities. While I do not believe there is a direct and exclusive association between a language, a type of knowledge, and a single, distinct nation or people, I nonetheless prefer the term *Quechua yachay* to other, more general and less precise ones. *Andean knowledge*, for example, at least in the Bolivian case, includes as well Aymara communities, while *indigenous knowledge* refers as well to the lowland indigenous peoples. Thus, *Quechua yachay* has a certain practical use.

To think of Quechua knowledge as oral also forces us to recognize the geopolitics of knowledge that has colonially subalter[n]ized certain languages, among them Quechua (Garcés 2005a). My understanding of

Quechua yachay as being fundamentally oral might seem to rearticulate the colonial imaginary within which indigenous languages were classified as "lower" because they did not express modern, abstract, or spiritual ideas (Mannheim 1991, 61–79; Mignolo 1999). On the contrary, I want to emphasize that colonial differentiation has also provided subalter[n]ized languages with a certain epistemological power reproduced at the margins or in the interstices of colonial power (Rivera 1987; Mignolo 2002). While there has been a history of permanent contacts between orality and the world of written communication, from colonial times and in a much more intense way in the contemporary period, the vast majority of the Andean world continues to privilege oral knowledge in everyday communicational spaces. As I will show, this is because Quechua yachay and its oral production and reproduction are counterhegemonic responses to a global colonial epistemology.

My final clarification has to do with the *pacha* from where I think and articulate my own intellectual and political practice with regard to Quechua.[5] My connection with the Quichua and Quechua languages is rooted in my involvement with diverse bilingual education programs, my support for local research projects, and my relationships with the newspaper's editorial team. Through these experiences I have found myself in a growing struggle with my own personal history of colonization, aware that my ability to partake of this process of reflection and intervention places me in a position of power. I thus develop my ideas about Quechua and Quechua yachay in a highly charged context of struggles over representation in which I myself am a participant (Castro-Gómez 2000).

In this text, as I attempt to map politically the environments in which the power of knowledge and languages moves, I necessarily involve myself in struggles over power and over different positions concerning Quechua and its yachay. I speak, then, from a location marked by my own subjectivity and history: as a white intellectual, male, native Spanish speaker, and as full of contradictions. At the same time, I constantly labor to insert myself into a learning process marked by crisis and rupture, a process that is the product of interaction with other women and men also displaced in the act of speaking and knowing. This essay emerges from a kind of frontier, a position where I know myself to be part of the system of power yet am also in constant conversation with other forms of knowing, thinking, speaking, and silencing.

Background on the Conosur Ñawpagman

The *Conosur Ñawpagman* newspaper was created in 1983 in association with the Portales Center of the Simón Patiño Foundation.[6] Financed with Swiss aid, the newspaper served to promote reading in Mizque, a province of the Department of Cochabamba. The newspaper was created through an agreement with the San José de Mizque Cooperative, under the name *El Mizqueño*. Initially, the paper was geared to the people of the Mizque community and supported the work of the popular libraries that the Portales Center had created in different provinces of the department.

The year the *Conosur* was born was one of significant drought in the valleys of Cochabamba and marked the arrival of many nongovernmental organizations (NGOs) that brought with them large quantities of money for peasant communities. The *Conosur* began publication in an attempt to analyze the impact of development projects in the communities. The first issues of the newspaper addressed the supposed benefits that development institutions brought to the countryside and the opinions of peasants who opposed the institutions' overwhelming presence. The following year, in an agreement with the Moyopampa Agricultural Union (Totora, Carrasco province), *El Totoreño* emerged and essentially reproduced *El Mizqueño*'s content but with different headlines. *El Totoreño* sought to be a more direct nexus with the communities and separate itself from the small-town sector to which it was initially linked.

The *Conosur* newspaper explored the issue of appropriate technologies and began to conduct research in different communities to test the hypothesis that the introduction of modern technology, instead of benefiting the communities, actually accelerated the erosion of peasant knowledge, just as it eroded the soil (Gonzalo Vargas, interview, 09/10/01). In Raqaypampa, for example, research demonstrated that peasants developed their own strategies, in which families and local grass-roots organizations acted together to counter the effects of introduced technologies and the constant, overwhelming assault of the market. It was possible to observe the cultivation of crops linked to each other, the use of diverse ecological niches, highly precise weather forecasting, seed varieties, and so forth.

At a meeting in 1986 of the trade union centrals of the three southernmost provinces of the Department of Cochabamba (Totora, Mizque, and Carrasco), the participants asked that each province have its own newspaper.

Taking stock of limited institutional capacity, the participants decided to create one newspaper linked to peasant organizations, especially the Mizque Provincial Trade Union, the Moyapampa Union, and the Departmental Peasant Federation itself.[7] At the same meeting, the newspaper was given the name *Conosur Ñawpagman* because it dealt with the provinces in the department's southern cone.

In 1988 the Andean Communication and Development Center (CENDA) considered the possibility of focusing on radio communications. As a result, the *Conosur*'s publication was suspended for almost a year, and the newspaper underwent an evaluation. Pressure from organizations and the political climate created by the upcoming general elections drove the editorial team to resume publication of *Conosur* and to define the newspaper's political stance. The paper's initial regional focus thus became connected with national concerns. The newspaper resumed publication in 1989, the same year the Unified Confederation of Bolivian Workers and Peasants (CSUTCB) was born at the Tarija Congress. At the congress, the delegates also discussed the possibility of creating a political mechanism to support peasant organizations.

The PCÑ has gone through a gradual process of self-definition that affected its stated objectives. By 1992 there was increasing discussion about the issue of a political mechanism, and a proposal was made to render the union organization independent of traditional political parties. The *Conosur* also made explicit its objective and defined itself as a tool of the peasant movement's critical intellectuals, not of the movement's leadership. Starting with the promotion of Quechua reading and writing and its transcription of speakers' testimonies, the newspaper began to define itself as part of a greater political objective. This objective, as stated earlier, was to be a tool for discussion among critical thinkers in the department's peasant movement. The editorial team's question was: Where is that sector of critical thinkers? From what it understood, the sector never took shape, not even after the Movement toward Socialism (MAS) was formed as the desired political mechanism.[8]

The role the newspaper played within the Quechua peasant movement was therefore not as an immediate means of communication, but as a space for reflection that linked the PCÑ to the particular conjuncture of peasant mobilization. The sale and distribution of the paper became massive at times of social mobilization in general and of peasant mobilization in particular. It was at these times that the *Conosur* responded most closely to its objectives, serving as the repository of memory and as an instrument of reflection for the peasant political movement.

Initially, the paper was aimed at the leadership sector. Starting in 1989, as part of its institutional evaluation and renovation, it sought closer ties to the grass-roots among the department's peasants, in search of the aforementioned critical sector. That sector, in general, was composed of people with low levels of education in reading and writing. This, however, did not deny the presence of the leaders' voices, and rural teachers, merchants, truckers, and even semiurban neighborhood organizations requested copies of the newspaper.

The PCÑ is distributed in what can be called a personal manner, with representatives visiting the department's important fairs and attending the various events held by the department's peasant organizations. The moment of the newspaper's distribution is at the same time the moment of research through specific interviews and the recording of speeches at the events. The resulting articles are largely testimonials, recordings, and interviews. Rather than more usual forms of writing, they are constructed texts.[9]

The newspaper is published bimonthly (it might even be called a magazine), and it deals with such subjects as the Andean productive system; weather prediction; community history; education; events and resolutions sponsored by peasant and indigenous organizations at the local, regional, and national levels; community events; national and international news; and the ever-present personal story. Currently, its printing varies from thirty-five hundred to four thousand copies. About twenty-five hundred to three thousand copies of each edition are commonly sold, although at times of mobilization the issue sells out. An important fact is that approximately 40 percent of the issues are sold in Chapare, a zone of permanent tension because of government and U.S. efforts to forcibly eradicate coca. While the newspaper has a token price (3 *bolivianos* in the city and 1 or 1.50 in rural areas), it is never given away. Significantly, some readers, especially children, barter community products (grains, potatoes, and so on) for the *Conosur*.

The Politics of Written Orality in the PCÑ

One of the PCÑ's characteristics is to work with Quechua writing based on the orality of the speakers. This involves the politics of inscribing oral discourse (Marcone 1997) that is not limited to the simple reproduction of an act of speech but instead creates a new form of communication. To inscribe orality becomes a political act that involves a textual selection based on the editor's or inscriber's needs and interests. One example of this in the *Conosur* involves an expanded notion of intertextuality.

Literary and textual linguistic studies frequently use the concept of intertextuality to mean the construction of a text from a mosaic of references as well as the absorption and transformation of another text (Kristeva 1982). In this sense, intertextuality creates new texts through the re-elaboration of existing ones. For me, intertextuality has a different meaning with regard to the *Conosur*'s practice of inscription. I understand intertextuality not only as a textual interrelation fashioned on paper, but also as the construction of a series of plots that are *textual* (in the broadest sense of the word), where diverse visual, textual (in the sense of written), and oral codes are in figurative battle. Intertextuality is a conflictual process whereby diverse actors construct texts as they move in different cultural imaginaries. Intertextuality also considers the diverse contexts of textual production and conflictive and diverse reception.

Intertextuality can be exemplified in the newspaper's inscribed written (and visual) practice. The PCÑ publishes news and produces information in Quechua and in Spanish. On the one hand, the editors' explicit principal criterion is that events occurring in one language be described in that same language, be it Quechua or Spanish. On the other hand, anything that has to do with the world outside the communities and the organizations (for example, national and international news or agricultural technical subjects) is written in Spanish, while matters involving internal interests (community history, weather forecasting, evaluation of the agricultural cycle, stories, and so forth) are written in Quechua. This is the general tendency that emerges from the Bolivian diglottic framework in which the newspaper exists.[10]

One could also describe the PCÑ's textual-linguistic economy from the perspective of the confrontation between official and unofficial discourses. From this perspective, official and legal discourse and the expressions or relations of the discursive and hegemonic state environment are published in Spanish. For example, even if the agenda for discussion at an organization's local meeting is written in Quechua, its resolutions generally appear in Spanish. This occurs because said resolutions politically position the organizations and communities in relation to the mechanisms of state domination. In this way, the construction of news not mediated by orality also appears in Spanish. That which forms part of the organizational and communal (not necessarily local) discursive environment is treated in Quechua. Here, stories and weather forecasting are as much a part of the discussion as local peasant events and national and international news (Constitutive Assemblies, the Free Trade Agreement of the Americas (FTAA), the North Atlantic Free Trade Agreement (NAFTA), World Bank policies about agriculture, and so on).

Nevertheless, this spatial-textual distribution is not that simple, for there are also frequent intertextual games. For example, in a given news piece the title may be in Spanish and most of the information in Quechua (or vice versa). Within a given article, there may be changes or jumps back and forth between Quechua and Spanish.

According to the rules of inscription, there are three criteria to follow in the face of the Spanish written word: to the extent possible, recover endangered Quechua vocabulary; create neologisms for those terms that are not historically found in the language and that current communication demands; and, when necessary, incorporate a Spanish term by either keeping the original spelling in Spanish or providing a phonetic rendition in Quechua (Plaza 1995, 58). Under these criteria, resorting to Spanish is a last resort, reflecting an explicit policy of recovering and strengthening Quechua. The presence of Spanish terms is considered a lesser evil. I will later touch on the topic of the PCÑ's periodic effort to recover the ancient Quechua vocabulary, but for now I will focus on some examples of the newspaper's norm for dealing with Spanish terms.

The PCÑ does not have an explicit policy for the creation of neologisms in the sense that it is the editorial team that proposes new Quechua terms. Nevertheless, and as a result of the collection of oral information, I can offer a few examples that prove speakers' creativity. In some cases, that creativity involves the description of characteristics, while in others it involves the appropriation and conceptual reformulation of the original Spanish term. We thus have a physical place where a radio functions, *wayra wasi* (54:12) (lit. 'wind house');[11] for airplane, *lata p'isqu* (63:4) (lit. 'iron bird'); for handkerchief, *qhuña pichana* (61:11) (lit. 'snot cleaner'); for members of the Mobile Unit for Rural Patrolling, a repressive force charged with the aggressive eradication of the coca leaf, *p'alta uma* (46:3) (lit. 'flat head'); to refer to *gringos* or foreigners in general, *jawa puka kunka* (50:4) (lit. 'red neck from abroad').

Beyond the effort of lexical recreation through neologisms, it is common practice in the PCÑ to use Spanish terms, written according to Spanish grammar. This is observed at different levels, such as the following:

a. In entire phrases:

[. . .] *lluksinankupaq* **representantes** *genuinos de las provincias* **compañeros** (39:3).	For them to become **genuine representatives of the provinces, comrades.**

b. In the lexical-morphological combination of Spanish and Quechua:

Munayku **Escuela Fiscal** *kananta, mana* **privatizakunanta** *campesinos manachay* **escuelas privadasman** *pagayta atiykumanchurayku* (44:19).	We want that the **school be public**, that it be not **privatized**; we the **peasants** would not be able to **pay** for these **private schools**.

c. In the consignation of different types of acronyms and the institution's full name:

CSUTCB *uchhika q'ayma kachkan, imata nisun?* **Central Obrera Boliviana** *q'aymallataq, uraman yaykuyta munachkan* (79:6).	The CSUTCB is a little bit unenthusiastic (lit. 'insipid'), what would we say? The **Central Obrera Boliviana** (Bolivian Workers' Union) is also unenthusiastic and it is becoming down.[12]

Quechua in the PCÑ

Few studies deal with the presence of indigenous languages in the media (Albó 1998), even though there is a relatively strong presence of Aymara and Quechua on urban radio stations in La Paz and Cochabamba, respectively.[13] In the written press, the daily *Presencia* published one page in Quechua and another in Aymara every day for a year. Unfortunately, this experiment in the media ended because the newspaper closed. Albó and Anaya (2003) describe the experience of the newspaper *Jaima*. It initially published texts in Aymara, and now it also does so in Quechua and Guaraní as a weekly under the new name of *Kimsa Pacha Ara Mboapi*, which is distributed together with the daily *La Prensa*. The *Conosur* is thus one of very few means of diffusion outside of the academy that generates information in an indigenous language in Bolivia.[14]

The first issues of newspapers like *El Mizqueño* and *El Totoreño* distinguished themselves by their limited use of Quechua. Nevertheless, with the New Era of the *Conosur* (starting in 1989) the revaluation of Quechua became a priority. A new era of debate over standardization begins, which can be summarized as "do we completely normalize Quechua or respect the testimony?" (Julia Román, interview, 05/10/01). Asked in a more conciliatory way: how to achieve equilibrium between the norm and an inscribed written variety that readers could understand even without a high level of standardization? In the PCÑ, the basic criterion was to use a comprehensible Quechua even though it did not entirely conform to the current exigencies of standardization. This practice began from thinking through the writing from the actual words of the speakers. However, there was a moment (PCÑ numbers 44 to 55) when the newspaper explicitly intervened idiomatically to purge the newspaper's Quechua speech of excessive use of Spanish vocabulary.[15]

The PCÑ's thematic sections move, disappear, or reappear from issue to issue. There is, however, an inalterable section that is not subject to the political articulation of the moment: the story. In each issue the story appearing on the last page is unchanged not only in its appearance, but also in the linguistic code it represents. In the story, we find Quechua in its purest form, as if it managed to condense forms impervious to modern communication requirements.

I have carefully studied the PCÑ's greater or lesser observation of the norms of written Quechua (Garcés 2005b).[16] Overall, and in spite of the editorial team's effort during a specific period of time, I could generally not find orthographic consistency. The newspaper's editors have a basic knowledge of grammatical norms and rules, since they occasionally attend training seminars or courses on the normalization of Quechua, but they do not necessarily apply them directly. This is because the paper's unique strength is dealing with Quechua writing based on its informants' orality—the voice of those who offer their testimonies and *speak*.[17]

Traces of Orality in the PCÑ

Conosur is a space of textual production, starting from the inscription of oral discourse. In the hands of the newspaper's editors, this is a political practice that implies a process of textual selection and reconstruction. In my view, this practice responds to three main issues in the extensive literature about the relations between orality and writing. First, it contradicts the idea that orality is less valuable than writing, largely because it contributes little or nothing to the configuration of abstract thought and the development of intellect (Goody 1968; Olson 1994; and Ong 1982, 1992). Second, it problematizes the notion that there is rupture rather than continuity in the relationship of orality to writing, what Street (1984) and others have called the "great divide." And third, it provides an alternative to the quandary we face when elaborating written forms of subordinated languages from the model of the dominant languages, thus producing a functional and political copy that also reproduces the linguistic colonialism present in our societies (Garcés 2005a, 2005b). Indeed, through these interventions *Conosur* serves as an example of the political uses of subaltern sectors' writing, which some authors have noted can impart a sense of history to local struggles (Portelli 1989) or counter-hegemonize or negotiate with the written inscribed officiality (Rappaport 1990).[18] With the aim of contributing to the debates about linguistic politics and the practice of written interventions in Quechua and Aymara, I offer examples of the most frequent and important cases of the oral presence that I found in *Conosur*'s writing.

One example of the oral presence in *Conosur* is the appearance of conversational ties, including *í*, which in Bolivian Quechua allows the speaker to express uncertainty and doubt, while also asking the interlocutor to voice their own opinion on the topic in question (Herrero and Sánchez de Lozada 1979). In PCÑ 68:14, we find the following: *Nuqaykup lugarniykumanta papa muju í, Laqmu tarpuyku* ("It is a potato seed from our place, you see; we sow laqmu..."). The presence of *í* would be normal in an oral interaction, where one of the speakers demands the participation of the other speaker.

Another way in which the PCÑ reproduces the context of oral conversation in the written text is by trying to reproduce the performative aspects of the linguistic event. Issue 84:11, for example, details the experience of a Workshop for the Handling of Potato and Corn Varieties organized by the Women's Organization of Kuyupaya. The expert in distinct varieties of potatoes and corn seeds carried out a demonstration for the attendees at the workshop. The newspaper covered this presentation in the same way the linguistic event unfolded:

*Ñuqa apamurkani saritasta, papitasta riqsichinaykupaq. Riqsichisaykichiq: Yuraq sara waltaku, ranqhanapaq, sara lluch'usqapipis walliqllataq; Guinda sara nisqa jank'apaq; **kaytaq** Q'illu sara Lurivayu, lawapaq,*	I had brought some corn (maize) and potatoes for display. I will show them to you: the Waltaku white corn, is for selling; it is also good for being peeled; the purple corn (is good for) being toasted; and this one the yellow

jank'apaqpis, jak'upis sumaq, bajiyupi puqun, patapipis kallantaq. **Kaytaq** Uchpa sarita jank'apaq, ranqhanapaq; **kay** Yuraq sara rosada jina, tukuy imapaq; Phasanqalla sara, muchhaspa jank'anchiq. **Kaytaq** Yuraq sara, puka q'uruntañataq lluch'usqapaq, ranqhanapaq, tukuy imapaq . . . (84:11).	corn (called) Lurivayu, for soup, for being toasted, it is also good for flour; it grows in the lowlands and also in the highlands. And this one is the Ashes corn, good for being toasted and for selling; this white, pinkish one, is good for everything; this is popcorn corn, it is toasted getting the grains out from the cob. And this one is the White corn, it has a red corncob, it is good for being peeled, for selling, for everything . . .

The text is accompanied by a photo of a lady presenting different corn varieties. In this way, the newspaper attempts to insert the reader into the interactional context and moment of speaking. By reproducing the environment in which text is produced, this type of textual construction distances itself from the rules of objectivity that should mark a formal written text and that give writing its character as a technology of abstract intellectual development.[19]

Another important presence of orality in the newspaper occurs in its quotation system. In the following example we see reproduced the most common Quechua quotation practice:

gobiernopunicha kachamun "runasta maqamuychis" **nispa** *fruta sach'asta aqnata machitiyamuychis* **nispa** (72:15).	It is most possible that it was the government itself that sent them, "go ahead, go to beat the peasants," **saying,** "go and cut them down with machetes as if they were fruit bearing trees," **saying.**

In addition to the classic system of quotation unique to Quechua's discursive structure, in its testimonies the PCÑ often relies on a generalizing anonymity through constructions like "it was said," "a leader said," and "the peasant delegates said." On other occasions the testimony directly attributes the words to their speaker:

Compañera cocata puquchik **Eugenia Blanco** *jaqay Central*	The coca producer comrade **Eugenia Blanco** from the Copacabana Union

96 FERNANDO GARCÉS V.

Copacabanamanta kay jinata willariwayku: "Kay jinata cocaykuta t'irapuwayku, mana cocayuqta saqirpawayku, kunan imawantaq wawasniykuta uywasqayku. Coca mana kaptin imawan kawsasqayku, cocallamanta qullqi jap'ikuq kani, mana ni ima puqunchu kaypi" (85: 11).

has told us this: "That's the way they ripped off our coca plants, they left us without any coca, now how are we going to feed (raise) our children. If there is no coca how are we going to live, I only get money from (selling) coca, nothing else grows here."

But in a third example, in PCÑ 41: B6–B8, after a page and half of discussion on *Ch'iñi laqatu* (Andean weevil) in a clearly journalistic style, the article suddenly poses the following question: *Imata ruwaq kanku ñawpa runas chay khuruta pisiyachinankupaq mana anchá jatarinanpaq?* ("What did people used to do to control the bugs, so that they do not proliferate?"). An unidentified interviewee directly responds: *Bueno, yachasqayman jina...* ("Well, according to what I know..."). As of this moment, since the text contains no quotes or any other sign that divulges its production or authorship, we do not know with certainty what belongs to the newspaper's editors and what belongs to the interviewee.

A dramatic instance of orality's presence in the newspaper is the use of oral formulas. As mentioned earlier, one of the enduring features in the PCÑ is the concluding story. With an exception here and there, all of the newspaper's stories conclude with the explicit formula of oral narration. For example, PCÑ 46:19–20 states, *Kunan kuti chayllapi tukukun kay kwintituqa. Waq kutikama* ("On this occasion this little tale ends just there. See you."); or also *Kaypi tukukun kay willanita* ("This little tale ends here.") (49:16). In addition, attempts to reproduce oral onomatopoeic or interjective forms appear as often in the stories as in other testimonial texts: *yuthuqa,* **churrrrrr** *nichkaqta pawarikapusqa* (77–78:16) ("The partridge flew away '**churrrrr**' saying"); *Chaymantaqa compadren nisqa: —Ayyy kumpa, mana ajinatachu luz k'anchaytaqa wañuchina, kay botonllata ñit'ina, chaywan wañun* (91:12) ("Then his compadre said: —**hey** buddy, that is not the way to turn off the light, you just have to press this button, that turns it off"); or the important case of the cover of PCÑ 45: *Kunan uqharikuna... a.a.a...!* ("Now let us riseeee...!")."[20]

Everyday Metaphors and Similes in the PCÑ

"Our ordinary conceptual system, in terms of what we think and act, is fundamentally of a metaphoric nature," write Lakoff and Johnson (1980, 39). They show how the metaphor impregnates language, thought, and action. Metaphors are constructed and circulated in an everyday linguistic market. They are not the fruit of specialists, as the Western literary intellectual class would prefer. Indeed, we find in metaphors the key to understanding relations between language, culture, and the comprehension of reality.

In such a context, the fact that the PCÑ's metaphoric world is especially evident in sociopolitical discourse demands attention. In reference to the Law of Popular Participation, for example, whose negative implications for peasant movements could not be clearly understood, the newspaper stated, *Imaynatacha katarita ch'uskirinchik, kikinta kay kamachiyta ch'uskikurqa* ("Just as we peel off a snake, likewise we peeled off this law") (62:3). On other occasions, we see a much more visual comparison than traditional political parties are able to conjure:

Eleccionespiqa **imaynatachus** *ch'uspi leche mankaman urmaykun ajinata wakin partidos tradicionalespaq qhipanman urmaykunku, paykunapaq votos rikhurin* (84:5).	In the elections just as the flies fall into the milk pot, they fall into the rear of some traditional political parties, the votes for them appear.

And throughout different Quechua texts of the PCÑ, we see the popular comparison of different organizational situations of the peasant movement with the movement of ants (see, for example, 50:3 and 50:4):

Sik'imira **jina**, *ch'inllamanta tukuy warmikuna, wawa uqharisqa, uk runa jinalla, auto yankuna wisq'asunchis* (69:5).	As ants, quietly all the women, holding our babies, just as one single person, will close down the roads (will block the roads).

Perhaps one of the richest sets of metaphoric uses from Quechua involves elements of human corporeity: *uma* (head), *sunqu* (heart), *maki* (hand), and *llawar* (blood). *Uma* means, among other things, the center of desires and intentions as well as of ways in which ideas are received:

Kunitan **gobiernop umanpiqa** *campesinosta wich'uy munachkan jaqay*	Right now in the mind of the government they are thinking of driving the

Parque Isiboro Sécuremanta, chayman gringosta sat'inankupaq (64: 5).	peasants from the Isiboro Sécure Park, to place the gringos there.
Participación Popular, mana **umaykuman yaykunchu** (57:13).	The Grass Roots participation (idea) does not enter in our minds.

Starting with these first examples, we can better understand the fact that *uma* is in permanent relation with intentions, deceit, or confusion:

[. . .] uk yana uwija warmikunaq qutuchakuynin ukhupi rikhurisqa, **umaninkuta muyuchiyta** munaspa, jinamanta atuqman qarananpaq warmi masisninta (46:17).	A black sheep had appeared inside the women's organization, swirling their minds, thereby feeding the women to the fox.

Uma also metaphorically designates the leaders and important posts of peasant organizations:

Kunanqa musuq **umallichik** kayku, chaytaq jatun thaskiriy, Federacionqa manamin pukllakuyku (51: 3).	Nowadays we are the new leaders, this is a great step (for us), (for) the Union is not a game.

This is precisely why *uma* also refers to the lack of leadership of a determined social entity. We see this, for example, in critiques of the government for incompetent social leadership: *Kay gobiernoqta* **mana tiyanchu uman,** *qhasimanakaq* (88:3) ("This government has no head, it is there in vain").

The other organ of the body that is a key starting point for the formulation of Quechua metaphors is the heart. *Sunqu* is a very versatile word because of its many metaphoric connections to multiple realities, states of being, and situations. Through *sunqu*, it is possible to speak truthfully and not just with words:

Dirigentesta qullqiwan umata muyuchichkanku, chayrayku dirigentes kanku cuchillo de ambos filos, qullqirayku mayladomanpis kutirillanku, simillawan k'achituta parlanku, **mana sunqunkuwanchu** (94:8).	The leaders are swirling the minds with money, that is why the leaders are double edged knives, for the money they will go in any direction, they speak beautifully with their mouths, not with their hearts.

But *sunqu* also refers to the center of a given reality, in its conception of the "middle," "importance," and "clandestine" character. For example, with respect to the night, we find these types of sentences:

*Chawpi **tutaq sunqunpi** sublevacionta ruwarqayku* (suplem. 77–78:1).	We had made a rebellion in the middle of the night.

In terms of the earth:

*Chayniqta Reservas Fiscales, Parques nispa jallp'akunata Instituciones-Empresaspaq makinman jaywarapusanku. Imapaq? Astawan Pachamama **jallp'aq sunqunta** waqcha runakunaq pulmonisninta ch'irwanankupaq* (70–71:2).	That is why they are delivering the state reservations, the parks, the lands to the hands of the (private) enterprises. What for? For them to squeeze the heart of Mother Earth and the lungs of the poor people.

A group of important associations with the term *sunqu* relate to the fact this is an organ thought to be the seat of satisfaction, conformity, rest, and rejoicing. In contrast, to say that you are not with *junt'a sunqu* indicates you are disquieted, dissatisfied, and anguished:

Mana sunquy junt'achu *Instrumento Politicota vendesqankumanta* (73–74:3).	My heart is not happy due to the fact that they have sold out the Political Instrument (of the people).

In terms of calmness, tranquility, serenity, the effect is achieved through the formula *sunqu tiyaykuy*:

*Sindicatos p'utusqanmantapacha **sunquyku tiyaykun*** (suplem. 77–78:1).	Since the birth of the unions our hearts are in peace.

The pain of the heart vivifies situations of suffering, at the same time its absence indicates insensitivity:

*Gobiernuqta mana **sunqun nananchu** waqcha runakunamanta, payta nanan chay qhapaq runamasinmanta* (92:7).	The heart of the government does not ache for the poor people, it aches for the rich people.

The topic of social and political control is expressed by resorting to the metaphoric construction of "being in the hands of. . . ." In this sense, the formula *maki* + (nominal suffix of a person) +*-pi* ~*-man* is used to express the idea of having someone subjected to the power, control, and authority of another person:

*Tawa diputados indígenas basespaq **makinpi*** (75:1).	The four indigenous deputies are in the hands of the grass roots.

| *Estados Unidospaq makinpi* | They make us dance in the hands of |
| *tusuchiwachkanchik* (67: 3). | the USA. |

Additionally, adding the root *tusu* in this last example demonstrates that this control is manipulative, managing others as if they were puppets that could be made to dance on demand.

Another element of human corporality frequently used as a metaphoric base is *llawar*. "I do not have blood" indicates insensitivity, not feeling in the presence of the other:

| *Gobiernoqa k'ullu, uk rumi churakun* | The government does not listen to |
| *mana llawarniyuq gobierno* (67:4). | (the people), making themselves hard as a rock, it does not have blood. |

In contrast, to do something "with blood" indicates effort, suffering:

Federacionqa manamin pukllakuyku,	The Union is not a game, but we
manataq uk institucion jina qhawa-	cannot consider it just as any other
sunmanchu, ni Prefecturawan, ni	institution, neither as the Prefecture,
Alcaldiawan, ni Policiatawan, chay-	nor the municipality, nor the police,
kunaqa qullquiwan ruwasqa kanku,	those are made with money, but our
*Federacionninchiktaq **llawarwan***	Union is made out of blood.
***ruwasqa** kachkan* (51:3).	

A special type of metaphor found in the newspaper refers to the personification of nature. Quechua testimonials in the PCÑ refer to nature or its elements as entities that get tired, walk, know, predict, get angry.[21] Here are some examples:

*Pitaq juchayuq kay **pacha sayk'usqa***	Whose fault it is that nature is tired?
kananpaq? (46:1).	
Sach'akuna** waliq wata **waqyamuch-	The trees are predicting a good year
kawanchik (53:8).	for us [lit. 'calling for'].
*wakin **yakusqa phiñas** chullchuya-*	Some waters are mean, they might
chiwasunman (35:7).	make us sick.

In the same way, peasant knowledge is anthropomorphized because it exists, it grows, and it stays with the Quechua speaker:

***Yachayniykuqa** nuqaykuwan kashan.*	Our knowledge is with us. This
Wawita kasqaykumanta pacha kay	knowledge of ours has to grow (multi-
*yachayniykuqa **miranan tiyan***	ply) ever since we were children and

wiñaypaq wiñayninpaq, kay yachayqa ni jaykaq tukukunanchu tiyan (Seminario sobre Escuela Campesina de Raqaypampa, in 44: 6).	forever and ever, this knowledge cannot ever end.
Kawsayniyku, yachayniykuqa, unaymantapachapuni nuqaykuwan kawsan (Pedro Olivera, in 79:13).	Our life, our knowledge live with us from time immemorial.

Overall, the newspaper's metaphoric world offers many possibilities for idiomatic development. The role of bridge that the PCÑ's editorial team plays is significant given that its members are also Quechua speakers who move between the world of oral informants and that of the writing skills required for the newspaper's journalistic function. On the one hand, they intuitively use the Quechua metaphors mobilized by villagers and leaders and, on the other hand, they permanently struggle to render writing that is comprehensible to readers because it follows certain norms.

Yachayniyku, *or the Politics of Quechua Knowledge*

In the past, the knowledge produced by subaltern groups was used to think about them and formulate policies for them. Today we seek the revaluation of local knowledge and the active participation of the actors themselves in policymaking. Three factors have influenced these changes. First, the transformation of global capitalism requires the further expansion of transnational markets and access to new, often scarce, resources (Lander 2002a, 2002b). Second, postmodern discourses have highlighted the essentialist and binary character of modern knowledge, making its positivisms and absolutisms more flexible (Coronil 2004). Third, and in contrast, many counterhegemonic groups have made the defense of place a theoretical, political, and ecological project (Escobar 1999, 2000).

At the same time, we continue to exist within a framework that Mignolo calls the geopolitics of knowledge (2000, 2001). Eurocentrism (in its historical form) and North-centrism (in its current form), both characteristic of contemporary global coloniality, have canonized and validated one knowledge as legitimate and considered it universal. Local knowledge, that of the colonial and global peripheries, is dismissed as local, aboriginal, indigenous, or "ethnic" knowledge. It is useful but not legitimate—a knowledge that can be studied and learned but that is not worthy of incorporation into the paradigmatic knowledge of thinking and living (Garcés 2005a). What is forgotten in this context is that so-called universal knowledge is also a local knowledge, but one that managed to impose itself onto the emerging capitalist world-system. As a result, this knowledge defined itself as universal and led others to recognize it as such (Santos 2003).

In the *Conosur* newspaper, we see a space for the communication of a wide gamut of topics related with the yachay—local knowledge, in the deepest sense—in Quechua communities. Some are technical or agricultural in nature: types of soils; elements of Andean technology, including the construction of ditches and furrows; control of plagues such as the *saq'u* and the *ch'iñi laqatu*; weather forecasting; native seeds; water source management; forest management. Others involve the communal management of health, including traditional medicine, medicinal plants, and animal sanitation. And still others deal with sociopolitical or symbolic aspects: reciprocity institutions like the *ayni*; community history; the mapping of Andean territory; rituals associated with productive and spatial control like the *q'uwa*, the *ch'alla*, and the *pijchu*; local educational institutions; and narrative traditions like riddles and stories. Throughout the *Conosur*, four major themes emerge in relation to Quechua yachay: its value; its location in different physical spaces; its relationship to language; and its roots in community production and cultural practices. I will provide some concrete examples of each.

A basic affirmation in the *Conosur* is that Quechua peasant knowledge is better than Western or urban knowledge, that it is professional and should not be lost. These beliefs can be seen, for example, in references to knowledge about weather forecasting and tending the land:

Chay campesinoq yachaynin aswan sumaq kasan. Nuqaykutaq taripayku ñawpaqpi kanan chay campesinoqta yachaynin. Pay yachan tiempota qhawayta uj wata tarpuypaq. Imaynachus jamuq wata kananpaq señasta riqsillantaq. Mana chayqa, imaynatachus jallp'ata waqaychaq kanku achachisninku (37:7).	The knowledge of the peasant is better. We realized that, long before, peasants had knowledge. They know how to observe the weather for the yearly planting. They recognize the signs for the coming year. Or else, (they know) how their ancestors knew how to take care of the land.
Profesionales kanchiq yachayninchiqmanta (Clemente Salazar, in 46:4).	We are professionals in our knowledge.

Nuqanchis unaymanta pachapuni montesninchikta jallch'ayta yachaq kanchiq" (Zacarías Ortiz 76:4).	We knew from times past how to take care of our forests.
Nuqaykuqa mana munaykuchu yachayniyku wiqch'usqa kananta (54:14).	We do not desire that our knowledge be put aside.

Nevertheless, even though this expert knowledge has responded to the environment better than Western capitalist knowledge, it is met with disrespect and scorn:

"Tecnología cientificamanta" técnicos, instituciones, gobiernos, Estado ima ch'ipakullankupuni, comunidadpata yachayninta manaraqpuni walichinkuchu. Ch'irwarkullaytapuni munawayku (63:14).	The technicians, institutions, governments, even the State continue swarming around "scientific technology," (and) they do not value the knowledge of the community. They still want to squeeze us.

There is a contempt for peasant goods and labor which rests on a type of racism that values production and knowledge from a colonial point of view:

Campesinospata productonchis mana valenchu, trabajonchis mana valenchu; todavía chaywan mana contentakuwanchiqchu kay pueblopi kaqkuna kay khapaq runas, paykuna noqanchista millachikusawanchis, imatá yachan kay indio bruturi nispa compañeros (Valeriano Romero, 34:6).	Our crops are not appreciated, our work is not appreciated; not happy with that (work), the town people, the rich, are getting disgusted by us, — what does an ignorant Indian know — saying, comrades.

As a result, peasant production and knowledge are degraded as a result of changes introduced by modern technology and its ideology. Peasant *yachay* is subordinated to urban and scientific knowledge at the service of dominant sectors:

[. . .] *ñawpataqa allinta puquykunata apayqachasarqayku, jallp'apis sumaq kallpayuq kachkarqa mana kunan jinachu, chayman chayanapaqqa karqa rikhurimusqan chay kimiku, maychus jamun tecnología moderna nisqawan,*	In the past we knew how to handle the crops well, the soil was also very fertile, not as it is today. The chemicals that appeared led us to this situation, the so-called modern technology, the town people resort to this discourse.

llaqtarunakuna kay parlayta apayqachanku. Kunanqa jallp'akunaqa chuqruman tukun, compañeros rikunku kay kimiku jallp'apaq uk veneno kasqanta. Chaywanpis, llaqtarunaqa Universidad yachay wasipi yachaqkunaqa mana campesinota valechinkuchu, ninku: –imata campo runa yachanri nuqayku Universidadpi yachayku, yachaykutaq kimiku venenochus manachus–, ajinata paykunapis parlanku, jinapis compañeros, yachanchik imaptinchus parlanku chayta, mana kimikusta rantisunman chayqa, mana qulqi yaykunmanchu qhapaqkunapaq, chayta yachaspa paykunaqa, chay tecnicosqa, comunidadespi yachachispa kanku qhapaq runaq kawsayninman jina, paykunaqa qhapaq runaq kawsayninta jark'akunku (Florencio Alarcón, in 60: 4).	Nowadays the soil has become hard. Our fellow countrymen have seen that these chemicals are a poison for the soil. In spite of that, the ones who have studied at the universities do not value the peasant's knowledge. They said–what does the peasant know? We studied at the university, and we know whether the chemical (fertilizer) is poisonous or not. That is the way they speak, comrades. Thus comrades, we know why they speak like that. If we did not buy those chemicals, there would be no income for the rich. Because they know that, the technicians are teaching in the communities the ways of the rich, they defend the way of life of the rich.

The second major theme in the *Conosur* is that Quechua yachay is expressed and socialized in many places, but here I will limit myself to showing the tension of two locations: the school and the community. At its most fundamental level, education takes place within the community and the organization:

Sapa comuna ukhupi nuqayku pura yachachinakuyku (Fructuoso Vallejos, in 64:10).	Inside every community, we teach each other.
Jatuchik tantakuykunaqa chaqrarunakunapaqqa uk yachay wasipis kanman jina (67:6).	The large meetings [congresses and union leaders meetings] are like schools for us the peasants.

Likewise, there is a clear awareness that the family provides a better education than schools and that schools must respond to the community's way of life and productive system:

Yachayqa mana yachay wasi ukhullapichu (64:10).	Knowledge is not found only in the schools.
Aswan allin wasipi mama tataq yachachisqan, mana ni qhillqayta, nitaq ñawiyta yachan (64:11).	The teachings of our parents at home were better, (even) without knowing how to read or write.
Educación nuqanchikpaq kawsayninchikman jina, nuqanchikpaq llank'ayninchikman jina kachun (57:14).	Let education for us be according to our culture, according to our work.

A specific historical case that illustrates the tension between family and community on one side and the school on the other occurred in 1986 in Raqaypampa, in the Mizque highlands. The community criticized the teachers for being arrogant with parents and community leaders; for impeding the children's learning by teaching in Spanish instead of Quechua; and, perhaps most important, for not respecting the community's work calendar. In response, the parents took their children out of the school. The following year the community named "peasant teachers" to manage the school in the neighboring community of Rumi Muqu. In an experiment under the name Ayni School (Garcés and Guzmán 2006), the community paid these teachers with products and labor in their fields, and, in turn, the teachers taught in Quechua and worked from June 24 to September 24.

The conflict, which persisted until 1992, revolved around two central points: the school calendar and who had jurisdictional authority. On the first point, community members argued that if their children were in school when they were needed for agricultural work, they missed the opportunity to be educated by their parents (Arratia 2001; Garcés and Guzmán 2006). On the second point, the community felt that the school, being practically the only state representative in the community, had to submit to communal authority (Garcés and Guzmán 2006; Regalsky 2003). The *Conosur* articles from those years, therefore, emphasized that the schools responded to the interests of the rich, not to the desires and needs of the peasant:

yachanchik jina kunankamaqa educación qhapaqkuna yachakunankupaq jina, mana nuqanchikpaq munayninchikman jinachu (Florencio Alarcón, in 56:6).	As we know, up to this date (formal) education has been for the rich; it has not been (designed) according to our needs.

Building from this experience, people emphasize that *Educacionqa kawsayninchikmanta kawsayninchikpaq kanan tiyan* ("Education has to be [designed, implemented] from our life and for our life") (Garcés and Guzmán 2003). On the basis of this principle, the Educación Intercultural Bilingüe project (Intercultural Bilingual Education, or EIB) is criticized as being imposed from outside and as being unsuitable to peasant life because, even though the project is bilingual, it does not respect the community's time and rhythms. In that context, the experience of Rumi Muqu serves as a valid counterproposal.

Nuqa uchhikitanta niyta munani chay iskay qallupi yachanakuymanta (Educación Intercultural Bilingüe), nuqanchik chaqra llank'aypi tarikunchik manataq kay yachakuykunamanta mana nuqanchikpaq mana kawsayninchikman jinachu. Chaytataq nuqa kaypatamanta autoridadesninchikmanta mañakuni, nuqanchikpaq kawsayninchikman jina, calendario escolar ruwa kunanta. Ñawpaq watamanta pachaña nuqanchik aynipi uk campesino yachachik churakuspa llank'aynin chikman jina risan, kikillantapuni llank'ananta yachay wasin Rumi Muqupi munani, chaywan nuqanchik yachasqa kachkanchik (Nicolas Pardo in 52:4).	I would like to say a little about that education in two tongues (Intercultural Bilingual Education), we are peasants but those teachings (of formal education) are not for us, are not designed according to our way of life. I would like to request to our authorities up here, that the school calendar be designed according to our life. For a few years, we have placed a peasant teacher in ayni (reciprocity system), and he is teaching according to our work. I wish they work in just that manner, as in the Rumi Muqu school; we are used to that.

The central criterion is that the indigenous organization must control any educational proposal. School calendars, teachers, and curriculum must all respect community values. On the question of calendars, if the school functions during the seasonal peak of agricultural labor, it breaks the community's educational time:

Nuqaykupaq chay tiempo escuela kanan mana waliq kasqanta k'ala entero agricultorespaq. Nuqa qhawarqani mayk'aqchus ima tiempochus nuqayku llank'ayniykumanta llawqiyaykuman	For us, for all the peasants the school time is not good. I had thought that the time we relax in our farming, that's when the schools for the children should start. The fact is that our

Quechua Knowledge and Writings 107

chaymanta qallarinman escuelas wawaspaq... Nuqaykuqta kawsayniy- kuqawaqjinataq, llaqtaq kawsaynin waqjinataq (Luis Albarracín, in 38:13).	life is of one kind, and the life of the cities is of another type.

On the question of teachers and curriculum, for the school truly to belong to the community, it must have its own peasant teacher so that Quechua children can study according to their own knowledge and language and at the same time benefit from the knowledge of their elders:

Waturirqayku, imaraykutaq mana kanchu maestros campesinos wawakunata yachachinapaq? Waliq kanman wawakuna escuelapi yachakunanku imataq jallp'a patapi kapuwasqanchikmanta, yachayninchikmanta, organización sindicalmanta, kay tukuytaqa qhichwa qallunchikpi. Atillasunmantaq intercambio de conocimientos nisqata ruwayta, kuraq tatakunaq yachayninta uqharispa, chayman jina purinapaq (Un comunario de Tacachi, in 83:7).	We asked why are there not teachers to teach the peasants' children? It would be good that the children at school learn about what we have on the soil, about our knowledge, our organization as unions, and all of this in our Quechua tongue. We could also make an exchange of the so-called knowledges, resorting to the knowledge of our elders, so we could walk according to that (knowledge).

The third major theme in the *Conosur* on the subject of Quechua peasant yachay is its close linkage to the language in which it is expressed (Garcés 2005a). From the perspective of the geopolitics of knowledge, indigenous languages have been subalter(n)ized, or constructed as inferior, in the process of colonial differentiation. The knowledge expressed in indigenous languages has been dismissed as a knowledge that, in the best of cases, expresses the emotive environment of these communities of speakers (Ong 1982). EIB programs, on the other hand, have attempted to normalize and standardize indigenous languages, to give them an inscribed written form, and to revalorize indigenous knowledge. Among the psycholinguistic justifications for EIB programs has been the promise of better cognitive development and scholarly results through learning in the mother tongue (López and Küper 2000).

What we find in *Conosur*, however, is that the Quechua language cannot be studied in isolation from the power relations in which it is embedded. The discrimination experienced by the Quechua peasant is seen as similar to the discrimination Quechua suffers as a language:

Qhishwa parlayninchista k'alata kunankamaqa saruchisanku kastillanu rimaywan (33:12).	They are allowing our Quechua language to be completely stepped upon by the Spanish language.

Because of this, Quechua positions itself conflictively and in opposition to Spanish; to compete with Spanish means to defend, value, and develop one's own culture:

Qhishwata pataman tanqananchik tiyan maqanachinapaq waq qalluwan. Chantapis kulturanchikta astawan pataman uqharinapaq (Pablo Vargas, in 59:10).	We have to push Quechua upward so that it can compete with another tongue. Also to raise our culture higher.

The study of Quechua is never an end in itself. In order to serve as a tool of liberation, it must operate in tandem with other strategies, such as its written inscription according to its oral use and not according to what a group of planners says:

Tukuy campesinos qhishwa parlayninchispi rimaspa qhilqasunchis. Kunan manta ñawpaqmanjinamanta par layninchista uqharisunchis, kay KULLASUYU llaqtanchispi imaraykuchus kay phisqapachaq watana qhishwa parlaq runaqa engañasqa rikukuyku tukuy imapi. Chaymanta qhishwa rimayninchispi qhilqasunchis chayqa librostapis ruwasunchis parlayninchisman jina (Santos Albarracín, in 39:16).	All the peasants who are speaking in our language will also write. From now on, in this way we shall raise our language. Because in the Qulla Suyu, we the Quechua-speaking people have found ourselves deceived in every thing for five hundred years. That's why, if we write in our Quechua language, we will make the books according to our own speech.

In this sense, Quechua can be an instrument of liberation or oppression, as happened in the colonial period. It would seem that the key matter is not only to develop, inscribe in writing, or intellectualize the language, but to determine what practical purposes and sociopolitical practices the language can serve. In this sense, the language—like communal institutions themselves—can be put in the service of systems of state control:

Gobierno qallunchikpi apay munach-kawanchik paykunaq yuyayninllankumanta (Félix Santos, in 57:14).	The government is trying to lead us to their thinking in our own tongue.

This brings me to the fourth and final theme in the *Conosur* dealing with Quechua yachay, which is that Quechua peasant knowledge has two closely related roots that feed it: the peasant system of production and reproduction and the indigenous peasant community. In relation to the first root, the *Conosur* collects Quechua knowledge on such topics as how granaries are built, which varieties of corn seed are known, and what medicinal plants are present in a particular area and how should they be used. It also uses research CENDA has conducted in Raqaypampa over many years to demonstrate the benefits of the Quechua productive system.

Perhaps one of the most important topics is weather prediction, and the *Conosur* has dedicated abundant space to it. As a front-page headline in PCÑ 32 proclaimed, "Predicting the weather is peasant wisdom." Later on in the same issue (8–9), several community members' testimonies on the topic are presented in a section entitled, "The principal peasant art is weather forecasting." The section then concludes in Spanish: "The principal art of peasants continues to be predicting the exact behavior of the rains and, accordingly, to organize the planting of different crops in the best places and on the best soils to ensure the rains' maximum advantage" (32:20). This continuous concern is perhaps best represented in the annual Weather Prediction Contest. In 64:8, we find an annual announcement:

Kay wata 1995–1996 qallarikullannataq, imaynataq kay wata kanqa, watuna kachkan, amañana siñakuna qhawayta: sach'akuna, wayra, chiri, uywakuna, phuyukuna, waqkuna ima chayllamanta astawan waliq kanan tarpuyninchik. Kay watapaq para imaynataq kanqa, mayqin makistataq para yanapanqa, manachayqa luku parachu kanqa, imaynataq?	This year 1995–1996 has already begun, how is this year going to be? We have to ask, we need to predict how it will be, accustomed as we are to reading the signs: the trees, the wind, the domestic animals, the clouds and other things; for making our farm fields better. How will the rain for this year be, who will the rain help, or will the rain be a downpour, how will it be?

The newspaper interviews participating elders and publishes the different versions of their forecasts for the upcoming agricultural year. At the end of each cycle, the newspaper evaluates the cycle in relation to the readers' testimonies and selects the elder with the closest prediction. By means of this contest the newspaper seeks to preserve and stimulate the circulation of the Quechua yachay about weather prediction and hopes that writing will safeguard this yachay given that global climate change is endangering weather prediction:

Ñawpa kuraqkuna astawan yachaq kanku kay tiempo qhawaymantaqa. Kay tiempo runasqa mana anchata yachankuñachu. Yachaymanchus ñawiyta, qhilqayta imaqa, tukuy qhawasqayta sapa wata qhilqiyman papelpi mana qunqanapaq. Ikillapis tukuy yachankuman tiempoman jinañachu. Chaytaq qhasiman rin llank'anku (Fermín Vallejos, in 39:8).	The elders are the ones who know more about these weather predictions. The people of today do not know very much. If I knew how to read and write, I would write down all my predictions for the year on paper so that they are not forgotten. Probably, all would already know about the weather in that way (written down on paper). But they work in vain (if they do not observe the signs).

The newspaper works as well to preserve knowledges that serve to control plagues like the *ch'iñi laqatu* (weevils of the Andes) and degenerative diseases like the *saq'u*. As the newspaper affirms, *Yachayninchiqwan khurukunamanta jark'akuna* (104:14) ("With our knowledge let us defend ourselves from the plagues"). The topic of traditional medicine is covered in articles on the uses of traditional medicinal plants such as rosemary and horsetail (PCÑ 38:7).

The second root that sustains peasant knowledge is the social organization of the community. Because modern techniques often seek to destroy communal organizations by imposing a different rationality of production on them, one of the principal topics of the Quechua yachay deals with the subject and practices of development. PCÑ 32:8 reports that state institutions as well as agrochemical companies and their sales representatives pressure peasants to "modernize." According to them, peasant agriculture would benefit through the introduction of improved seeds, the increased use of chemical fertilizers, pesticides, herbicides, and insecticides, and the introduction of mechanization. Mechanization is also achieved through regularizing the size (*medianización*) of the agricultural plots. Afterward, the newspaper cites CENDA experiments that show a rather different reality, namely, that "the introduction of improved seeds or the increase in fertilizers and pesticides are of secondary importance and sometimes detrimental to crop yields; while traditional peasant knowledge about weather prediction (in relation to soils and plants) continues to be what defines the success or failure of a crop."[22]

CENDA, in agreement with a local organization, carried out a series of tests on fifteen plots of land in Raqaypampa community during the 1987–88 agricultural cycle. The results, presented in PCÑ 32, contained three main points. First, the local varieties of potato are more productive than the newly introduced "improved" variety, since they have the advantage of suitability to the type of rain and soils of the area. Second, fertilization does not ensure greater production because a hailstorm or lack of rain can reverse its positive effects. And third, the technological element of greatest importance is weather management, which implies weather forecasting in relation to suitable varieties for the types of terrain, the dates of planting chosen according to the types of soil and varieties, and the management of family members' labor. "In other words," the article concludes, "the most important techniques in the region's agriculture are based entirely on peasants' traditional knowledge and, by comparison, 'modern technology' can make few solid and effective contributions."[23]

A series of articles in the *Conosur* critiques patents, the appropriation of peasant-indigenous knowledge by transnational agro-food and pharmaceutical companies, and institutions that introduce into the communities technological packages inherited from the green revolution. Examples of the first case are found in PCÑ nos. 76 and 77–78, which discuss the patent of quinoa, the protest by the National Association of Quinoa Producers, and the patent's subsequent annulment. PCÑ 86:8 contains an article denouncing Monsanto's attempts to introduce transgenetic seeds into the country.

The link between the yachay and communal organization is a subject of great importance to the newspaper. It could be said that knowledge is valued because of the ways in which it contributes to strengthening communal organization. While individual knowledge may be more prestigious in a national imagined community, it does not work at the community level:[24]

ñawpata papasusninchik mana qillqayta, ñawiyta yacharqankuchu, jinapis organización sindical sumaq purichik kanku. Nuqanchik ñawpata jina uk runa jinalla purinanchik tiyan, sut'inta	In the past our parents did not know how to read or write, but in spite of this they made the Union function well. We have to walk as in the past, as one single man, speaking the truth;

parlana, nuqanchikqa uk chhika yachaytawankama ñapis politikuq chupanta jap'itawan purichkanchik, ukman ukman k'askachkanchik, chaywanqa mana ni jayk'aq kay llakiy kawsay sarusunchu (56:6).	knowing a little bit, we are already grabbing the tails of the politicians, sticking to one or another; in that way we will never overcome this life of misery.

Modern knowledge, therefore, is unable to offer organizational strength, and education cannot consist only in knowing how to read and write; rather, it must involve knowing local Andean technology and communal organizational forms:

Educacionqa mana ñawiriy- qillqariyllachu, kawsayniykumanta 'tecnología andina' yachayta, sindicalismota yachay wasiman churayta munaspa Consejo Comunal de Educaciontaqa jatarichirqayku (Florencio Alarcón, in 64:10).	Education is not only reading and writing. We created the Communal Council of Education because we wanted to introduce Andean technology and unionization to the school.

Quechua yachay and the social organization that sustains it are intimately connected: if unique organizational forms are lost, social knowledge is also lost. Consequently, it does not make sense to defend peasant knowledge in and of itself, but in close connection with the preservation of territorial autonomy:

Ñawpataqa yakuyuq jallp'akunapiqa karqapuni qarpanapaqqa, comunidad sindicatowan khuska apaykachaq kanku mit'asta, paykuna rak'iq kanku yakutaqa. Kay qhipamanri Instituciones de desarrollo q'alata tukuyniqman junt'aykamuwanchik, paykunataq comunidadespiqa ruwanku obrasta: canales de riego cementowan, jatuchik quchas tukuy imata. Kay jina obraswanqa comunidadpaq yachayninqa chinkan, sindicatopis manaña makinpichu jap'in, chay institucionesqa kamachinku jatarinanta Asociaciones manachay Comités de Riego" (68:11).	Before, there was water for irrigation and the community with the union organized turns for everyone. They would distribute the water. In recent times, however, development agencies put us all together and carried out public works in the communities: irrigation canals that are paved and blocked off. With public works like these, the knowledge of the community disappears, neither is this in the hands of the unions; these institutions ordered us to create new associations or committees for irrigation.

The link of the yachay with communal organization and territorial autonomy is, however, located in a broader context that seeks independence from the institutions and foreign nations attempting to change peasant life in order to incorporate it into capitalism:

Campesino yachan, tukuy imamanta experiencia tiyan: tiempota qhawan, jallp'ata llank'ayta, mujuta churayta, trojaspi mikhunapaq waqaychayta, vendenanpaq ima. Tukuy kayta organizacionninwan mana dependespa ni pimanta. Wakin Institucionesqa mana qhawankuchu, mana yuyankuchu. Mana kay culturasta respetaspalla, cambio socialta mask'anku nispa ninku. Jawa nacionesmanta dependenanta munanku chaywan culturanchista cambiananta (Dirigentes de Campero, in 37:11).	The peasant knows. He has experience with everything: he watches (predicts) the weather, works the soil, sows the seeds, knows what to store for eating and what to sell. All of this is done independently, with the organization, without depending on anyone. Some institutions do not see, do not think. Without respecting the culture they strive for social change. They want us to depend on other countries, to change our culture.

The communal organization of the Quechua peasantry, then, is not simply an administrative apparatus, but also the main line of defense and control of territory in order to preserve political autonomy in the face of attempts at destructuring by the state and transnational capital. As the fundamental element in the historical continuity of Quechua communities, it also oversees other entities present in the community, such as the school, and controls access to resources. It is for this reason that the resolutions of a peasant congress in Campero province (PCÑ 42:5) prohibit merchants from cutting trees in the forest and selling the wood; request that the CSUTCB guard the communities' forests by, among other measures, ensuring that the lumber companies do not profit from the sale of communal forests; and prohibit merchants from stealing and selling trees that belong to the communities.

Conclusions: Rethinking Power, Knowledge, and Linguistic Practice

Historically, Quechua's process of inscription and system of writing have been unable to get beyond their use for specific ends, such as religious conversion and training, education, and so on. In general, linguistic policy in relation to minority or oppressed languages basically exists solely to promote the written inscription of these languages. In the Bolivian case, over the past few years the main effort has been to develop a process of the inscription of Quechua through two fundamental mechanisms: the standardization of Quechua writing through a unified orthographic normative, the creation of neologisms and the establishment of a certain morpho-syntactic normative; and the diffusion of this generalized system through the Educational Reform.[25]

Bolivian linguistic policy toward Quechua, even if supposedly a policy of recovery, is being formulated on the basis of four arguable assumptions: (1) that the maintenance and revitalization of Quechua must be built from its inscription in writing and through teaching it in the schools; (2) that a pan-Andean unification of Quechua will promote the empowerment and the destigmatization of Quechua speakers; (3) that the written form's standardization is key to the language's development and fortification; and (4) that historical criteria are the best guide for developing a standard form when faced with existing dialectical variation (Luykx 2001). As Luykx notes, these assumptions emphasize a linguistic policy that (a) directs efforts to situations in which Quechua is at a disadvantage with Spanish; (b) prioritizes the preoccupations of language and educational planners above those of the Quechua-speaking majority; and (c) links dialectical variation to the prestige and hierarchy of one class, which stigmatizes nonstandardized varieties.

This policy starts from a set of criteria developed with reference to Spanish and the interests of policymakers, including criteria of inscription in writing, scholasticization, pan-Andean standardization, and historicism. In an attempt to overcome diglossia, policymakers are elaborating a prestige-based, academicist model that prioritizes intellectualization and writing. They do not begin from the linguistic reality of the majority of speakers or from their concrete communicational interests and necessities. In the end, they do not pay attention to the language's own sociocommunicative capital, but instead seek to impose its standardization through a comparison with the practices of the language and the group in power.

What I have attempted to show here is that the *Conosur Ñawpagman* newspaper offers a way to research writing as it emerges from concrete linguistic practices. This is especially interesting because it deals with an extra-scholastic experience that seeks to inscribe speakers' oral discourse. I think that in this process there is potential for developing a written inscription that has not received much attention in terms of linguistic planning, one that seeks to overcome normative and elitist visions. The very creation of neologisms would benefit from the incorporation of speakers' everyday metaphors, rather than resorting to desktop creations or to the resurrection of obsolete historical forms which, even if passionately sought after by the linguist, sound strange to contemporary speakers.

As for the topic of the Quechua yachay, I think it is important to reflect—even if hypothetically—on the relations between knowledge and territoriality. As the topic of local, indigenous, or native knowledge has become central to the academic agenda of many intellectuals, whether indigenous or not, we risk building a decontextualized, abstract discourse about indigenous knowledge that can be managed by global capitalism. If this happens, indigenous knowledges would be disqualified in the name of science and progress even as global capitalism sought, through legal mechanisms, to appropriate and pillage those very same knowledges.

Within the current system of globalization, the development of biotechnology and the appropriation of the collective knowledge of indigenous-peasant communities could constitute an important resource for capitalism when faced with crisis. We are on the verge of a qualitative leap in how knowledge can be linked to relations of neocolonial domination in the contemporary world, in the sense that it can "*immediately* and *directly* create new forms of subordination and new relations of domination and exploitation" (Lander 2002b, 73).

For those who have created the global order, Western knowledge is objective and universal and therefore worthy of protection through private property rights. Other knowledges are nonknowledge and can therefore be appropriated through pillage and piracy. Scientific and entrepreneurial knowledge is *the* knowledge, meaning it has to be protected by exacting payment for its use. Here we have "one of the most important methods for the concentration of power and the increase in the inequalities that characterize the current globalization process. For that reason, it constitutes one of the more significant dimensions in the geopolitics of contemporary capitalism" (Lander 2002b, 74).

The development of biotechnology has recently seen impressive advances with experiments in cloning, genetically modified crops, and the decoding of the human genome. To realize such development, biotechnology requires legal and commercial-economic security mechanisms, designed over the course of several years, to allow it unfettered accumulation. In recent international agreements and treaties, such as NAFTA, the creation in 1995 of the World Trade Organization, efforts to subscribe to the Multilateral Investment Agenda, and now attempts to formalize even further "free trade" negotiations such as the FTAA and the Andean free trade agreement, the topics related to agriculture and intellectual property rights receive a great deal of attention.

It was no accident that in these agreements and treaties the concept of intellectual property rights was expanded; it no longer is limited to that which is invented, but now includes that which is discovered. As has been true for over five hundred years, colonial modernity continues discovering and conquering. Before, colonial modernity *discovered* America, meaning it became aware of that which was previously unknown to it, and that awareness translated into conquest, domination, and accumulation. Today, colonial modernity *discovers* genetic diversity and privatizes the rights to access and use of the planet's genetic-biological wealth. In both cases, previous knowledge—collective, orally circulated, and indigenous—does not count or even exist. Only colonial-imperial jurisprudence has the power to create and to give the ability *to be* to nature, to human beings, and to their knowledge.

A few years ago during the triumphant green revolution, which promised to abolish world hunger, the knowledge of allegedly ignorant Indians and peasants was denied in the name of a modern scientific perspective that boasted objectivity, precision, and veracity. Driven by this denial, missionaries of development poured into peasant and indigenous communities to teach Indians how to sow, what seeds to use, and how to increase production. Today, people continue to deny that Indian knowledge is knowledge (*conocimiento*)—at most, it gets to be wisdom (*saber*) or ethnic wisdom—but community knowledge is surreptitiously usurped, robbed, plundered. The knowledge of Indians is not worthy of written legal protection, but it is very useful to unfettered capitalist accumulation.

In the PCÑ, indigenous peasant knowledge and Quechua yachay are linked to the political and territorial autonomy of communities and their organizations. Quechua yachay defends the indigenous peasant way of life and is a weapon to combat governmental and nongovernmental development policies. In this sense, *yachayninchik ~ yachayniyku* ("Our knowledge [inclusive] ~ knowledge [exclusive of second person]") is related to *kawsayninchik ~ kawsayniyku* ("Our life ~ life") as an expression of a territorial presence. In the voices represented by the newspaper, almost everything must be *kawsaynichikman jina* ("According to our life"): the organization, education, environmental management, health, and so forth.

As such, it does not make much sense to speak of local or indigenous knowledge in the abstract. Defending it makes sense only in the context of the struggle for the territorial revindication of Bolivia's indigenous peasant movement. This knowledge is linked to the control of territory understood as a defense of communal jurisdiction and peasant autonomy before the state and a defense from the attacks of global capitalism.

This struggle against racism is expressed in multiple ways and has inspired don Roberto Albarracín to say:

Maypi yachayninchiq, rimayninchiq, wich'usqa kasanman karqa. Nuqanchiq yachananchiq karqa. Nuqanchiq qhiswaruna kanchiq. Nuqa chayta tapurikuni, yachayta munayman (Roberto Albarracín, in 46:1).	Where have our knowledge and our words been wasted? We were supposed to know. We are Quechuas. I ask myself that, I would like to know.

The ideas presented in this essay run parallel to the question don Roberto asks from within his community. Taking as a pre-text the voices of the *Conosur Ñawpagman* newspaper, I have attempted to understand, through continual discussion with community members and leaders in Raqaypampa and Ayopaya, where and how the knowledge and words that are uncomfortable for global capital are being lost. I am conscious that, as a *q'ara*, and since I am known to belong to this space of academic power, I can be a discursive tool and act as a *jawamanta yachay* ("knowledge from abroad"), enabling the interstitial resistance of Quechua's yachay. In this way I seek to convey the idea that don Roberto's question is not final, that such knowledge and such words have not been entirely lost. They are worth the impertinence of continuing to live, the impertinence of continuing to bloom, as Tata Fermín knew so well:

Kay pata chiri jallp'akuna pampas ñuqanchikpata, ñawpa tatakunanchik saqisqanku, kaypi tiyakunchik. Chaytaqrimana chinkaq, mana tukukuq, kunankamapis kawsachkallanchikpuni, kay kikinpi saqisqas, kikinpi wañuq, kikinpi kawsaq. Mana waq llaqtamantachu rikhurinchik, kay kikin llaqtayuq	These high and cold lands are ours, our old ancestors' inheritance, we live here. And that is nondisappearing, never ending, we continue living even to this day, left (to live) here, to die in the same place, to live in the same place. We have not appeared in another land, we belong to this land,

kanchik, qhurajina kanchik mujumanta	we are as weeds that return from the
watanpaq watanpaq kutirin mana	seeds year after year, never ending, we
tukukuq, qhura jina mana tukukuq	are as weeds that die out not.
kanchik (Fermín Vallejos 1995:3-4).	

Notes

I thank Florencia Mallon, not only for inviting me to the conference that provided the framework for this paper, but also for her comments on my work. I also thank Pedro Plaza, who helped me with the translation of Quechua texts into English, and Soledad Guzmán, who helped me shorten the presentation. I dedicate this article to my brother, Armando Muyulema, who knows the creative and transformative power of language, both in its oral and its written forms.

1. Throughout this essay I opt for using the phrase *inscription in writing* and the word *writing* in place of *literacidad*, ever more common in the existing bibliography as a loanword of the English *literacy*. In spite of Zavala's justification, I think *literacidad* evokes in Spanish the world of literature, marked by its elitist and academic (*ilustrado*) character. I agree with Zavala's definition of the term: "A social phenomenon that is not restricted to technical learning in the educational arena" (Zavala 2002, 15). I will refer to this publication as the *Conosur*, the PCÑ, or *the newspaper* throughout the text. *Ñawpagman* means "go forward."

2. *Yachay* can be translated as "knowledge." However, it is the basis of an entire semantic field related to knowledge, learning, teaching, and even to a way of life. For an ethnographic study on this concept, see García (2005).

3. The Cuna peoples use the term *Abya Yala*, meaning "mature and fertile earth," to name America. Many countries' indigenous organizations have adopted this term to refer to a geographical space. If to name is to struggle, as Muyulema states (2001, 328), and if America and Latin America result from naming policies that partially implanted the conquistadors in this communication, then I insert myself in that struggle. I thus opt to use *Abya Yala* to refer to what has usually been constructed as America or Latin America.

4. In two of the regions that witnessed recovery of territory in Cochabamba Department, peasant organizations stated their organizational position in their legal documents as "Unified Regional Trade Union of Indigenous Peasants of Raqaypampa" and "Unified Regional Trade Union of Indigenous Peasant Workers of Ayopaya."

5. The term *pacha* is one of the richest, most complex terms in Quechua's semantic universe. It refers to the entire and very ample spectrum of space and time in which we are located.

6. This section is a synthesis of a previous discussion (Garcés 2005b, 82–104).

7. The same group that started the newspaper had created CENDA, a nongovernmental organization, the previous year. At first, CENDA worked on the issue of introduced technologies and their effects on peasant communities, primarily the community of Raqaypampa.

8. Evo Morales, leader of the Peasant Federations from Cochabamba's Tropical Region, founded the MAS political party. In June 2002 MAS participated in national elections and won 20 percent of the votes (1 percent less than the Movimiento Nacionalista Revolucionario, Gonzalo Sánchez de Lozada's party) and thirty-five parliamentary seats in the Congress (Postero, 2005).

9. At one point the newspaper carried out an experiment in which the readers themselves wrote the articles. The experiment did not work because, among other things, leaders critiqued it for wanting to create a select group of writers.

10. *Diglottic* is a sociolinguistic term referring to the conflictive coexistence within a territory of two or more languages or variants of a language in asymmetric conditions of use and value. One of the languages appropriates to itself all the uses and functions, while the rest restrict their uses and functions to domestic and agricultural arenas. For the term's technical specificities, see Albó (1998), Fishman (1995), and Luykx (1998).

11. I cite texts of the PCÑ by indicating the number of the issue followed by the page numbers.

12. These examples are merely illustrative and intended to support the assertions I make.

13. For the case of Aymara in radio, see Condori's work (2003). Currently, Soledad Guzmán is investigating the broadcasting of Quechua in a Cochabamba urban area as part of her master's thesis at the PROEIB Andes (Guzmán 2005).

14. In addition, CENDA publishes a Children's Supplement in Quechua called the *Añaskitu*. It is a monolingual magazine that seeks the socialization of children's Quechua knowledge through interschool correspondence and the valuation of community knowledge.

15. On the strong presence of Spanish in Bolivian Quechua and especially Cochobambino, see Sichra (2003, 105–16).

16. The Quechua alphabet currently used in Bolivia is based on the *Alfabeto Único para el Idioma Quechua* (Unified Alphabet for the Quechua Language), made official and published in the Supreme Decree No. 20227 (*Gaceta Oficial de Bolivia* 25:382, 10 April 1984) by President Siles Suazo. Bolivian Quechua's normative written inscription is developed on the basis of scholasticized Pan-Andean standardization and historicized criteria (Luykx, 2001). This development seeks to recover the etymological forms of Quechua's previous states. It takes into account regional variation as a way of diagnosing current forms of usage, but these usages absolutely do not impact the norm's definition.

17. The topic of writing with an oral base is not an entirely novel phenomenon.

For the case of Spanish, see the studies of Oesterreicher, Bustos, Cano, Eberenz, and Stoll in the edition of Kotschi, Oesterreicher, and Zimmermann (1996).

18. This last one is a practice with a long tradition in the Andean world (Guamán Poma 1615; Pachacuti Yamqui c. 1613; Yupanqui 1570; Lienhard 1990).

19. Virginia Zavala (2002, 62) questions whether objectivity is in fact an intrinsic characteristic of writing, or instead a part of the imaginary created by the scholastization associated with it.

20. Beneath the heading on the cover there are two photos of the indigenous peasant mobilizations of 12 October 1992.

21. See Pari (2005, 77–79), who posits that nature is one of the teachers of peasant knowledge.

22. See PCÑ 51, which has a four-page (9–12) critique of chemicals in relation to "natural" peasant production.

23. What I am interested in showing with these data is that the NGO that publishes the newspaper uses the same tools of Western technological knowledge to delegitimize it. Moreover, it shows the singular interaction between the NGO's political positioning and peasant knowledge in an effort to validate this knowledge. This means that for the *Conosur* or for CENDA, knowledge is a tool used to struggle against development and prepackaged technology rather than an end in itself.

24. A connection with this topic can be found in the research of Romero (1994). He shows that the *ch'iki* makes reference, in the community of Titicachi, to a type of social intelligence adults value positively. The ch'iki is the intelligent child who knows how to behave socially in the proper context. By contrast, *saqra* refers to children who dazzle others with their individual cognitive intelligence, but who do not receive positive reinforcement from the community because their individualized behavior locates them just outside its borders.

25. On this last aspect, see Arnold and Yapita (2000). The authors propose that writing promoted by the Bolivian Education Reform fulfills the same dominating role as that implanted by the colonial evangelization model.

JOANNE RAPPAPORT AND ABELARDO RAMOS PACHO

Collaboration and Historical Writing

Challenges for the Indigenous-Academic Dialogue

More than three decades ago, Delmos Jones proposed that a "native anthropology" would become viable only when it developed "a set of theories based on non-Western precepts and assumptions in the same sense that modern anthropology is based on and has supported Western beliefs and values" (1970, 251). Jones was thinking of minority scholars in the United States who, armed with the double consciousness afforded by their position straddling the boundary between the dominant society and their own subordinated groups, could potentially develop what W. E. B. Du Bois (1989 [1903], 2–3) called "second-sight," a privileged minority vantage point from which to analyze social life.

While Duboisian concepts resonate in very specific ways within the Afro–North American context, the notion of double consciousness provides fertile ground for the interpretation of the role of intellectuals within Latin American ethnic movements, where efforts have been made to develop what might be called an indigenous second-sight: in other words, the discovery from within Native cultures of those conceptual elements that may enable new interpretations of reality consonant with the epistemologies and political priorities of indigenous organizations.[1] Theorization—the creation of such conceptual tools—is one of the fundamental objectives of intellectuals affiliated with Latin American indigenous organizations.[2] This process ranges from the development of narrative models that decenter Western notions of historical chronology (Fernández Osco 2000; Vasco, Dagua, and Aranda 1993) to the use of concepts in Native languages as frameworks for adapting Western concepts to indigenous ends. But such conceptual tools not only function as models for interpreting experience; they also assist indigenous organizations in acting politically upon the social realities in which they live. In other words, the "second-sight" stimulated by these intellectual practices is aimed at transforming reality, not only analyzing it.

In this essay we probe the nature of this moment of indigenous theorizing, inquiring into the intellectual conditions of its emergence and its epistemological character. For us, this process is more than the simple appropriation of primordial values in a modern context. Indigenous theorizing emerges within a multiethnic social sphere, a reality that impacts both its epistemological nature and the ways in which it is put into political practice. It emerges out of a process of appropriation of knowledge systems framed by indigenous thought and sustained by a critical appreciation of other cultures. Such strategies originate in the political context, given that the indigenous movement seeks to build what could be called a radically pluralist democracy (Laclau and Mouffe 1985), a national imaginary in which social justice is constructed through the infusion in the social process of a multiplicity of ethnic demands and political practices.

What this means is that it is not always easy to identify the indigenous in Native theorizing by distinguishing its components as belonging to one indigenous culture or another. Much of the conceptual matrix employed by indigenous organizations has been appropriated from progressive academic scholarship in education, anthropology, history, linguistics, and political science as well as from the methods and concepts developed by popular movements and nongovernmental organizations (NGOs). There is a desire to create conceptual vehicles that do not privilege a specific Native culture over the others that comprise indigenous organizations, which are frequently multiethnic. What makes this theorizing indigenous is the space in which it is appropriated—the indigenous organization—and the fact that it is filtered through indigenous languages and, through translation, is transformed. It is more the locus of theorizing and its linguistic practices than its contents per se that are at stake here.

The process of creating conceptual vehicles is at once methodological (in the sense of providing new research tools) and political (because these methodologies make possible the establishment of Native autonomy in specific areas). In this sense, indigenous theorizing is somewhat akin to feminist research, which is simultaneously academic and political. But what is different about the indigenous theorizing we describe here is the fact that it takes place at a great distance from the academy. While it is true that Latin American academics and a small number of foreigners collaborate on an intellectual level with indigenous organizations, their numbers are far smaller proportionally in comparison to the collaboration of academics with the feminist movement or, in the United States, of African American scholars with black organizations. Perhaps the discrepancy is due to the fact that the results of indigenous research rarely appropriate academic formats for their dissemination, being instead directly absorbed into the projects of Native organizations. Moreover, feminist scholars, particularly female academics, have a direct stake in the feminist movement, which is not as true of the mostly non-Native academics who work with Latin American indigenous organizations; the nature of Latin American universities has largely excluded the hiring of Native and African-descended faculty, producing a marked ethnic or racial difference between the academy and grass-roots organizations. In some ways, then, the research currently under way in Latin American indigenous organizations is sui generis.

We examine the process of indigenous theory making through a critical analysis of a recent research experience in which we studied the history of the Bilingual and Intercultural Education Program (PEBI) of the Regional Indigenous Council of Cauca (CRIC), a Colombian indigenous organization that over the course of the past thirty-one years has come to occupy an important role as an interlocutor between the indigenous population and the Colombian public at large. In the course of our collaboration, which included bilingual teachers, CRIC activists, and three researchers—one from the Nasa ethnic group, a nonindigenous collaborator with CRIC, and a North American anthropologist—we came to realize that indigenous theorizing finds significant sources in the culture of the indigenous organization, which in itself is a kind of intercultural microcosm, including not only different Native ethnic groups, but non-Native collaborators as well. Several methodologies and key concepts informed our research.

Translating Theory

Indigenous theorizing in Cauca arose out of the intersection of various circumstances. On the one hand, in the mid-1980s a Master of Arts degree in ethnolinguistics was offered for the first time at the Universidad de los Andes in Bogotá to indigenous students sponsored by ethnic organizations. This development afforded activists the opportunity to discover the possibilities that language holds as a source of theoretical frameworks.[3] On the other hand, the experience of translating the Colombian Constitution of

1991, which includes provisions regarding the rights of Native peoples (Van Cott 2000), into Nasa Yuwe, the language of the Nasa of Cauca, created a political context in which the linguistic methodologies acquired in the course of graduate study could be appropriated by Native leaders.

Translation presents an innovative strategy through which Nasa activists appropriate concepts originating in the dominant society and reconfigure them in an indigenous framework. Nasa-speakers frequently reflect upon the possible array of meanings of a term in their own language, with an eye toward adjusting its significance to bring it in line with their own objectives. This strategy is engaged when translators encounter, for example, terms like *development, interculturalism,* and *culture* whose significance has limited resonance within the Nasa sphere, but whose meaning can be adapted to the politico-cultural project of the movement. Following the suggestions of the film critic Rey Chow, we believe that the translating of such words into Nasa Yuwe *improves* the original Spanish term, injects it with a new Nasa significance that liberates it from its original limitations (1995, 186).

The strategy originated when CRIC set out to translate the Constitution of 1991 (Ramos and Cabildo Indígena de Mosoco 1993; cf. Rojas 2000). The intercultural team that was formed to undertake the task was composed of the traditional authorities of the indigenous community of Mosoco, bilingual teachers, indigenous and national linguists, and a range of professionals from the national society, among them lawyers, sociologists, psychologists, philosophers, and economists. The team was forced to confront the challenge of rendering a series of universal political concepts in Nasa Yuwe. The exercise transcended one of preparing a simple translation or of creating mere neologisms. The team sought to rethink these concepts from a Nasa perspective, and the result was something that went far beyond a glossary of new terms in Nasa Yuwe: the exercise in translation opened up the possibility of reconceptualizing the notions of justice and nation from the vantage point of indigenous cultures and organizational needs. That is, the Constitution was not simply translated; instead, its fundamental precepts were *reimagined* from a Nasa subject position, offering a Nasa critique of the Colombian state (Rappaport 2004). In this sense, translation into Nasa Yuwe, as a research—and political—methodology, provided the movement with the philosophical foundations of its pluralist political proposal.

At the same time, the introduction of translation as a methodology fostered new approaches to the indigenous study of social reality, a new form of Nasa "autoethnography." Two decades ago Talal Asad suggested that ethnography is a kind of translation, "addressed to a very specific audience, which is waiting to read *about* another mode of life and to manipulate the text it reads according to established rules, not to learn to live a new mode of life" (1986, 159). Translation is equally crucial to the indigenous project, but its function is the inverse of what Asad proposed for ethnography. When Nasa activists engage in cultural translation they do it "to learn to live a new mode of life": they appropriate external concepts within an indigenous political matrix with the aim of introducing new strategies for cultural survival. In other words, their objective is to take hold of cultural potentialities, not to textualize cultural differences. This autoethnographic methodology can be better comprehended as one of a series of intercultural approaches that the indigenous movement employs to negotiate a multiethnic milieu.

Interculturalism

The translation of the Constitution sheds light on a fundamental aspect of indigenous theorizing in Colombia: it emerges from an intercultural dialogue. The translation process was, in fact, a double intercultural dialogue: between indigenous activists and professionals from the national society as well as between Nasa philosophies and Western jurisprudence. Indigenous organizations are themselves intercultural contexts in which indigenous militants and non-Native collaborators interact daily, constantly exchanging ideas originating as much in national and international spheres of theorizing as in Native cultures. Although these organizations were intercultural from the moment of their inception—CRIC, for example, was founded by Guambianos, Nasas, and mestizo activists—in the past two decades, as the concept of interculturalism was promoted by Latin American educators, its contents were appropriated within indigenous organizational practice.

Interculturalism developed in Latin America alongside the popular struggles of the 1970s and 1980s, when grass-roots organizations posed concrete alternatives to traditional notions of electoral democracy (López 1995). In the case of Colombia, where the Constitution of 1991 established the legal potential for the creation of a pluralist nation, interculturalism provides a radical alternative to the concept of multiculturalism. The latter poses a threat to pluralism insofar as it promotes a simple tolerance for ethnic minorities, fostering their participation in an electoral system that dilutes their impact upon the nation (Hale 2002). By contrast, interculturalism (on paper, at least) seeks new forms of establishing conditions of equality and consensus by enhancing the contents of minority voices (Heise, Tubino, and Ardito 1994). The objectives of interculturalism transcend those of multiculturalism because interculturalists seek more than a cross-cultural encounter framed by hegemonic relations. Their objective is to create new horizontal relationships (Gottret 1999) within a pluralist state (López 1999). In addition, interculturalists aim at injecting cultural difference within the demands of the Left for a radically pluralist democracy (Laclau and Mouffe 1985).

Interculturalism is an emergent project, not an existing social reality. It originated in Latin America within indigenous education, where radical educators built local bilingual programs based upon its precepts. Intercultural education makes cultural difference explicit through its aim of fostering the incorporation of new ideas within emergent Native cultural constellations (Mengoa 1999). We emphasize the emergent nature of indigenous cultural projects because the notion of cultural revival is oriented not toward the retrieval of customs from the past but toward the future (Heise, Tubino and Ardito, 1994). Interculturalism transcends the task of schooling children in a culturally sensitive manner. It presupposes a link between education and social change, suggesting that the school is a critical scenario for the construction of democracy. The promotion of self-esteem and the creation of nonhierarchical interethnic relations can provide firm foundations for building political pluralism beyond the schoolhouse (Heise, Tubino, and Ardito 1994; Gottret 1999; López 1996, 1999).

Indigenous theorizing is an example of putting interculturalism into practice. Interculturalism provides the conceptual tools needed to create indigenous theory, but it does more than that: it has a political objective. Intercultural dialogue is valued by indigenous organizations in Colombia precisely because Native people are also Colombians; they recognize that their participation in popular struggle must transcend purely indigenous demands. But while ethnic organizations participate actively in the construction of a new nation—the best current example is the organization by the indigenous movement of a popular referendum on Colombia's acceptance of the Free Trade Area of the Americas and indigenous rejections of neoliberal policy—the creation of new conceptual tools also impacts upon local efforts at cultural revival, nourishing the emergence of new indigenous cultural forms.

Culture and Political Autonomy

In this essay we problematize the nature of theorizing within the indigenous movement, analyzing it from an intercultural perspective. Frequently, as was the case in the translation of the Constitution, the theoretical vehicles are the product of linguistic research, but cosmological knowledge is also an important source of theory. One of the models most frequently employed by indigenous organizations is the spiral motif, an icon that appears on petroglyphs, is reproduced in the hand movements of shamans during ritual séances, and has been adduced in the grammatical structures of various Caucan Native languages (Muelas Hurtado 1995). Adoption of a spiral sense of time allowed the Guambiano History Committee to generate an alternative to linear chronological narration, permitting them to reorganize historical events by privileging mythic heroines and sacred space as anchors for a political history of the Guambianos (Vasco, Dagua, and Aranda 1993; cf. Rappaport 2005).[4] But it is also possible to ground theorization in the organizational culture of the indigenous movement, where activists have appropriated universal concepts like autonomy and territory as the primary interpretive threads for historical and sociological research (Allen 2002; Field 1999), transforming their contents so that they are in accord with the principles and demands of the organization.[5] The discourse of political autonomy feeds simultaneously upon the work of cultural activists and on the demands of nonethnic social movements. The notion of territory, for instance, which has come to replace earlier demands for land, implies a degree of sovereignty over a population and its landscape. But territory also emerges out of a cosmological relationship with that landscape, thus merging political universals with specific Native notions of space.

In reality, discourses of cultural difference and political autonomy operate in tandem within indigenous organizations. As Bruce Albert explains so convincingly in his interpretation of the discourse of the Brazilian Yanomami leader Davi Kopenawa, the indigenous movement must negotiate an ethnically heterogeneous political field. Ethnic organizations survive thanks to their simultaneous appropriation of political universals and cultural specifics: "If the indigenous political discourse were limited to the mere reproduction of white categories, it would be reduced to empty rhetoric; if, on the other hand, it remained in the exclusive sphere of cosmology, it would not escape from cultural solipsism. In any case, the lack of articulation between these two registers leads to political failure" (Albert 1995, 4). The nature of the indigenous project spans both universal political discourses and Native cultural specifics, its objectives interweaving various constructions of pluralism that originate as much from inside as from outside indigenous communities, established through intercultural dialogue among indigenous ethnic groups and with members of the national society. In short, if we are to understand this project, we need to take a dual approach that can infiltrate the interstices where universal and specific discourses meet.

In reality both poles of this equation are heterogeneous. After more than four centuries of colonization and in the wake of decades of dialogue between indigenous organizations and sympathetic popular movements, one cannot speak of two totally incommensurable logics. The process of cultural resistance has forced the ethnic movement to develop contestatory cultural forms that are deeply modern and are in dialogue with national forms. As Paul Gilroy indicates, echoing Du Bois, the power of minority cultural forms "derives from a doubleness, their unsteady location simultaneously inside and outside the conventions, assumptions, and aesthetic rules which distinguish and periodise modernity" (1993, 73). In the process, minority forms are *reimagined*, mixed with appropriated cultural forms from the majority society in a dynamic antiphony (1993, 74). What Gilroy suggests is essential. Minority theorizing appropriates concepts and methodologies from dominant paradigms and reconfigures them within a minority conceptual space, at the same time that indigenous cultural forms are reimagined within the space of struggle. In this sense, there is a certain urgency to maintaining the balance between culture and autonomy, so that one register does not erase the other.

In recognition of this challenge, indigenous theorizing in Cauca centers on the relationship between an inside and an outside. Native researchers have reflected on the meaning of the process of constructing cultural difference within the social system that surrounds them. They seek to define, through research and political action, ways to maintain a cultural inside different from the outside of the national society (Rappaport 2005, chap. 1; 2008). The inside is not a cultural essence as traditional anthropology would have it, although it is based on constellations of values and structures of behavior; the cultural forms of the inside articulated by the indigenous movement do not correspond to an observable cultural reality. After four hundred years of colonial domination, the cultural topography of Cauca is heterogeneous and syncretic, something activists not only recognize but appropriate into their field of action. Yet there are a few localities that demonstrate the constellation of values that the movement seeks to revitalize and project across the vast expanse of indigenous territory. For this reason, the inside is not really located in a concrete site, but in the utopias that the movement hopes to build on the basis of models generated by their researchers.[6]

Collaborative Theorizing

In what follows we reflect upon the complexities of indigenous theorizing on the basis of our collaborative work on the history of the PEBI, a program of the CRIC. Two members of the team, Abelardo Ramos, a Nasa linguist and PEBI member, and Joanne Rappaport, a North American anthropologist, are the authors of this essay; a third member of the team, Graciela Bolaños, is a non-Native collaborator with CRIC and a member of PEBI.[7] Since our work assumed the form of an interethnic dialogue—what in the movement is called a *diálogo de saberes*, an exchange of epistemologies—the remainder of this article is written as a script. Our two voices are marked by different fonts.

Joanne: Indigenous theorizing is the product of the complex negotiation of the ethnic movement's priorities and discourses aimed at bridging different epistemologies and methodologies so that they are not incommensurate. Thus, as we have argued, the task of the collaborative researcher presupposes a conversation between several subject positions, in particular, between representatives of national society and indigenous groups. But we haven't yet touched upon the organization of the production of such knowledge, which is inseparable from its theoretical qualities. In distinction to academic practice, which in anthropology is generally a solitary endeavor or organized into a relatively homogeneous group of researchers, in the indigenous movement research is profoundly collective; this presupposes a distinct methodology. Given that indigenous organizations include a range of activists, not only Native people from various ethnic groups but also nonindigenous collaborators, the research groups that coalesce within these organizations are also culturally—and epistemologically—heterogeneous.[8]

When external researchers collaborate in such enterprises, their methods and theory are subordinated to those created by the group (Vasco 2002, 449). This implies an acceptance not only of the equality of the different forms of knowledge, but also of their partial commensurability. Above all, it means that indigenous priorities must provide the general framework for research, although external theory also enters into discussion. That is to say, the contributions of external researchers are appropriated and transformed just as the movement refashions external cultural and political elements in its everyday activities.

It is imperative to understand that a collaborative dialogue is not between two monolithic poles—non-Native academics and indigenous researchers. Given that the research taking place in indigenous organizations emerges out of the joint work of indigenous actors and non-Native collaborators, who construct their research methodology as a team, it might be more fruitful to comprehend this process as a dialogue between activists (both indigenous and nonindigenous) and academics. I have discovered that the epistemological differences between my vision and that of my indigenous interlocutors is easily bridged, thanks to the anthropological training I received, which focused on Native epistemologies. However, I was not trained as an ethnographer to decipher the differences between activist and anthropological methodologies, where distinctions can be considerably more subtle.

Research in an indigenous organization frequently takes place in workshops, whose collective methodology presupposes that the community itself, and not just the researchers, participate in framing the project and analyzing its results. In this sense, workshops are exegetical spaces where theory is produced, not simply occasions for collecting data (Vasco 2002). Under such conditions, theory emerges out of a process of "co-theorizing," in which activists, the community, and external researchers all play a role. What makes this theorizing indigenous is its articulation with the priorities of the organization, which are developed collectively by traditional community authorities, the organizational leadership, shamans, bilingual teachers, non-Native collaborators, and others. In other words, what makes this knowledge indigenous is the particular way in which it is created and transmitted.[9]

Abelardo: The process of co-theorizing can be conceptualized in terms of local indigenous practice, through the application of the metaphor of the *minga*—collective work activities that benefit the community or a family—to the organization as a whole. It was in the experience of translating the Constitution of 1991 into Nasa Yuwe that we began to reconceptualize research as a minga in which various groups of people participated: the bilingual teachers of the community of Mosoco, cultural and political authorities recognized by the community (the cabildo, shamans, artisans, midwives), students from the local high school, and specialists in linguistics and in law, the latter being non-Native. The work done by this collective had a concrete result, a book that could be read by both Native people and members of the national society (Ramos and Cabildo Indígena de Mosoco 1993). Our metaphor merged physical labor, which is what is generally done at a minga, with intellectual work.

Frequently, local indigenous community members do not understand that intellectual labor is also a kind of work. Like work in the fields, intellectual work requires effort, produces fatigue, and creates results. But the comparison goes further than that. In Nasa Yuwe, both types of labor are referred to as majï, a term which is also used to describe the ritual activities of the shaman and the collective work of the cabildo in the building of territory (in particular, the walking of boundaries). Intellectual labor, when framed by the political priorities of the indigenous movement, fits neatly into this amplified notion of majï. The metaphor of the minga transcends the simple definition of collective labor, because it allows us to recognize that the notion of work is multifaceted.

Majï is a concept that unites various interests and collectivities. Similarly, collaboration cannot be reduced to a simple dialogue between individuals belonging to different cultures. The institutional interests of the participants are always in the background—the interests of the university or of academic theory, the objectives of NGOs, the program of the indigenous movement. That is to say, collaboration and co-theorizing involve much more than interpersonal dialogue; they promote a conversation in which individuals articulate the collective interests of the groups they represent or of which they are members. This distinction is important because in some instances such interlocution can lead participants, especially academics, to transcend the interests of their institution and merge, perhaps temporarily, with an interethnic and nonacademic collectivity. When research funding has been acquired by the movement itself, the academic is at liberty to function independently of her or his institution in order to embrace indigenous priorities.[10]

The profile of the researcher is equally significant. He or she must recognize that research is not a neutral process, that one must choose dialogue. It is not just a question of respecting indigenous positions, but also of entering in active conversation with them. This is difficult for academics to accept since they are accustomed to treating indigenous ideas as ethnographic data, not as potential conceptual tools.

Despite the generosity of the participants, such a dialogue cannot but produce tensions. These may be due to the prejudices each member brings to the table, to the underlying sense of competition, and to the epistemological differences between them, whether academic or organizational epistemologies or those of the Native culture. Such conflict requires that participants act responsibly. Tensions can easily turn into nonnegotiable conflicts, or they can be fruitful. It is the responsibility of the participants to aim toward negotiation, not toward rupture.

The balancing of institutional and cultural interests involves a highly complex process. There are cultural differences even among the members of indigenous organizations, since they include representatives of different ethnic groups and non-Native collaborators. This is to emphasize that conflicts will arise not only among academics and activists, but also in the movement itself.

Collaborative research, with all of its institutional conflicts and cultural differences, is like two roads that cross each other, even if ultimately they are headed in the same direction. That is to say, difference is not necessarily negative, nor is it something that must be transcended. Assumed with responsibility, difference can produce new approaches to social reality, if the participants commit to the objectives of the indigenous organization. In other words, an intercultural framework, not the academic appropriation or concealing of indigenous ideas, must guide the research. The academic, who has been trained through a model of individual intellectual production, must recognize two fundamental realities: that collaborative work cannot be individual and that indigenous elements cannot be subsumed under an academic model. The two paths must nourish one another, being always conscious of their difference but also aware of their common goals. In the course of the research process, individual participants will be enriched intellectually by learning from one another. In the end, collaboration makes a contribution not only to the collectivity, but also to each of the participants.

The History of PEBI: *Collaborative Research at the Grass Roots*

In the case of the history of PEBI, collaboration was not grounded exclusively in the dynamics of our three-member research team, but also required initiating dialogue with the broader group of activists.

PEBI was founded at the end of the 1970s as an initiative of the Fifth Congress of CRIC and, particularly, of its vice president, Benjamín Dindicué. PEBI was conceived as an organizing space in which communities in struggle could be mobilized around regional demands.[11] Although PEBI is an educational program—including curricular design, historical and linguistic research, the generation of theory, and teacher training—its central objectives focus on the creation of schools as a vanguard for the organizing of political, social, and cultural activities in indigenous communities in conjunction with cabildos and other traditional authorities. In other words, from the start PEBI's objectives have transcended pedagogy, and its members characterize their project as contestatory, nourished by a critical and politicized appreciation of intercultural pedagogical methods. In contrast to other popular education projects in Latin America, PEBI originated not from within an educational movement, but in a political organization. Schools were founded in those communities that exhibited intense involvement in political organizing, and the first teachers were chosen from a pool of the most committed activists, irrespective of their level of schooling. Community members served as evaluators and advisors, developing their ideas in workshops and community assemblies. More than a space for training children, the school was conceived as the pivot of the entire community.

In its more than three decades of existence, PEBI has entered into dialogue with educators across Colombia and Latin America, contributing innovative cultural and curricular projects that have served as models for ethnoeducation at the regional and national levels. It has trained a significant number of indigenous teachers and political leaders in Cauca. Its intercultural and culture-specific proposals for the construction of ethnic pluralism have permeated CRIC as a whole, and increasingly CRIC's leadership has drawn upon PEBI members to fill important political roles in the organization.

Around 2000 PEBI undertook the task of researching and writing its history. The project was conceived as a learning experience and a space for collective analysis, requiring the broad participation of program members in the research. To this end, a series of workshops and meetings were held in 2000 and 2001, gatherings at which activists, including staff members in the regional program as well as local bilingual teachers and leaders, compiled a list of fifty-one questions meant to orient the research process and prepare grass-roots activists for collecting relevant information in their localities. PEBI's program is crystallized in these guiding questions. The questions exhort researchers to illustrate how education is a political vehicle, how it leads communities to develop a cosmic and historical relationship with their territory, how this project lays the basis for forging political autonomy, economic reconstruction, and community development. The questions emphasize the centrality of intercultural appropriation of ideas within a project that is not merely educational, but political. They outline how PEBI objectives are directed at the entire organization and not just at its educational sector. They illustrate how the program acts as a vanguard promoting indigenous content in the organization at large.

However, almost all of the questions engage PEBI's current policies. They are not at all retrospective, in part because so many of the workshop participants were young, most with a scant decade of experience in the organization. Their presentist cast posed a challenge for the research team, which was charged with writing a history of the program.

Abelardo: For me, those fifty-one questions were challenging methodologically because I felt that they constrained the nature of the project, forcing us to focus on current organizing strategies instead of engaging in a political-historical analysis. The latter was my primary political interest. For some of us who are Nasa-speakers, the idea of doing history was appealing because it would help us to trace the educational process retrospectively. We wanted to study the political nature of the process over time. In particular, we hoped to communicate to future generations the hopes of the elders who founded CRIC and PEBI at the end of the seventies: how they fought to build a feeling of dignity as a people and how they gained their rights by building an educational system based upon our own culture. Doing history would permit us to engage in a dialogue with those first generations. In the final workshop we built a consensus in favor of the history project, with testimonies collected from the protagonists in the process.[12]

The truth is that the guiding questions were composed before we made the decision to write a history of PEBI. As a result, our team was forced to adapt them to the historical framework we had chosen. This meant we would have to engage in a negotiation, using the questions as conceptual guides for thinking retrospectively, and in the course of this reflection we would have to find a way to engage and foreground the voices of the narrators. I think that the questions helped me to see that a history of education was of necessity a political history. We would need to interpret the testimonies within this framework, bring together today's political priorities with the memory of the past.

Joanne: The workshop participants did not seek answers to their questions in a historical narrative that highlighted the earlier experiences of PEBI but hoped to resolve them through reflection on their own experiences, which, on the whole, went back only a decade. In a sense, their questions contained the answers they sought, calling up accepted discourses instead of historical explanation. But although the questions expressed the concerns of the present, they would have to serve as a fulcrum around which we could organize our interpretation of the past. At the outset I resisted this arrangement because I did not fully comprehend it.

The three-person research team began to debate the ways in which we hoped to frame this history. In numerous PEBI meetings, ranging from curricular planning and program evaluation to political meetings, I had observed that local teachers frequently made use of the spiral motif to organize their presentations. At one curricular meeting, the teachers from the experimental school in the community of Juan Tama presented their pedagogical projects—community history, organic agriculture, the school garden, Nasa literacy—in a chart organized into a spiral. PEBI's magazine, *Çxayu'çe*, published a board game to stimulate use of Nasa Yuwe among schoolchildren, also organized as a spiral (Anonymous 2000).[13] I enthusiastically recommended that we consider the spiral as an organizing motif for our history project.

The lukewarm response I received indicated that PEBI hoped to produce a document whose analytical character and sphere of circulation would be considerably wider than that which the culturally specific spiral motif could assume. There was a great desire to produce an intercultural history that incorporated the experiences of the various ethnic groups under the CRIC umbrella, despite the fact that the bulk of PEBI's work had been with Nasa speakers. Such a set of objectives obviated the possibility of employing the spiral as a conceptual model. I was confronted with the naiveté of my understanding of indigenous theorizing as something that could arise only out of Native cultural forms. The regional space of indigenous politics, where concepts originating in national and international debates could be appropriated, was a more apt space for theorizing the history of PEBI. Despite their presentist orientation, the fifty-one guiding questions provided us by the workshops supplied useful tools for conceptualizing movement history from the vantage point of a discourse of political autonomy, as opposed to one with a culturalist perspective.

Community Control, Interculturalism, and Cosmovision

Joanne: In my three decades of ethnographic research in Colombia I had never followed such a conceptual itinerary: a research agenda that was more political than academic, a research plan for historical study based on presentist referents, a project whose conceptual framework originated outside of the academic community and whose objectives were determined by a group of nonacademics who were not directly involved with the research team. I quickly learned that when a social movement conducts research, its methodology is vastly different from that employed by academics.

However, the broad participation of PEBI members in the establishment of our conceptual framework does not mean that activist research lacks rigor. In the course of collecting oral narratives from early indigenous activists and collaborators, I discovered that activist researchers have access to a much more extensive range of information than academics, and they are constantly submitting these data to collective evaluation and analysis. Where they differ from us is in their objectives, which lead them to produce analyses based upon explicit political criteria, whereas the politics inherent in academic research is frequently made imperceptible by academic discourse.

The book that resulted from our research (Bolaños, Ramos, Rappaport, and Miñana 2004) draws its three conceptual threads from the political program of PEBI: community control (an educational program that stimulates community organizing), interculturalism (the construction of an intercultural dialogue framed by indigenous values), and cosmovision (the need to maintain harmony in the universe). All three guiding ideas have been embraced throughout the continent by ethnic organizations and NGOs; however, we instrumentalized them in our narration of PEBI history by emphasizing the specific constellation of political contexts in which they were articulated. Community control provided the conceptual framework for a chapter dealing with how and why education is politics for CRIC. The concept of interculturalism allowed us to take a critical look at relations over time between nonindigenous collaborators and Native activists. Cosmovision, embodied in a creation story generated through collective research by PEBI with almost two hundred shamans, provided us with an alternative historical chronology rooted in how notions of culture evolved within the organization.

Joanne: The way I visualize the interaction of the three conceptual threads we selected is that community control provides the political foundations for the educational activities in which PEBI has always engaged. Interculturalism allows for an outward-looking orientation, permitting educational activists to never lose sight of the larger picture, the fact that education is part of a general political struggle for recognition as participants in the construction of the Colombian nation. Cosmovision provides the tools for an introspective orientation that values indigenous lifeways and ideologies, providing a specific cultural framework for interculturalism and, ultimately, for political action.

Abelardo: Our organizing strategy has always consisted in strengthening an indigenous cultural identity that has been impacted by colonization. This objective cannot be undertaken without the participation of the community, yet it also permits us to relate to other peoples and resolve our problems in conjunction with them. Our concept of identity is intimately related to one of community power. This is a principal axis in our political work and must necessarily mediate our analysis of our historical experience. The notion of interculturalism is related to the conceptual thread of community control. Cauca is a multicultural province, one in which the future of the Nasa people can be strengthened only by forging links of cooperation with other indigenous groups as well as with the rest of the social fabric, including mestizo peasants, Afrodescendants, and popular urban sectors. This means that we must stake out a clear intercultural position founded in respect and the sharing of survival strategies. Interculturalism is profoundly political for us: it leads us to demand that we be recognized as culturally different peoples and as national actors. Cosmovision is the accumulation of ancestral knowledge that, from our point of view, affords us important tools for interacting with others. Cosmovision defines our cultural difference, marking our participation in a diverse nation. It is only through recourse to cosmovision that we can put interculturalism into practice because cosmovision provides us with the conceptual model that permits us to act as Natives.

Joanne: Each of us experienced conceptual conflicts in the course of the process. Once having constructed our conceptual framework, we began the task of historical interpretation. It was not an easy process. Having opted for a retrospective approach, as opposed to a systematic organizational analysis, we had to construct a narrative of the evolution of the three unifying concepts. That meant accepting that some of these concepts, particularly cosmovision and interculturalism, were only incipient during the first decade of the organization, not full-blown as we observe them today. Cosmovision was a particularly difficult concept to historicize. As it is articulated today, cosmovision is the product of an intensive research process that was undertaken in the 1990s, giving rise to an integrated cosmology and ritual complex that is being adopted by Nasa communities throughout Cauca. It is thus a recent arrival on the scene in the sense that although much of this knowledge existed among shamans, it was piecemeal and had never been verbalized in a coherent narrative. Cosmovision is an attempt to integrate cosmological knowledge and to give it a didactic form that can be internalized by the indigenous population. The challenge for us, as historians, was to explicate the origins and evolution of this concept without denying the millenarian existence of cosmological knowledge. But cosmovision was not the only sticking point we encountered.

Abelardo: My personal preoccupation, as both an actor in and an interpreter of the process, was with transcending anecdotal narrative. This meant negotiating the constant tension I felt between these two roles, which implied a movement between orality and writing. The founding leaders of CRIC eloquently expressed their political thought orally. With the exception of Manuel Quintín Lame, the elders had no experience in writing down their ideas.[14] Therefore, in the development of a contestatory political process writing was not necessarily a task of the leadership, although they controlled the written production of other indigenous activists and of the nonindigenous collaborators. I was educated in such contexts, not as a leader, but as a cultural activist, a role that implied a command of written communication. Because Nasa Yuwe was my first language, my entry into the activity of written reflection has been an ongoing process, one in which my training as an activist unfolded parallel to the development of my literate sensibilities. I have written works in various genres, including educational documents, texts inspired by Nasa mythology, and linguistic analysis. But this was the first time in my experience that I was to participate in the production of a historical narrative, a story in which I was also an actor.

For me, writing the history of PEBI has been a process of confronting the difficulties of thinking retrospectively in dialogue with other team members. I had to strive to transcend a recounting of everyday experience, which was what I, as an actor, could most easily narrate. Instead, I had to attempt to elaborate an interpretation that included, simultaneously, my own experience, the objectives of the bilingual teachers and PEBI activists who formulated our guiding questions, and the evaluation of the actions of the elders.[15] To weave all this into a written narrative that was pleasing to read and at once preserved the voices of the protagonists and situated them in their historical contexts: all of this forced me to be attentive to my responsibilities within the team. I could not adopt the role merely of an informant but had to exercise political and cultural responsibility, not only as a member of PEBI and of the indigenous movement, but also as a Nasa. I needed to transcend the biases that indigenous actors generally felt toward academics and collaborators, but in addition I had to ensure that what we wrote reflected an indigenous ideology. This was my role: to ensure that in the course of the project the intercultural team maintained the transcendence of the indigenous discourse.

Conclusion

What did we learn in the process? That collaboration necessarily implies being open to other modes of thought, to different ways of formulating research questions, to the possibility of political analysis. But these differences do not always arise out of the fault lines between Western academic culture and the radical cultural alterity of an indigenous researcher; they more frequently result from the disparities between academics and activists, whose cultural differences are more subtle and not as easily recognizable. We must also understand that the political aspirations of cultural activists are frequently embedded within a cultural discourse that obscures their political nature—at least, for the external observer, but not for the internal participant. What we must accomplish is to build methodological and conceptual bridges across divergent but not always completely apparent positions. This can be achieved only by adopting a framework in which academic analysis occupies a secondary position that respects and does not violate organizational priorities; even if academic contributions introduce concepts external to the indigenous culture, the objective is to internalize them by resignifying them through translation. If an academic accepts these rules, she or he also accepts the intercultural orientation of the project.

Such are the priorities that determined the nature of our work. When we entered into conversation, we came to realize that the guiding concepts of PEBI history would have to assume a discourse of political autonomy, not one of indigenous culture and much less one of an academic nature. To theorize from an indigenous perspective does not always mean that cultural alterity is foregrounded, but it does mean that cultural difference must be grounded in an intercultural perspective.

Rey Chow (1995, 180) distinguishes between ethnography and autoethnography by suggesting that the autoethnographer is simultaneously the subject and object of her research: as she engages in study she is cognizant of the fact that others have studied her, something that Chow calls a state of "being-looked-at-ness." Autoethnography is thereby more contestatory than conventional ethnography. In a way, our history of PEBI arose out of a sense of being-looked-at-ness: the fact of being an *object* of conventional education influenced CRIC's desire to achieve indigenous protagonism, to become a *subject* in education. Equally, the three members of our history research team experienced being-looked-at-ness. This was certainly the case for Abelardo, who, as actor and analyst, was simultaneously a subject and object of historical research. But by virtue of the collaborative nature of the project, Joanne and Graciela also came to experience this effect, as each of us was exposed to the gaze of the other team members and of the PEBI collective whose questions guided our work. The complex dialogue that arose out of this exercise helped us understand the deep and multifaceted meaning of collaboration and interculturalism.

Notes

Acknowledgments: The German foundation Terre des Hommes funded CRIC in its efforts to write a history of its bilingual education program. Joanne Rappaport's research was funded by an international collaborative grant from the Wenner-Gren Foundation for Anthropological Research during 1999–2002. We thank Florencia Mallon and the University of Wisconsin for inviting us to participate in the "Narrating Native Histories" conference, where this book originated. Portions of this essay were published in chapter 5 of Joanne Rappaport's *Intercultural Utopias: Public Intellectuals, Cultural Experimentation, and Ethnic Pluralism in Colombia* (Duke University Press, 2005); in this essay, however, the republished sections appear in dialogue with the observations of Abelardo Ramos, thus transforming their intent.

1. The Duboisian notion of double consciousness arose at a particular moment in the history of interracial relations in the United States and out of the very specific intellectual trajectory of Du Bois himself. But notwithstanding its origins in the highly polarized racial atmosphere of the United States in the early twentieth century

and its insertion into a discourse of racial pride, the concept of double consciousness presupposes a complex and heterogeneous experience, not a simple essence (Chandler 1996, 85). In this sense, it is a metaphor that can be fruitfully applied across geographic and historical contexts. In a workshop with some forty bilingual teachers affiliated with the CRIC, the concept was reconfigured according to indigenous political priorities as "a revaluing of our own culture as difference." One of the participants offered the following rereading of the concept: "The pain of being indigenous, with all of the implications of rejection to which we are subjected and, at the same time, pride in being different, with a clear and defined identity" (Chocué Guasaquillo 2000, 14). For an analysis of this exercise, see Rappaport (2005, chap. 1).

2. Theory is a major challenge today, when Native groups across the Americas have proposed the creation of indigenous universities (Pancho Aquite et al., 2004).

3. Abelardo Ramos graduated from this program.

4. There is not sufficient space here to describe other attempts at indigenous theorization in Bolivia (Fernández Osco 2000); Guatemala (Montejo 2002, cf. Warren 1998, chaps. 5, 6); and New Zealand (Bishop 1994; Smith 1999), which also present rich sources for the creation of Native conceptual tools.

5. Both Allen and Field employ the term *sovereignty* in their analyses because it is a fundamental demand of Native Americans. However, in a country like Colombia, where indigenous communities exist on the basis of colonial royal titles instead of treaties, the notion of sovereignty is not as relevant as that of autonomy, which permits them to think of themselves simultaneously as Native people and as Colombians.

6. Our use of *utopia* to signify a dream that is partially attainable comes from the usage in CRIC itself.

7. The final product of our research (Bolaños, Ramos, Rappaport, and Miñana 2004) was also coauthored by Carlos Miñana, an anthropologist at the National University of Colombia in Bogotá who has worked on a number of PEBI projects; Carlos assisted in the writing of the final chapter on PEBI's pedagogical activities.

8. We refer specifically here to CRIC, whose various programs in education, health, agricultural production, and gender operate with interethnic personnel. In the Indigenous Authorities of Colombia (AICO), a parallel indigenous organization that works in Cauca, there are no non-Native collaborators. Instead, nonindigenous supporters formed a distinct solidarity movement parallel to AICO; however, even in this case, research takes on the character of an interethnic dialogue, as the two organizations enter into collaboration (Vasco 2002).

9. The term *traditional authority* is used in Cauca to refer to annually elected reservation councils (*cabildos*). The executive council of CRIC was recognized recently as a traditional authority after a protracted struggle with the national government, entitling them to carry staffs of office, as cabildo members do. However, in practice there is an implicit distinction made between community authorities and *líderes* (leaders) in the organization.

10. Joanne: Colombian academics are frequently constrained by their institutions in ways that are unfamiliar to those of us who work in U.S. universities. For instance, their research must be approved by the university administration if they are to conduct it during the academic year—which extends for considerably more weeks than in the United States. The constraints that operate upon academics in the United States are more subtle, generated by the venues in which we publish our research. Nevertheless, Abelardo, who has an M.A. in linguistics from a major Colombian university and was trained by French academics, is acutely aware of the ways in which the international academy limits the activities of its members.

11. Until 2004, PEBI was called PEB, the Bilingual Education Program. As a result of research into PEBI's history it was decided that interculturalism was a critical component of the program, and so its name was changed to the Bilingual and Intercultural Education Program.

12. Joanne: Until the last of the three workshops, the general membership of PEBI did not have an opportunity to discuss the nature of the project. Many of them assumed that it would take the form of a *sistematización*, a collective analysis of current goals and objectives, evaluating their progress in the different components of the education program. In fact, the guiding questions were prepared with a sistematización in mind. It was only at the third workshop that the idea of writing a history was broached and subsequently chosen as a viable option by the Nasa-speakers at the meeting, who were in the majority. For more on these negotiations and on the nature of the guiding questions, see Rappaport (2005, chap. 5).

13. A universal orthography for Nasa Yuwe was adopted in 2000. In an earlier alphabet used by CRIC, *Çxayu'çe* was written as *C'ayu'ce*. We will cite articles in the magazine that were published before the adoption of the new orthography in the earlier alphabet.

14. Manuel Quintín Lame was a Nasa leader who, in the first half of the twentieth century, organized indigenous communities in the provinces of Cauca and Tolima. His demands form the basis of CRIC's political program. Lame wrote a treatise, *Los pensamientos del indio que se educó dentro de las selvas colombianas* (Thoughts of an Indian educated in the Colombian forests), which has become a foundational text for the Colombian indigenous movement (Lame 2004 [1939]).

15. Graciela Bolaños, the third member of the team, also had to confront this challenge, given that she was a founding member of CRIC.

JAN RUS AND DIANE L. RUS

The Taller Tzotzil of Chiapas, Mexico

A Native Language Publishing Project, 1985–2002

Between 1976 and 2002 the Taller Tzotzil (Spanish for "Tzotzil Workshop") published more than thirty booklets by indigenous authors in Tzotzil-Maya, a language spoken by some four hundred thousand people in Mexico's southernmost state of Chiapas. The Taller followed the model of the Brazilian educator Paulo Freire (for example, 1969), and the original purpose of the publications was to put on paper the reflections of Tzotzil-speakers as they finished literacy courses in their own language as an exercise in *concientización* (consciousness-raising or empowerment.)[1] Typical themes were the importance of communal labor, the revitalization of local fiestas, and the achievement of indigenous control over schools and town halls—topics that essentially focused inside of indigenous communities and reaffirmed their solidarity and continuity. Beginning in the mid-1980s, however, as Mexico's economic crisis made life within traditional communities more and more precarious and drove increasing numbers of people into cities and distant labor migrations, the Taller began providing a space in which to examine Tzotzil people's place in the larger society and economy, to discuss economic and organizational alternatives, to explore alternate indigenous-centered histories, and then to share those discussions with other Tzotzil-speakers. Publications began focusing outward, taking on contract labor on coffee plantations, the struggle for land, organization of artisan and agricultural cooperatives, indigenous rights in the city, undocumented migration to the United States, and reactions to the Zapatista Rebellion.

This essay is a reflection on the course of the Taller in this second period. Most of the questions addressed could be asked of any publishing project: How were topics chosen? How were the texts composed and edited? How were the publications distributed? Beyond the extraordinary historical circumstances of the 1980s and 1990s, however, the fact that the Taller was in two senses an intercultural project adds additional levels of complication to these questions.

On the first level, because there was no recent precedent for written as opposed to oral communication within the larger community of Tzotzil-speakers, the very fact of publishing raised questions about new versus old culture among Tzotzils themselves.[2] Who, for example, had the authority to be an author? Although they are increasingly a thing of the past, in the 1980s there were still deeply felt disagreements over the right to write—to express a public opinion—of the young as opposed to the old, women as opposed to men, and people who had not achieved offices within their communities as opposed to people with socially defined status. What dialect and orthography should be used? What formats, themes, and audiences were appropriate? That is, was it better to publish monolingually for an indigenous audience or bilingually so nonindigenous people could listen in? Were there themes too sensitive to share with nonindigenous people or with indigenous political rivals—or to write about at all?

On the second level, questions arose from the fact that the Taller's coordinators—that is, we, the authors of this essay—were nonindigenous participants in what otherwise aspired to be an indigenous project. Just whose culture and politics came into play in making choices about form and content, even when these were made collectively with indigenous colleagues? How much did our presence affect the way in which people participated in the Taller—their comfort with themes, linguistic forms, and processes of production—or even their willingness to participate? How much, finally, was a publishing project, as opposed, for instance, to a project of community discussions without a written record, "our thing," itself a cultural artifact, not to say an imposition?

By the time we went to work in the Taller we had lived for extended periods in indigenous communities in Puno, Peru, and in highland Chiapas and were not naive about our status as outsiders. At the same time, Rigoberta Menchú's *I, Rigoberta* had appeared only a year and a half before we began our project, and the arguments about *testimonio*, representation, and whether the subaltern could ever speak in a supposedly colonial form such as writing, with all the exquisite self-consciousness these arguments would eventually evoke within the academy, had barely begun.[3] During the 1970s we had done extensive oral history and ethnohistory interviewing in

Tzotzil and had also established many personal relationships and alliances with members of Tzotzil communities. Thus we knew that among Tzotzil-speakers speaking in Tzotzil there was an internal, indigenous conversation about history and politics that was not only different from, but also opposed to the ways those same themes were talked about in Spanish, even by the same people. Through stories and gossip, people discussed and analyzed exploitative labor conditions, repressive government, and discrimination against Indians as well as ways to combat these ills. These conversations had always existed and had just as certainly almost always been kept within the community of those who spoke Tzotzil, secret from ladinos (non-Indians). Our proposal, in all its straightforward simplicity, was to help disseminate some of this internal, face-to-face analysis; to encourage communities to talk with each other in their own language across the region, with us acting temporarily as "midwives" for what they had to say.

If our goal was to help Tzotzil-speakers express themselves in print, however, it should also be clear that we had interests and points of view of our own. From the beginning of our time with the Taller, we continued to study and write about the deep economic and political changes occurring in rural Chiapas. We were critical of the inwardly focused community studies characteristic of most Chiapas anthropology through the mid-1980s, and although we appreciated the efforts of others to publish in native languages, we were also impatient with the tendency of many writing and literacy projects to stay at the level of myths and animal stories. To us it seemed obvious that Tzotzil-speaking people were struggling with the same worldwide forces that affected us as well. Virtually all of the books published by the Taller from its inception had been preceded by extensive conversations and seminars within communities about their own history; about the exploitation, repression, and discrimination they had experienced; and about how they had dealt with them. As much as we hoped to continue these local discussions and to connect them to wider conversations involving others who might pick up and read a book in Tzotzil, we also looked forward to participating in them ourselves, to being part of what Andrés Aubry (2005) called the "co-production of knowledge."

It seems to us that the most natural way to get to these questions is to take them on chronologically, as we came upon them, or tripped over them, in the course of working in the Taller. The following essay thus takes the form of a sort of diary, describing in order the projects created by the Taller during the years of our participation and then probing the evolution of our practice with each new project—that is, the puzzles that arose, and, as best we can reconstruct them, the discussions and thinking behind the Taller's solutions.

Chiapas in the Mid-1980s: Beginning Considerations

When we started our collaboration with the Taller in late 1985, it had been eight years since we had finished our long ethnographic fieldwork in Chiapas in the mid-1970s. The first change we discovered, although it took us a few months to recognize it, was that which we had formerly thought of as indigenous communities' dissenting, critical, often angry private conversations among themselves had become increasingly public. By that point, Chiapas's indigenous communities were deeply immersed in the economic depression, *la crisis*, which officially dates from the Mexican financial collapse of 1982 but which in fact had begun in the countryside almost a decade earlier. The seasonal, often migrant, agricultural labor on which indigenous communities depended for their livelihoods had stagnated in the mid-1970s, and by the mid-1980s the demand for workers was actually slightly less than it had been in 1975.[4] For a while Mexico's borrowing against its oil reserves had underwritten construction projects that took up some of the employment slack, but after 1982 that work also disappeared. Under these circumstances, indigenous people made radical changes in their lives to support themselves. Tens of thousands abandoned their ancestral communities in order to homestead land in the Lacandón jungle. Many tens of thousands more moved into shantytowns around Chiapas's cities, cities that had never before had sizable indigenous populations. Economic choices also changed life within families. Men began migrating greater distances to find work and staying away for longer periods once they had found it. Given men's absences and their families' pressing needs, women, in turn, began looking for ways to make money outside of their homes. For the first time, many women became agricultural wage laborers in regions near their homes. Many others turned their traditional weaving and embroidery into artisan goods they could sell to tourists.

Most of all, indigenous people throughout the state, previously renowned for the insularity of their communal social and cultural lives, increasingly joined new regionwide associations, some of them independent political and economic organizations, others religious groups, both Catholic and Protestant (Harvey 1998; Rus, Hernández Castillo, and Mattiace 2003, 1–26; Collier 1994). Some of these groups helped resettle those who migrated, others helped with the production and marketing of new kinds of goods, and still others organized protests about injustices and in some regions even led land invasions. The rising reorganization and reorientation of the state's indigenous population are beyond the present discussion, except to the extent that they are a theme of many of the Taller's books. What most interests us here is that by the mid-1980s people all over the state had begun to say publicly things that in the past they had said only among themselves. Without quite understanding the extent of this break or even, at the beginning, that it was a break, we clearly had come into a very different political and cultural environment from the one in which we had lived during the 1970s.

For its part, the Taller Tzotzil had already begun responding to the change even before we arrived. The first history of the Mexican Revolution in the Tzotzil highlands produced by Tzotzil-speakers themselves, with acute, biting commentary about the behavior of landowners and the government during the decades after the Revolution (*K'alal ich'ay mosoal / Cuando dejamos de ser aplastados*; When we were no longer crushed), was coordinated by Andrés Aubry, the Taller's founder, and published in Tzotzil and Spanish in 1982. This was followed in February 1985 by a deeply felt book by the Taller's principal Tzotzil editor and translator, José González Hernández of Zinacantán, and his great-uncle Antonio López Pérez, Zinacantán's first Native municipal secretary. The book (*Ja' k'u x'elan ta jpojbatik ta ilbajinel yu'un jkaxlanetik / Cómo escapamos del control de los ladinos*; How we escaped the control of the ladinos) was about their community's successful fight at the end of the 1950s to overthrow the state government's custom of imposing nonindigenous municipal secretaries to supervise the community's local council. Neither of these stories, about the Revolution of the 1910s and the fight for local self-government in the 1950s, was a new one, but in retelling them, *publishing* them, in the 1980s the authors of the two books were holding them up for reflection during a new period of doubt and vulnerability.

We did not fully realize the extent of the changes that had already begun when we arrived in the fall of 1985, nor could we have predicted that a new historical period was beginning. In the new configuration, most Tzotzils would no longer be occupied full-time in agriculture, and cultural and political leadership would increasingly swing from local communities to city and even regional organizations. After a couple of months of talking with our Tzotzil friends, however, we did begin to understand the urgency of their economic worries. In the 1970s, as a couple with a small child, we had studied migrant labor, accompanying Tzotzil workers to coffee plantations, sugar-cane fields, and corn haciendas, staying and working alongside them for brief periods. We knew that mention of such labor had been left out of most ethnographies of the highland Tzotzils. It occurred away from the communities that were the sites of research, and in any case was not, according to most anthropologists, an item of Native culture.[5] We also knew, however, that among Tzotzils themselves that work had been an important topic of conversation in the 1970s, when it was a mainstay of their families' incomes. If anything, it was an even more important topic in the 1980s, when it was disappearing. We thus decided that our first booklet should be about seasonal migrant labor, specifically, coffee labor, and the ways it was woven into community life.[6] Everyone had a story about working, and not working, in coffee. As a theme that might spark discussions of work and economic change, it seemed ideal. And so in early 1986 we began interviewing for *Abtel ta Pinka* ("Labor on Coffee Plantations").

1985–1986: "Turning Talk into Paper"

Abtel ta Pinka was published in a monolingual Tzotzil edition in September 1986 and republished in a bilingual Tzotzil–Spanish version in 1991. It consisted of selections from the testimonies of coffee workers from the *municipio* of Chamula, three men and a woman, plus the wives of the men, who had felt the effects of *enganche*, contract labor. In all, the texts spanned the period from the late 1930s to the early 1980s. The sections were organized by theme: the planters, labor contracting, the coffee workers' union, life on the plantation, what it was like to be the wife of a worker who stayed behind in the village, what it was like to be a woman coffee worker, and so forth. After recording and transcribing the open-ended testimonies, several of which were done over several days, the members of the Taller—the two of us and two colleagues, one from the community of Zinacantán and the other from Chamula—edited the texts and then submitted them to the authors for approval. In all but one case, this meant reading the entire manuscript aloud for those who could not read, checking both content and language. Finally, we added photographs, both historical and recent, and provided captions with additional information about the plantations, such as the dates they were founded, the nationalities of the owners, the value of Chiapas's coffee production through the years, and so on. The final booklet was twenty-eight pages long.

Following the precedent of earlier Taller publications, we printed two hundred copies. Most were sold for thirty cents, far less than the cost of printing them, but we felt it was important that the books have a value.[7] Copies were given to the authors and their families, and many more (some forty) were distributed to Tzotzil schoolteachers and catechists for sharing with their classes or community discussion groups (*grupos de reflexión*). To our surprise, the largest single market, however, consisted of the mostly Protestant settlers in the *colonias* surrounding San Cristóbal, who bought seventy to eighty copies for the full price. Smaller numbers, perhaps twenty-five, were purchased by residents of other rural Tzotzil-speaking communities.

The second edition, published in 1991, was, as noted, bilingual and consisted of four hundred copies. Most of the edition was sold through bookstores, where it was still available at the beginning of the Zapatista Rebellion in 1994. Soon thereafter, as one of the few publications that described indigenous people's lives in their own words, it sold out. Over the next several years, parts of the text were published multiple times in Spanish and English (for example, Paz Paredes, Cobo, and Bartra, 1996; Womack 1999, 111–18; see also Collier 1991).

Practice: Initial Decisions

Voices: From the beginning we set out to counter the homogenizing tendency of typical ethnographies and histories, with their single narrative voice. Beginning with this test publication, all but two of the Taller's publications after 1986 had a variety of voices: men and women, old and young, and, if possible, individuals from more than one community. In the specific case of *Abtel*, we hoped to convey the testimonies' message that the system of migrant labor affected not just the migrants but their entire families, and not only during the months migrants were away at work but throughout the year. Life in coffee workers' communities, hundreds of miles from the plantations, was organized around the calendar of coffee. Scheduling of community work days, planting, fiestas, marriages, and baptisms had to take into account the prolonged seasonal absences of adult men. Everyone's life was affected, even those who never left their home *municipios*. By letting a variety of people speak, *Abtel* tried to demonstrate the variety of ways in which this impact was experienced.

On women's participation: With only two exceptions, we believe, women's voices were not present in native language books in Chiapas before *Abtel*, either in the state projects, or among Protestant and Catholic missionaries' books, or even in the early Taller Tzotzil publications (1975–85).[8] Nor, as far as we know, had scholarly writing about coffee work and other migrant labor in Chiapas ever mentioned the impact of such work on the women and children who stayed at home. As it happened, however, including women seemed as natural to our collaborators as it did to us. Men and women both knew that labor migrations affected the entire family, and both understood and accepted that the point was to explore the experiences and hardships of men and women alike. Indeed, one of the former coffee workers encouraged his wife to come forward with the painful story of her fights with her first husband every time he had to depart for the *fincas*. Another woman talked about the economic survival strategies she learned during her husband's long absences. Still a third told of the difficulties of being a single mother and one of the very few women who hired on as a coffee picker.

Monolingual vs. bilingual publication: Because we started with the idea that these were to be indigenous books, we worked solely in Tzotzil on the first two projects only, *Abtel* and *Lo'il yu'un Kuskat* (see below). One unexpected effect of this choice was our almost immediate popularity with urban Protestants. Many adult converts had become literate in order to read the Bible in Tzotzil, and by the early 1980s they were probably the largest single category of Tzotzil readers. Having learned to read, they were continually searching for new material, and when it appeared, word spread quickly through their congregations and colonias. A side effect of this popularity, however—and a paradoxical one, given that we had decided to work in Tzotzil precisely to emphasize traditional language and culture—was that many traditionalists became quite suspicious of us. By the mid-1980s municipios throughout the highlands were riven by bitter and bloody conflicts between traditionalists and Protestants. Many traditionalists, seeing *Abtel* (which most of them could not read), concluded that we must be Protestant missionaries. Were we not gringos, like the missionaries? Were gringo missionaries not the main producers of books in Tzotzil? Were our books not widely read in the Protestant settlements? Given the bitterness of the religious struggle, this assumption could have closed some communities to us, particularly Chamula, where we had hoped to concentrate our efforts. Luckily, two of the families that had contributed to *Abtel* were themselves leading traditionalists. Although at first they were discreet about their participation in the book, eventually they helped dispel suspicions of us. For our part, we attempted to counter gossip against the Taller by giving Chamula's leaders free copies of *Abtel* as well as copies of some of the book's historic photos. More than that, we made a conscious choice that the Taller's second publication would be an account of a Chamula uprising in the nineteenth century by one of the community's most traditional religious leaders.

Editor-written introductions vs. letting the books speak for themselves: To avoid intruding into the content of the books, we resolved at the beginning to try to keep editorial introductions to a minimum. We limited ourselves to stating the time period, the locations in which the books were set, and perhaps brief descriptions of the authors. The only exception to this rule in all of the books was the second book, *Lo'il yu'un Kuskat*.

Orthography: Spelling and alphabet in Chiapas's indigenous languages are still not settled. Since 1988 government and secular groups have been using conventions chosen in meetings called by the National Institute for Adult Education (Instituto Nacional de Educación Adulta, INEA), in which we participated. Publishers of Protestant materials, on the other hand—successors of the Wycliffe Bible Translators and Summer Institute of Linguistics (WBT/SIL)—who have the overwhelming majority of native language readers, use an orthography developed fifty years ago in consultation with the Instituto Nacional Indigenista of the Ministry of Education. The WBT/SIL orthography is more similar to Spanish and was thus presumed to be more appropriate for literacy programs seeking to use Tzotzil as a transition to Spanish reading. Against our largely Protestant market, we chose to use the simplified government alphabet rather than the Protestant one. Although the actual differences between the orthographies are slight, the symbolic importance of the choice was enormous. In practice, we found that readers who were comfortable with the WBT/SIL orthography had little trouble with the INEA variety. Nor did they seem to care. Choosing the SIL's "missionary writing," on the other hand, would have clinched our association with the Protestants and made it almost impossible to be accepted in other communities.[9] In the long run, the acceptance of a conventional orthography will be decided by writers and readers.

Dialect choice: There is considerable difference among Tzotzil's still mutually intelligible dialects. As a result, a major concern of some anthropologists and education specialists when we were beginning to work in the Taller was which dialect we would use and whether that would privilege some people over others. Would we pick a central dialect, supposedly accessible to more speakers and readers, participate in the development of a standardized one, or, our preference, transcribe dialects as people spoke? In the INEA meetings on orthography in 1988, Jacinto Arias Sojom, a Tzotzil-speaker from Chenalhó who had studied anthropology at Princeton and is still the most accomplished Tzotzil writer, argued that this would be worked out by the writers themselves as they chose a language in which to write—just as had happened long ago in Spanish and other European languages. In practice, we discovered that sophisticated speakers of all the dialects not only understood, but took great delight in mimicking the others, in the process playing with different communities' stereotypes. Indeed, far from pushing for standardization over the past twenty years, writers appear to have found the differences among dialects to be a real resource: after reading three or four words most readers can tell where the writer or character is from, and often how old they are, whether they are male or female, and even, from the incidence and shaping of words borrowed from Spanish, where they stand with respect to modernization and politics.

Photographs: We set up a darkroom and were able to take new photos as well as copy historical photos to illustrate the Taller's books and to present as gifts to our collaborators. Almost no one had ever seen late nineteenth- and early twentieth-century photographs of Chiapas, many of famous indigenous leaders, so they were a great conversation opener.

Authorship: While we made no secret of who participated in the Taller, our initial decision was not to attribute authorship to particular passages or their translations. Authors, editors, and helpers were all listed alphabetically, by the Tzotzil versions of their names, at the back of the books. In retrospect, we probably were trying to downplay, perhaps even disguise, our roles: we were identified in the lists of names as Xalik Kurus and Tina Kurus, the names by which we have always been known in Chamula.[10] In addition to the two of us, the Taller consisted of a very small permanent team who moved from one project to another. Both of our long-term collaborators, Chep Ernantes (José Hernández) of Zinacantán and Xalik Kusman (Salvador Guzmán) of Chamula, had worked as translators and field assistants for ethnographers before working with us. As for pay, the Taller offered all of us slightly more per day than rural schoolteachers made.

1987–1988: Publishing and Politics

In the months after *Abtel* appeared two reactions were common among those who read it or heard it read. First, many exclaimed, "Yes, that's the way it was! That's my story too!" After a little probing, it turned out that they had seen school texts and other books about "ladino things" and may also have seen religious texts in Tzotzil. But few seem even to have imagined books in their own language about their own lives. Indeed, many proceeded to ask why schoolbooks never told history from their perspective and expressed pleasure that "their own" history might be saved for their descendants. Second, and often almost simultaneously, many went on to say that it was a shame that ladinos and Indians who did not speak Tzotzil could not read the book and learn about the "Tzotzils' truth." Perhaps, some suggested, *Abtel* could be printed again, in Spanish. Even better, said others, would be a bilingual edition so that while others could read it, it would still be clear to them that it was the Tzotzils' history.

Our next project began in early 1987 with a suggestion from colleagues in our umbrella nongovernmental organization (NGO) who wondered if we would be willing to undertake a collaborative history with the members of the *ejido* (landholding collective) of Los Chorros in the municipio of Chenalhó, north of San Cristóbal, as a way to help heal what had become a bitter factional fight. Perhaps the process of recalling what they had in common might draw the two factions back together. We agreed to initiate the project, and late in the spring of 1987 we made several overnight trips to the community. After the first trip, we took along historical documents, agrarian reform files, and maps as well as our tape recorder and began talking about the past with small groups of elders on both sides of the split. But the factionalism was brutal: people on one side would see us talking with members of the other and either grill us about what they had said or angrily refuse to speak to us. There seemed no way to get the leaders of the two sides together, but because they were leaders, it was also hard to work very long with anyone else without their help.[11] After many visits and some initially very fruitful recorded conversations over the course of four months, we reluctantly gave up on any hope of finishing a history as a community project.

Earlier in the 1980s one of the factions, looking for support against its rivals, who ruled the community in the name of the state party, the Partido Revolucionario Institucional (PRI), had affiliated for a time with the Partido Socialista de los Trabajadores (PST). Following the Zapatista Rebellion in 1994, young men from the dominant faction used their connections to the state government and security forces to expel many of these formerly PST, now presumably pro-Zapatista, neighbors. Trained by the army as paramilitary forces, some of these same young men participated in the massacre in the neighboring community of Acteal in December 1997 (see Arias 1984; Aubry and Inda, 1998, 2003).

The first group of urban Tzotzil to approach us on their own, in the summer of 1987, were representatives of San Cristóbal's mostly Protestant Tzotzil colonias. Expelled from their native communities by their traditionalist neighbors beginning in the mid-1970s, often following beatings and destruction of their property, the first of these migrants had by the end of that decade begun to establish themselves on rocky hillsides and former pastures on San Cristóbal's periphery (see J. Rus 2005). Following Mexico's financial collapse in 1982, these original settlers were joined by surging numbers of other indigenous people displaced by the economic crisis. At the end of the 1970s, there were perhaps two thousand indigenous "exiles" in San Cristóbal, people who were accepted as refugees by most of the city's Spanish-speaking residents. By the second half of the 1980s, however, there were as many as twenty thousand, and Cristobalenses had begun to react xenophobically to the so-called invasion. In newspapers, through political campaigns, and even to the migrants' faces, ladinos told them they should go "home" to their own municipios and leave the ladinos with "theirs." Invited to a meeting of urban Tzotzil activists, Jan took along copies of *Abtel ta Pinka*, which most had already seen, as well as historical photographs from as early as the 1880s of indigenous men doing the construction work on the city's most important buildings. In response to questions, he mentioned that not only had the valley land been part of Mayan states when the Spaniards arrived, but also that in the colonial period indigenous people had built and paid for the city's many churches as well as providing the workers, tribute, and food that made the city's existence possible. Several of those in attendance became quite enthusiastic about the pictures and asked if a book could be made to show this history and justify their presence in the city today. And so *Buch'u Lasmeltzan Jobel? / ¿Quién Hizo San Cristóbal?* (Who Made San Cristóbal?) was born. Unlike any of the Taller's other productions, this one was composed by the members of the Taller in consultation with the council of urban migrants. Published in May 1988, it was a brief, illustrated account, in Tzotzil and Spanish, of indigenous people's contributions to the history of San Cristóbal. Three hundred copies were printed, and, at thirty cents each, more than one hundred were quickly sold in San Cristóbal's colonias. Most of the rest went to the city's two bookstores and by the end of 1988 were sold out. For a brief period there was intense interest in the city about who had been responsible for *tal provocación* (such a provocation.) As in other Taller publications, the contributors' names, including our own, were listed in the back in Tzotzil.

During the preparation of *Buch'u Lasmeltzan Jobel* close questioning about the book and about the pattern of distribution of *Abtel* by friends in Chamula finally led us to realize that we were becoming identified with Protestant activists in the city and that this might jeopardize our ability to continue working in the more traditionalist countryside. By this time the expulsion of Protestant converts had spread from Chamula to indigenous municipios throughout the highlands, and as the Protestant urban colonies became more established and successful and their attractiveness to unemployed rural families grew stronger, animosity deepened (Rus and Vigil, 2007; Rus and Morquecho, 2008). Since one of our goals at the Taller was to encourage reconciliation within communities by getting them to think about their common histories, we began looking for a way to keep the doors open to both sides.

The solution we hit upon was another book, to appear at the same time as *Buch'u*. Entitled *Lo'il yu'un Kuskat: Sk'op mol Marian Koyaso Panchin* (Kuskat's Story: The Words of Marian Koyaso Panchin; in Spanish, Mariano Collazo Panchín), it was an account of the Chamulas' brief, rebellious attempt to found an autonomous market and political center in the late 1860s and the ensuing massacre of its participants by the state militia (Bricker 1981, 260–72). In succeeding years, ladino histories and folklore had turned these events on their head and sensationalized them as an *indigenous* bloodletting, with fanatical, crazed Tzotzils killing innocent ladinos. By publishing Koyaso Panchin's very accurate oral history of these events, we hoped to counter the inflammatory version that was still current in state textbooks, serving as an implied warning about the dangers of indigenous government. At the same time, mol Marian ("elder Marian") was a respected, conciliatory figure among Chamula's traditional leaders. By doing a little book with him, to be published concurrently with *Buch'u Lasmeltzan Jobel*, we hoped to establish that the Taller welcomed traditionalists; that it was not a Protestant activity and we were not missionaries. We printed one hundred copies, and most were distributed with Koyaso Panchin's help in the head town of Chamula—often as part of a two-book set with *Buch'u*. The Tzotzils who had built San Cristóbal over the course of several centuries and who had struggled for autonomy in the 1860s were, after all, the ancestors of traditionalists and Protestants alike.

Practice: Refinements

Bilingual Editions: Both of the communities where we worked through most of 1987 specifically requested books with bilingual or Spanish texts. In the case of the urban Protestants, the reason for this was precisely that they wanted ladinos to read their history and recognize their legitimate claim to a share of the city. In making *Buch'u Lasmeltzan Jobel* our first bilingual publication, we determined that if we were going to use two (or more) languages, they were going to be on facing pages and strictly parallel, sentence-by-sentence, paragraph-by-paragraph.

Meanwhile, for those in Los Chorros who would participate in our conversations, the text was going to have to be Spanish alone because one of the rifts in the ejido (although not the only one) was between Tzotzil-speakers and Tzeltal-speakers who had been forced to live together decades earlier. In fact, both groups understood both languages, and after their long coexistence had even intermarried. But if we could not publish in both Tzotzil and Tzeltal as well as Spanish, they preferred that neither indigenous language be used.

Practices and politics: If *Buch'u* was, in its bilingualism, more like later publications, the simultaneously published *Lo'il yu'un Kuskat* was in several ways an anomaly. Because an important reason for publishing it was to broach the idea of books in Tzotzil to the Chamula traditionalists, it was monolingual, like *Abtel ta Pinka*. At the same time, unlike *Abtel* and *Buch'u* but like the later books, it credited mol Marian as the author and even included a photo of him on the title page. In part, this was the result of a changing view of authorship within the Taller (a point to which we shall return below). However, it was also a political decision, to make as public as possible that we and mol Marian had worked together. Finally, unlike the books that came before and after, we composed an introduction in Tzotzil to enumerate the ways in which Koyaso Panchin's oral history of the events of the late 1860s—like those of other Chamula elders—differed from the dominant, ladino version and was more true to the latest historical reconstructions (J. Rus, 1983, 1989).

1988-1990: Community Collaborations

By the spring of 1988 we had begun to understand more fully the extent of Tzotzil communities' adaptation to the post-1982 crisis. Beyond colonizing the jungle and moving into cities, beyond developing new ways of making a living, from flower growing to producing textiles for tourists, highland Tzotzils were also experimenting with new forms of organization. Most visible were the independent regional organizations and urban councils mentioned earlier. However, even within apparently settled municipios still considered traditional, the structure and orientation of extended families and local hamlets were shifting, challenging age and gender hierarchies, and eventually entrenched political power.

Many of these local changes were not apparent from outside. By the time *Buch'u* and *Kuskat* were published in the spring of 1988, however, we had been drawn into a series of new projects that would place the Taller at the center of the conversations about these changes. Diane had begun to interview women in Chamula about their responses to the economic crisis, eventually completing a survey of household economics in a Chamula hamlet in collaboration with the women of the hamlet (D. Rus 1990). At the same time, she undertook in-depth conversations with the women about how their lives and families had been changed by the fact that their husbands and fathers had trouble finding work. This led to a book on the life history of one of the women, Maruch Komes (María Gómez), and her role in building a local, independent artisan cooperative, *Ta jlok'ta chobtik ta ku'il / Bordando Milpas* ("Embroidering Cornfields," a beautiful wordplay on the fact that since she and her husband had stopped planting corn she had begun embroidering stylized corn plants on blouses for tourists).

As Maruch's story revealed, the cooperative had begun in the mid-1980s, as women began gathering to watch their children collectively as they wove and embroidered. Within a few months they were purchasing thread together and soon thereafter were starting to take turns carrying products made by the group to the city to sell. By the time they came to the attention of artisan organizations run by state and national governments in 1988, they were a functioning, independent cooperative (for comparison, see Nash 1993; Eber and Rosenbaum 1993; Eber and Tansky 2001). Unlike other texts about indigenous women artisans, in *Bordando Milpas* Maruch talked not only about her art and its meaning, but also about the difficulties indigenous women encountered in working with external organizations and traveling to distant markets without knowing Spanish or being literate. She also discussed the profound changes in household dynamics when women took leading, entrepreneurial roles. Finally, she described the dire economic circumstances that forced her to sell her goods to *coyotes*, intermediaries, fully aware that by doing so she was underselling her own products in the cooperative store.

This was the history captured by *Ta jlok'ta chobtik ta ku'il*, which was published in 1990 with a print run of four hundred copies. One hundred of these were distributed immediately to other artisans through Maruch and her cooperative. Almost simultaneously the book also came to the attention of the Fondo Nacional de Artesanías (FONART), the federal government's agency for promoting folk art, which informed us that Maruch's testimony was the first they had seen of a native artisan in all of Mexico. Somewhat contrary to our intentions for the book, FONART bought fifty copies to distribute to its employees and member cooperatives and invited Maruch, Diane, and our Chamula collaborator, Xalik Kusman, to Mexico City to present the book in the national artisan store. To promote indigenous art and also FONART, they arranged for Maruch to be interviewed on the morning culture program of the national network Radio Educación. Within a short time, *Ta jlok'ta chobtik ta ku'il* was republished in Spain, France, and Italy.

Jan, meanwhile, at the suggestion of the agronomist of the Instituto de Asesoría Antropológica para la Región Maya, A.C. (INAREMAC), Alain Retière, began a two-year collaboration with five constituent communities of the Unión de Uniones (UDU), an independent peasant organization concentrated in the Lacandón jungle and adjacent lowlands. The UDU had a history of aggressively confronting ladino planters for control of the land and of farming and marketing collectively on the lands they acquired (Harvey 1998; Legorreta 1998; Leyva 2003). Taking advantage of a government loan-guarantee program that enabled peasants to buy ladino haciendas (a program which, not incidentally, bailed out wealthy owners whose failing farms no one else would buy), the five communities had bought, in 1986, the combined coffee and cattle plantation on which their families had served for generations as indebted workers. By 1988 they wanted to produce a memoir of their passage from debt servitude to co-ownership of the planation, from suffering forced labor to dreams of starting a cheese factory and founding a peasant university (*universidad campesina*) to teach agricultural science and humanities to the next generation of the UDU. At the same time, they also wanted a step-by-step account of the process of labor organization and strategic land invasion by which they had finally convinced the owner to sell. They felt that the UDU could use it to proselytize other indigenous rural laborers. The result was *Kipaltik: K'u cha'al lajmankutik jpinkakutik / Cómo compramos nuestra finca* ("Kipaltik: How we bought our plantation"), published in 1990. An eighty-page book based on the testimonies of men and women members of the cooperative, with photographs of collective labor and governance, half of *Kipaltik*'s four hundred copies went to the members of the collective and the UDU. One hundred of these were for the members themselves, so that someday, as one of them put it, "our grandchildren's children could read about how we got our families out of poverty." Several dozen more were distributed through the Taller itself and San Cristóbal bookstores. The rest were for internal promotion in other UDU communities and to use in organizing campaigns, often clandestine, on other plantations.

Practice

Authorship: After 1988 we decided to attribute authorship and editorship more overtly, namely, on title pages. The problem with not naming those responsible for texts was that, in the absence of obvious attribution, journalists had several times commissioned translations of passages from *Abtel* and then cited them without mentioning the source. Unfortunately, even when authors' names were given, as in *Ta jlok'ta chobtik*, such pirating continued. In the most egregious case, a self-described proindigenous solidarity group in Europe republished the entire text and included the photo of the author, Maruch Komes, without mentioning either her name or where the text had come from. It seemed to us that indigenous "artifacts," including stories and testimonies, were viewed as "naturally occurring objects" that, like rocks or flowers or birds, could belong to whoever "found" them. When we complained about the failure to attribute authorship, we and the author received a formal apology. But we also heard from mutual friends that the reason no credit was given was that "indigenous people aren't contaminated by ideas of individualism and property" and that the preoccupation with naming authors was ours alone.

More on translation: Publishing *testimonio* bilingually also led to questions about what level and tone of Spanish should be used. In the past, representations of indigenous speech in Chiapas, whether in fiction or translations of testimonies, had often used a rural, backwoods Spanish, suggesting an equivalence between rural indigenous people and poor, rural ladinos. Some texts even mimicked the grammatical errors Tzotzil-speakers commonly commit in Spanish, suggesting a sort of minstrel-speak. We decided that since our Tzotzil texts were in perfectly proper and sometimes elegant Tzotzil, the Spanish translations should be straightforward and correct.

Beyond these concerns, each of the two new projects, *Ta jlok'ta chobtik* and *Kipaltik*, brought its own demands. From the beginning of our publishing project the editing we did was aimed primarily at cutting repetition.

Tzotzil language, particularly prayers and formal or ritual speech, frequently coupled words and phrases, and occasionally repeated whole passages in different words. To make the texts read smoothly and to achieve economies in the printing process we had to edit out such duplication before the translations were made. We always read the edited texts with the authors, many of whom were unlettered, and never considered them finished until they had agreed to the changes. But we did cut.

An amusing result of such editing was that during the national radio interview about *Ta jlok'ta chobtik*, the interviewer asked Maruch Komes to say the weaver's prayer that appeared at the end of her book so the radio audience could hear Tzotzil being spoken. When praying, Maruch always closes her eyes and chants, composing the phrases as she goes along, and they often last fifteen to thirty minutes. The prayer in the book, however, had been abbreviated to thirty-six short lines. When Maruch's prayer on the radio began to run beyond two minutes, then three heading for four with no sign of ending, the interviewer began to panic. How to make it stop? Eventually, Maruch understood why the interviewer was nervous and brought the prayer to an end. With the help of Diane and Xalik Kusman, she then explained that there was no set prayer, that what she did was enumerate and repeat in different ways the help she would need with her work and ask for guidance and patience from God and the saints. Although on this occasion everyone finally understood what had happened, in some sense the original prayer had been violated by being shortened for publication, truncating what the author might have thought the most important part of her book. Given the expense of making books and the need to be concise, we were unable to find an alternative that would meet everyone's ideas of what mattered.

Soon after work began on *Ta jlok'ta chobtik*, the women's artisan cooperative described in the book began to receive offers of loans and grants from the government. Although they had not sought these funds, the women of the co-op, including Maruch Komes, were more than willing to accept them. Traditionally, such government resources would have been brokered through the regional indigenous caciques (political bosses) in the head town of Chamula rather than contracted directly by community members, much less women community members (Rus and Collier 2003). Although the production of a book was an entirely separate project from the organization of the cooperative that was attracting government funds (in fact, when we were asked our opinion, we advised caution in accepting government help), by the time the caciques became aware of the cooperative's funding the book had appeared, and the women were able to use the book as a calling card to maintain their independence from cacique control.

After 1990 Maruch and her group also used the book as an entry point to make contact with NGOs, ever hopeful that such contacts would broaden their support and perhaps help them establish their own store. At the same time, Maruch's published and therefore public explanation of why her group sold items outside the cooperative stores, in the process driving prices downward, could have endangered her ties to the government agencies and NGOs that sponsored those stores. As it turned out, however, they found her analysis instructive.

Finally, outside of their immediate families women had rarely expressed themselves about how their insertion into the market economy had affected their relationships with their husbands. Maruch's admission that at first her husband and other women's husbands had tried to destroy the women's work and end their participation in organizations that brought them into relationships with mestizos in town potentially made her subject to marital problems. What actually happened was that the appearance of the book and her subsequent invitation to visit Mexico City helped legitimate her and the women's new roles in their husbands' eyes.

Our work on *Kipaltik* brought up other questions, most notably in regard to editing. Previously, editing had been done for reasons of style and economy of expression. In the case of *Kipaltik* we were faced for the first time with the problem of editing as censorship. The story of *Kipaltik* is one not only of the triumph of a group of Tzotzils in buying the plantation on which they had been virtual slaves, but also of their families' century-long fight to recover their land, expropriated in the late nineteenth century. After the Mexican Revolution, from the 1920s to the 1970s the struggle was rarely an open one. Debt-laborers sabotaged production and resisted work when they could, but the landowner had overwhelming force on his side and with impunity could beat, expel, and even kill those who defied him. The balance of power between the two sides began to change in the 1970s, when declining agricultural prices led landowners to expel resident workers and turn cropland into pasturage for cattle. Simultaneously—and not by chance—independent peasant and indigenous organizations arose and became increasingly militant as they pushed back against the landowners' attempts to expel them from land that had belonged to their ancestors (see Harvey 1998; Toledo 2002; Bobrow-Strain 2007; Garza and Toledo 2008). Violence between the two sides escalated throughout northern Chiapas, with indigenous workers cutting fences, killing cattle, and invading land, while owners responded by getting the state police and army to repress their former workers and hiring private gunmen, *guardias blancas*, to do the job when the state would not. Some of the passages we transcribed in preparing *Kipaltik* described the first real attack on landowners and their ladino employees in this isolated region in 1974.

After they had invaded a neighboring finca, men from the communities that eventually bought Kipaltik beat the overseer, who had cheated them of wages and treated them brutally for two decades, and then assaulted his particularly cruel, arrogant wife. The description is a raw one. Those of us in the Taller and others working in the region who we consulted did not know what to do with it. The acts it described were ugly and certainly illegal. Yet the men who had participated were quite open about their deeds as justified vengeance for decades of mistreatment. It was an example of the kind of revolutionary violence described by Frantz Fanon. As editors and sympathizers, we were especially concerned about preserving the anonymity of those involved — of the perpetrators but also of the victim, who still lived in a small town nearby. During a long, at times contentious discussion, Jan finally convinced the men that the story should be cut on the grounds that it described the details of a crime, and it was impossible to predict what would happen if we committed evidence of it to paper. Caution prevailed, but we still wonder whether we denatured history in the process. Could, or should, a different decision have been made?

Elsewhere in *Kipaltik*, as in the Taller's other books, individuals and places were identified: landowners, politicians, settlements, and plantations. The risk, faced more often by journalists than by academic writers, was not only that many of those who were named or were identifiable from their landholdings were still alive (certainly their families were), but also that they were still likely to be in powerful positions in the region. Publishing accounts of their deeds might have had negative economic, political, or personal repercussions for the actors themselves, for community members, or for the Taller should they take offense. Nevertheless, the Taller's purpose was to try to present for analysis history as people had lived and remembered it, and if such details had been omitted discussion would have been impossible. Only in the case in which someone could be hurt gratuitously was a name suppressed.[12]

At the beginning of the *Kipaltik* collaboration, the community made it clear in an assembly that it was to be a collective product, none of which could be published until it had been read and approved in subsequent assemblies. Nor were we to interview anyone separately and represent them as spokespeople for the group. Accordingly, all the interviews were conducted with groups of at least four or five and on occasion as many as fifteen or twenty. Jan and Xalik Kusman interviewed the men over the course of half a year, often during rest periods on communal workdays. Diane interviewed the women in the schoolyard. In fact, a handful of senior men and women did most of the talking but never apart from the group.

This sharing, or diffusion, of authorship—and, in a sense, of responsibility—seemed to us another expression of the UDU customs of collective, consensual decision making and of protecting the identities of leaders, practices that have become well known through the Zapatistas. During demonstrations, scores and even hundreds of demonstrators would huddle tightly when they had to make a decision so that no one from outside could see who was talking or identify the leaders. Given the assassinations of some 195 indigenous and campesino activists in rural Chiapas between the mid-1970s and late 1980s, this precaution was well warranted (Burguete and Montero, nd.).

1991–1994: Transitions

As publishing ventures and even as political projects *Ta jlok'ta chobtik* and *Kipaltik* were successes: widely read by the measure used in indigenous Chiapas, where print runs number in the low hundreds, and useful as representations of their authors' projects. Even as they were being printed, however, Mexico and rural Chiapas alike were entering a new political and economic environment, one that would eventually undo the successes of both Maruch Komes's cooperative and the collective farm of Kipaltik.

At the end of 1988 Carlos Salinas de Gortari became president of Mexico and immediately accelerated the pace of the neoliberal economic reforms that had begun in the early 1980s. Over the next six years he would privatize most of the remaining state enterprises, remove controls on foreign investment, and dismantle the laws on communal landholding that had been one of the triumphs of the Mexican Revolution. Almost unremembered among these sweeping reforms is that during the first weeks of his term Salinas undermined the International Coffee Agreement, the cartel that maintained the stability of world coffee prices. One of Salinas's overall goals was to help the administration of George H. W. Bush convince the U.S. Congress and public opinion in the United States of Mexico's worthiness as a partner in the North American Free Trade Agreement. From Salinas's perspective his act was little more than a token of his commitment to free markets. For producers around the world, however, including those in Mexico, it was a disaster. By spring 1989 the international coffee market had collapsed, plunging millions into poverty. Among those whose plans for the future were dashed were the members of the Kipaltik collective, who lost the coffee income they had counted on to make their mortgage payments. For the next two and a half years, the collective managed to survive by obtaining emergency credit from various government agencies. The condition for securing the last of these loans, in early 1992, was that the elderly president of the collective, a former debt-laborer who had fought all of his life for the land, had to stand behind President Salinas with two other historic peasant leaders, in native dress, as Salinas signed the end of agrarian reform. When the news photos of the event appeared, Kipaltik fractured, and even some of the leader's sons refused to speak to him or face him. With no credit forthcoming for the fall harvest of 1992, Kipaltik's members and the UDU's officers divided the land among themselves before the bank could foreclose. The collective was dissolved.

Although the mechanism was different, the impact of Salinas's reforms on the artisan cooperative was no less destructive. Concerned with the independence and the increasingly oppositional stance of the grass-roots organizations that had taken up much of the burden of sustaining the poor during the years of government neglect after the financial crisis of 1982, the Salinas government came into office with a plan to buy back their loyalty: the Programa Nacional de Solidaridad (National Solidarity Program—PRONASOL) (Dresser 1991). In return for affiliating with government organizations and confederations of organizations, PRONASOL funneled to so-called popular groups a share of the profits from the privatization of state-owned businesses. In the case of Maruch Komes's cooperative, this aid came in the form of a large loan composed of inferior materials and a complicated scheme tying repayment to government participation in the commercialization of the group's products. To cement the relationship, women in the cooperative were also compelled to participate in PRI electoral campaigns in 1988 and 1991, for which purpose they were bused around Chiapas with other brightly costumed indigenous groups so that they could take a prominent place in the front row of televised events. Unfortunately, the women's production was not sufficient to pay back the loans that had been foisted on them, and in mid-1992 the state held back both the pay they were due for products they had turned over on consignment and the fees they had paid to incorporate as an official cooperative. The two losses added up to far more than they had ever received in loans. Their protection as members of a favored cooperative now removed, the PRI bosses of their municipio, who resented them for having made contracts with the state over the heads of the municipio's supposedly legitimate representatives, prevented them from sharing in any of the local PRONASOL funds to which they were entitled. As a result of what they considered a swindle, many of the women and their families became staunchly anti-PRI after 1992. But their group, which had come together out of common need and grown into a powerful force in the women's lives through the 1980s, broke into factions that blamed each other for their losses (Rus and Collier 2003).

If the Salinas government's goal had been to rein in the organizations of the poor, by the end of 1992 it had succeeded in the cases of the Kipaltik collective and Maruch Komes's cooperative: both had ceased to exist. Although every case is different, similar fates befell independent organizations across Chiapas. If this was "success," however, the eventual cost to the government was a high one. Those whose painfully organized projects failed often became bitter opponents of the government and the PRI, and those whose organizations survived were usually more determined than ever to maintain their independence.

At the beginning of this period of renewed government intervention, in the fall of 1988, our family moved back to California. We still had projects and grants, so through 1992 Jan spent half of each year in Chiapas over two or three visits, and Diane two and a half months during the summers. *Jlok'ta chobtik*, *Kipaltik*, and a third book, *Slo'il cha'vo' kumpareil / Cuento de los dos compadres* (Story of the two compadres), were finished under these conditions and published in 1990.[13] While we did begin two new publishing projects between 1990 and 1993, the increasing distress of the communities and organizations with which we had collaborated led us to spend much of our time with them, talking about the rapidly changing conditions and discussing alternatives. Before any of us could act on them, however, these conversations, like almost everything else in Chiapas, were overtaken by the Zapatistas' invasion of San Cristóbal on New Year's Day, 1994.

Post-1994: Zapatismo

After the economic depression and official neglect of the 1980s, and then the assault on indigenous organizations of the early 1990s—not to mention the centuries of exploitation and humiliation that had gone before—the armed rebellion of 1994 was almost overdetermined. Following an initial period of confusion on the part of those who were not Zapatistas, within a few weeks of January 1 indigenous people throughout Chiapas, indeed, throughout Mexico, remember feeling a surge of pride that others like them had occupied a mestizo city and defeated the Mexican army in initial encounters. Friends of ours say that for months afterward upon encountering other indigenous people on the sidewalk they smiled knowingly at each other, proud of their identity.

Although they pale next to the other effects of the Zapatista Rebellion, the impacts of the revolt on independent projects like ours were also profound. While there was more than enough to learn, talk, and write about, for several years working on publishing projects within communities became problematic. By the summer of 1994, as the state's reaction to the Zapatistas became organized, there began to be paramilitary patrols, assassinations, and random shootings throughout rural Chiapas. As a result, whereas formerly it had been our practice to stay overnight in people's houses and participate in local discussions, now we worried about bringing unwanted attention to those with whom we collaborated. Aside from any danger to ourselves—which we actually judged to be slight[14]—we worried about how this surveillance and violence and the reaction to them might affect our friends and hosts. Would someone mistake us for government representatives or *subversivos* and take it out on our collaborators?[15] As for native language publishing itself, in the highly polarized atmosphere of the second half of the 1990s everyone was forced to choose sides. In the summer of 1994 the government held meetings of native language writers and publishers and soon after began subsidizing many as a way of promoting the idea that the state was "with" indigenous people. The Ejército Zapatista de Liberación Nacional (EZLN) and the generally pro-Zapatista independent political organizations, meanwhile, also published manifestos and newsletters in indigenous languages—both sides demonstrating, parenthetically, that in just a few years writing in native language had become a well-established means of communicating across entire regions.[16] There was no question of which side our NGO, INAREMAC, was on in this division. At great personal risk, those members of INAREMAC who were resident in Chiapas traveled to the most conflictive parts of the state and documented human rights abuses.[17] As summer visitors, however, the two of us were not in a position either to sustain a contestatory publishing project or to encourage indigenous communities whose dangers we did not share to do so. Instead, over the first several years after 1994 we continued to make open, public visits to places where we were known, concentrating less on publishing than on documenting economic deterioration and political change (see Rus and Rus 2004).[18]

Nevertheless, two Taller Tzotzil productions did appear during this period. The first was a pair of translations for nonindigenous audiences of Tzotzil-language accounts of the rebellion of 1994 and its aftermath: "Los primeros meses de los zapatistas" ("The first months of the Zapatistas") (1995) and "Conversaciones interrumpidas" ("Interrupted conversations," 2000), by Mariano Peres Tsu (the pseudonym our partner Xalik Kusman had chosen for himself). The two translations present vignettes of indigenous life in Chiapas after 1994. The first told of the emotions and reactions of different groups immediately following the rebellion, and the second of events in an urban colony in the late 1990s as the state tried to reassert control and the inhabitants tried to evade it. Both chronicles have been published several times in four countries and in 2002 were published together as "A Tzotzil Chronicle of the Zapatista Uprising" in Gilbert Joseph's and Timothy Henderson's *Mexico Reader* (Duke, 2002.) Unlike earlier publications of the Taller, most of which were transcribed oral histories, these essays were written in Tzotzil by a native writer; we provided only the translation and editing.

The second publication, *Jchi'iltak ta Slumal Kalifornya* ("Chamulas in California"), which appeared in 1996, originated from one of the two projects we had begun between 1990 and 1993 and grew out of our contact with some of the first undocumented Tzotzil workers to arrive in California. Four hundred copies of the testimonies of the brothers Manuel, Salvador, and Pedro Pérez were printed, and they were distributed largely through NGOs and churches working in the Tzotzil region. "Going north" was still almost unheard of in rural Chiapas in the 1990s, and in addition to telling a story the book attempted to offer counsel to those planning to make the trip. In addition to the brothers' adventures getting to and crossing the border and learning to survive in the United States, woven into the story was advice about obtaining and safely using false identification, avoiding being cheated by employers or caught by the *migra* (border patrol), and getting help after being detained and dumped back on the Mexican side of the border without money or documents. In appendices which were later copied separately as flyers, *Jchi'iltak* also provided information in Tzotzil and Spanish about groups along both sides of the border that offered aid to migrants and about the rights of undocumented workers.

The biggest difference between the projects undertaken after 1994 and those before is that in the later projects authors' identities were sometimes hidden. In the case of *Jchi'iltak* we had conducted the interviews in California, and neither we nor the interviewees were sure what pressures the brothers' families might experience in Chiapas if their absence and dollar income were publicized. To be safe, we all agreed to mask their identities. When the brothers returned to Chiapas after the book's appearance, however, and realized that it was circulating in the shantytowns and that Xalik Kusman of the Taller had been interviewed about it on a Tzotzil-language radio program, they were proud to claim authorship. One brother later used it in his campaign to be the first indigenous member of San Cristóbal's city council, and in radio interviews elaborated on the book's account of his experiences. In the case of Xalik Kusman's own vignettes of the Zapatista Rebellion, on the other hand, the disguise has been maintained for years because of Xalik's well-founded fear of reprisals from the ladino authorities he so humorously portrayed.[19]

In general, our practice had been to keep from intruding in the texts with introductions and explanatory footnotes. In the case of *Jchi'iltak*, however, where the purpose was in part to warn readers about the hardships of undocumented migration, we felt it was necessary to say something about why people migrated and to elaborate on the conditions migrants faced. We also wanted to explain that most U.S. citizens were the descendants of migrants. A brief socio-politico-historical section was added. In the case of the translated chronicles, introductions were provided to explain the unusual origin of the documents.

This brings the story of the Taller up to the present. Although the Taller never formally closed, its activity waned after the 1990s. One project is still in progress: a Tzotzil-language history of San Cristóbal's shantytowns. Undertaken in collaboration with the Tzotzil writer Xalik Kusman in 1990, it had, by the summer of 2009, generated more than thirty-eight hundred handwritten pages of testimony and stories. All that remains to be done is editing and organization.[20]

Final Reflections

As economic and then social and political conditions deteriorated during the 1970s and 1980s, the tradition of critical historical narrative and analysis that had always existed within Tzotzil and other indigenous communities increasingly transcended social and cultural borders and spread across Chiapas. What native speakers talking to each other in their own languages had formerly said only among themselves was now increasingly expressed to indigenous people beyond their local groups as well as to Spanish-speakers. Information traveled the other way as well, deepening Tzotzil-speakers' knowledge of the changes affecting all Mexicans, not just themselves. By the second half of the 1980s all of indigenous Chiapas was engaged in an earnest intellectual and political debate, as within every family different members tried new ways of making a living, organizing themselves, and even thinking about life. What was the news from those who had moved to the city; had they found work and places to live? What of homesteading in the jungle, did clearing land and planting coffee seem to offer a safe future? What about the many independent organizations and cooperatives, what did they offer? Were Protestantism, in its many varieties, or liberation Catholicism better ways of organizing and thinking about life than traditional communities and religion?

Native language writing and the birth of media controlled by indigenous people were among the by-products of this effervescence. The plantation economy and the community structures bound to it were swept away so quickly that people who spoke Tzotzil and Chiapas's other native languages had little choice but to talk about the change and discuss alternatives in their own tongues. In the process, they made Tzotzil—including written Tzotzil—not only a means of communication, but also a basis of solidarity in the new urban and national environments they were entering. If we and others helping with communications projects found receptive audiences, in turn, the reason was not so much our own persuasiveness as this changed context. By the early 2000s, in a region where only thirty years earlier native language speakers were only beginning to write, university theses are now being completed in indigenous languages; the international and national news are translated daily into Tzotzil and circulated in xeroxed "newspapers" in the market; unregulated, low-power FM radio stations broadcast in Tzotzil from San Cristóbal's shantytowns; and the number of government institutions, churches, NGOs, independent organizations, and private presses that publish in Tzotzil and other indigenous languages continues to multiply.

Thinking about indigenous people in developing societies from the comfortable, urbanized North, it is possible to despair. "Our" world is systematically squeezing theirs out of its environmental and economic niches, in the process unraveling their societies and ways of life. Seeing how one-sided this change is and always has been, one might well believe that the people of small cultures and languages do not see what is happening to them, and that even if they do, whether through our fault or theirs, they cannot make themselves heard. Those of us who have had the opportunity to be in direct contact with people in places like Chiapas, however—to have experienced both their eagerness to communicate and the power of their ideas—are probably more hopeful. Writing and publishing in native languages cannot roll back the current global order. But by giving as many people as possible the means and the confidence to express their views, they do make it possible for ever more voices to join our common conversation, for the subaltern to speak.

Notes

Acknowledgments: We would like to thank John Burstein, George Collier, María Elena Fernández Galán, Edward Fischer, Christine Kovic, Ámbar Past, Pedro Pitarch, Stephen Lewis, and Juan Pedro Viqueira for their comments and suggestions. Particular thanks to Florencia Mallon for her careful readings and editing. The essay is dedicated to the memory of Andrés Aubry and Angélica Inda, who founded the Taller Tzotzil in 1974 and entrusted it to us in 1985. From then until the ends of their lives they shared friendship and counsel and always their fullest support. We never stop missing them.

    1. The Instituto de Asesoría Antropológica para la Región Maya, A.C. (INAREMAC) was founded by Andrés Aubry in 1973 with the sponsorship of Bishop Samuel Ruiz, who felt Chiapas's liberationist Catholic Church needed independent anthropological advice. Following the Congreso Indígena of 1974 (Morales 1992), in which it played a role, INAREMAC acted as host for experimental, community-directed projects in organic agriculture, health education, a furniture cooperative, and the Taller Tzotzil. In its first years the Taller organized language classes for clergy and social workers. Under the direction of the anthropologist John Burstein, however, it soon turned to providing literacy courses in Tzotzil communities. The first booklet to follow these courses was published in the fall of 1976 (Aubry 1988). During our own time in the Taller, funds have been provided by the French Comité Catholique Contre la Faim et Pour le Dévellopement, the European Community, INAREMAC's French support group, INAREMAC's Chiapas board of directors, headed by Amado Avendaño and Carlos Rodríguez, and the Jacobs Research Fund of Bellingham, Washington.

2. There are no known documents written in Tzotzil by native speakers to be read by other native speakers from the arrival of Europeans (1524) through the 1940s. During the 1940s writing was reintroduced in Tzotzil, as in Chiapas's other Maya languages, by the missionary linguists of the Summer Institute of Linguistics/Wycliffe Bible Translators (SIL/WBT). After 1951 SIL/WBT linguists produced the materials for the bilingual education programs of the Instituto Nacional Indigenista (INI), which became the source of Chiapas's new indigenous literacy. The first publishing by native writers appeared after the mid-1970s. Among those who produced this material in addition to the Taller Tzotzil were Taller Leñateros (1979-) (see note 8); Sna Jtz'ibajom (1982-), founded by former language assistants to anthropologists with help from Robert M. Laughlin; the writers' project of the state government (1982-88), led by Dr. Jacinto Arias Sojom; La Castalia, advised by Gudrun and Carlos Lenkersdorf, which published in Tojolabal from the mid-1970s through the 1980s; the Instituto de Estudios Indígenas of the Universidad Autónoma de Chiapas, which has published occasionally in native languages since 1985; and various irregular projects of independent organizations, churches, and Mexican universities with programs in Chiapas. Since the mid-1990s, the native writers' own organization, CELALI, has also published native language texts or placed them with other publishers. (For more, see Laughlin 1993; Benjamin 2000; and Past 2005.)

3. Menchú (1984 [1983]), in reaction, see Stoll (1999), J. Rus, ed. (1999); Chakravorty-Spivak (1988), Gugelberger (1996).

4. Chiapas's commercial agriculture required some 125,000 seasonal workers in the early 1970s, and only a few thousand more in the mid-1980s. Meanwhile, the number of indigenous men looking for such work almost doubled between 1970 and 1990, from 150,000 to more than 300,000 (see Collier 1994; J. Rus 1995).

5. This was true of virtually all studies published before the 1980s. The exception was Ricardo Pozas (1952; 1962), whose *Juan, the Chamula*, although classified as a novel when it first appeared in 1948, was arguably the Maya region's first *testimonio*. See J. Rus (2004).

6. Originally we intended to produce both booklets and tape cassettes of sound documentaries blending the interviews with music. Thinking about all the time people spent in minibuses and *colectivos*, with their omnipresent tapes of ranchero music, we thought tapes would broaden our audience. After a first experiment, however, we realized that recording, mixing, producing, and distributing tapes was beyond our capacity.

7. At a panel entitled the "Current State and Future Prospects of Maya Language Literature" at the Congreso Internacional de Mayistas in 1989, there was an energetic discussion about the distribution and sale of native language materials. Minimum wage in Chiapas is regularly adjusted to remain at approximately three dollars per day, with agricultural workers typically making half to two-thirds of that wage, often paid in kind. Potential readers' ability to pay is severely limited. INI has historically

given away its materials, while the SIL/WBT and most of the writing projects charged low, highly subsidized prices. For example, both editions of *Abtel* sold for the equivalent of twenty cents in indigenous communities, and the second edition for five dollars in bookstores.

8. The exceptions both involved Ámbar Past (1989; 1980), and in Burstein, Past, and Wassestrom (1979). Past began collecting women's stories and lore in 1975 and has helped indigenous women publish continuously since 1979 through Taller Leñateros. Since the late 1980s there have been a number of other writing, theater, and media projects managed by women and dedicated to women's themes, among them Fortaleza de la Mujer Maya (FOMMA) (1992–), inspired and advised by Miriam Laughlin; and the Proyecto Fotográfico Maya, founded by Carlota Duarte.

9. The principal differences between the orthographies is INEA's use of "k" versus SIL/WBT's use of "c" and "qu" for the same sound, and slight differences in conventions about glottal stops. Ironically, in discussions with Maya writers from Guatemala at the Congreso Mayista of 1989, it turned out that the Academia de Lenguas Mayas de Guatemala chose to use "c/qu" over "k" because in Guatemala the latter was associated with the despised national government. In Chiapas, the SIL/WBT orthography received a boost as a universal convention at the end of the 1990s when Bible translations in Tzotzil and Tzeltal, originally undertaken by the Protestants, were approved by the progressive Catholic diocese of San Cristóbal (e.g., Sociedad Bíblica 1997).

10. Our Tzotzil names since our first summer in Chiapas were Xalik for Jan, and Tina for Diane. When we added "Rus," Jan's name sounded to Tzotzil-speakers like "Xalik Kurus," Tzotzil for "Salvador Cruz." Kurus thus became our last name.

11. Most of those on one side were descendants of the ejido's original Tzotzil-speaking community, dispossessed by a ladino planter in the mid-nineteenth century. Most of the members of the other were Tzeltal speakers whose ancestors had been brought to Los Chorros as debt laborers after the 1890s. In all the years of inhabiting the same space, many on each side spoke the other side's language, and there were even intermarriages. But since the 1970s they had joined rival political parties and by the mid-1980s were locked in conflict (see Arias 1984; Aubry and Inda 1998; Hernández Castillo 2001).

12. In the United States, whether to use names or not is still debated among oral historians and the university and government officials charged with protection of research subjects. See the website of *Perspectives* of the American Historical Association for the range of views: www.historians.org/Perspectives (accessed 30 January 2006).

13. *Slo'il cha'vo' kumpareil / Cuento de los dos compadres* was a Zinacanteco folktale transcribed by our colleague Chep Ernantes. Edited as a bilingual children's story by Chep and Diane, with illustrations by Elizabeth Ross, it was later translated into French by Isabelle Duquesne of INAREMAC for distribution to Taller supporters in France. A fourth book from this period was *Historia de un pueblo evangelista: Triunfo*

Agrarista (1993), by Ricardo Pérez. A ladino campesino from Chiapas's Central Valley, Pérez read the Taller's books and then wrote his own history of his Protestant refugee colony, illustrated it with his own snapshots, and presented it to the Taller for publication.

14. Aside from expulsion for interfering in Mexican politics, occasional heavy-handed surveillance and interrogation, and a handful of cases of official assault, foreigners were largely immune to the repression after 1994. The hope that this would be so was the basis for stationing foreign citizens in Peace Camps in the midst of threatened communities. That none have been killed does not in any way diminish the courage of peace campers, who still, as this is written in 2006, face the prospect of violence.

15. This did not apply to our "home" hamlet in Chamula, where our sons' godparents resided and everyone knew us. Even there, however, although it had nothing to do with us, a paramilitary patrol surrounded and menaced a primary school graduation we attended in 1997 until local men calmed them down.

16. For the larger context of this shift, see Benjamin (2000).

17. Angélica Inda, one of INAREMAC's six members, was the EZLN's secretary at the San Andrés Peace Talks. Andrés Aubry worked full-time writing and editing the summaries and communiqués of Bishop Samuel Ruiz and the mediators at the talks. At great personal risk and eventually cost to their health, they also documented and spoke out about human rights abuses throughout the period after 1994 (see Aubry and Inda, 2003). Still a third associate, Michel Chanteaux, a resident of Chiapas for more than thirty-five years, was expelled from Mexico two days after the Acteal massacre in December 1997 for having been the source of the first news reports that the army was nearby and did not intervene (Chanteaux 1999).

18. Outside of Mexico we felt freer and lectured and were interviewed frequently. We also helped organize an international campaign in 1998 to keep Chiapas open to scholars and human rights observers and to free a Mexican scholar who had been swept up in a military raid.

19. In confimation of the continuing power of Xalik's words, in Subcomandante Marcos's speech celebrating the fifteenth anniversary of the Zapatistas' rebellion of 1994, he quoted directly and at length from "Los primeros meses de los zapatistas" (Subcomandante Marcos, "Siete vientos en los calendarios y geografías de abajo," reprinted in *La Jornada*, Mexico City, 4 January 2009).

20. Meanwhile, beginning soon after the San Andrés Peace Accords of 1996, Andrés Aubry supervised the translation of the accords and related documents, more than one hundred pages, into ten indigenous languages spoken in Chiapas, including Tzotzil (*Los Acuerdos de San Andrés* 2003).

PART THREE *Generations of Indigenous Activism and Internal Debates*

IN THE FIRST decade of the twenty-first century, as globalized indigenous movements completed their fourth decade of struggle, a new generation of Native intellectuals took shape and found its own voice. As the two essays in part 3 make clear, these younger Native intellectuals are well versed in postcolonial theory as well as indigenous methodologies. They straddle the line between activism and academic work, committed and aspiring to both. Brian Klopotek and Edgar Esquit are both committed to building what is, in essence, an "insider's critique" of the accomplishments and limitations of Native political and intellectual production. But neither wishes this critique to stay only inside Native circles. In a sense, they demonstrate that in the new generation it is important to eschew false unities in order more fully to build true and enduring ones.

In addition to these generational similarities, however, Klopotek and Esquit exhibit the differences generated by their distinct locations in the American hemisphere. While both aspire to a place in the academy, Klopotek is more firmly placed within it given the comparatively greater presence that Native intellectuals have carved out in academe in the United States. The political and historical context in which each has lived is also quite distinct. Klopotek has come of age in a time of antiracist activism that is attempting to build coalitions across the distinct experiences of various ethnic and racial minorities within the United States. Esquit, on the other hand, is part of the first generation of Maya intellectuals to come of age after the Guatemalan civil war of 1962–96, when more than 83 percent of the approximately two hundred thousand victims of violence were Maya.[1] He is attempting to place the Maya struggle for self-determination that emerged most strongly as a reaction to this civil war into historical context. For each, then, the meaning of multiculturalism is different, and, as we shall see, for Esquit it cannot be separated from questions of neoliberalism.

Basing his work on that of the Maori scholar Linda Tuhiwai Smith, Klopotek reflects deeply on the double meaning of the phrase "decolonizing methodologies." Not only do some methodologies decolonize research and knowledge, he argues, but we must also learn to decolonize the methodologies we use. In addressing the very sensitive issue of racism against blacks among southern Natives in the United States, Klopotek sees opportunity within the danger of "speaking secrets." While recognizing that for many years subaltern people have reacted to academic researchers by closing ranks and not being open about internal issues, Klopotek also considers the possibility that speaking the truth about internal divisions may be a form of activist healing.

For his part, Esquit is interested in who speaks for whom in the Maya movement. He explores the historical dynamics and origins of the pan-Maya movement across the twentieth century, focusing on prosperous, educated Maya elites in certain urban regions and among certain Maya linguistic groups, most notably the K'ich'e and Kaqchikel. Esquit demonstrates that the use of Mayanist discourse to claim space in particular worlds, such as national politics, that were previously closed to the Maya has a tradition going back to the end of the nineteenth century. He shows that this form of Maya empowerment has been used by Maya elites in relation to both ladinos and to poor and uneducated Maya. What is different in the post–civil war period, he suggests, is a discourse of peoplehood which, one might presume, has a new ethnic inclusiveness to it. Taking this inclusiveness seriously, Esquit concludes, means being attentive to all sectors of the Maya people and finding ways to get beyond internal class, gender, and ethnic differences. And it is in this sense that the economic problems exacerbated by globalization must take center stage. Unless the Maya movement takes account of the ways in which globalization hurts all the poor, Maya and ladino alike, then educated Maya who participate in the government will ultimately become complicit in the deployment of multiculturalism as a tool of state control and in the continued oppression and exclusion of the poor more generally.

Taken together, then, these two essays suggest that a more open and self-critical perspective on indigenous cultural and political issues, when formulated from within indigenous intellectual circles themselves, can provide new insights about the past and new clues for the future of indigenous activism. This combination of unity and loyalty to one's group, yet a willingness to criticize from within and to do so openly, with eyes on the future, is an important mark of the new generation of indigenous activist-intellectuals taking shape across the Americas.

Note

1. *Guatemala: Memory of Silence*, Report of the Commission for Historical Clarification, http://shr.aaas.org/guatemala.

BRIAN KLOPOTEK

Dangerous Decolonizing

Indians and Blacks and the Legacy of Jim Crow

For the past ten years I have been doing ethnological and historical research in the southeastern United States that revolves around federal recognition of Indian tribes. One of the thorniest issues to negotiate with people I interview has been the place of blackness in southern Indian communities. The subject quickly raises hackles because of the ways in which the presence of blackness undermines claims to a distinct Indian identity; as a result of this and other factors, antiblack racism remains an unresolved internal and external conflict in the South. As a Choctaw with roots in Louisiana and an activist for racial equality, I feel obliged to discuss the matter publicly to counter antiblack racism and free indigenous communities from what is ultimately a self-defeating support of white supremacy. By doing so, however, I am forcing other southern Indians to talk about the matter against their will and discussing a history that sometimes reflects poorly on us. On the basis of the conflicts and methodological problems I have encountered in this process, I suggest some revisions to indigenous methodologies and discuss the implications of this knowledge for indigenous studies as a field.

This essay addresses the stories we are not supposed to talk about, a thought that gives me pause. Decades of subaltern groups talking back to academics have made it clear that colonial gazing, airing dirty laundry, and treating indigenous people as laboratory animals undermine the safety and integrity of the communities being studied. In light of these critiques, indigenous peoples and scholars have developed a new model based in collaboration with and respect for indigenous sovereignty, and scholars try to be self-critical and self-aware, ensuring that scholarly work benefits the community in some direct way. Collaboration, mutual benefit, and scholarly support of tribal endeavors are central both to indigenous methodologies and to my ethical concerns as an indigenous researcher.[1]

But the problem of antiblack racism in Indian communities presents a theoretical oversight in indigenous methodologies in a couple of ways. First, indigenous methodologies need to be able to account for indigenous peoples as entities with blurred boundaries and internal heterogeneity rather than as discretely bounded, homogeneous communities. While scholars have often acknowledged the blurred boundaries between indigenous and colonizing populations that result in mestizaje, middle grounds, and colonial domination in American Indian studies, we have only recently become more careful about accounting for the ways in which Indian communities have come into contact with other marginalized groups and at times reproduced systems of oppression from the colonizers within our own communities. Moreover, we too rarely account for the multiplicity of social and political positions within a community, preferring the simplicity of well-intentioned declarative statements about supporting tribal sovereignty that carry a secret, homogenizing, nationalist "conceptual prison" for Indians within them.[2] Indigenous methodologies in some ways depend on a presupposition of a tidy power relationship between a tightly bound, oppressed subject group and a separate, oppressive external world, and a presupposition that all of the values of the indigenous community are worthy of upholding and in line with the values of the researcher. So what should we do when that is not true? Or, more accurately, what do we do once we understand that it is, in fact, an impossibility? Can we classify as collaborative work that which seeks to change the values of a community? In this case, I view it as part of a painful process of decolonization and a conversation long overdue in Indian country, but it raises the question of how to make these ethical considerations fit into a collaborative model.

That leads to the second area of concern, which is that in the context of U.S. indigenous studies, we need to have a better infusion of the study of race more broadly than simply in the Indian–white context. In many ways, the native–white relationship is unique. We need to keep this in mind because as a field U.S. ethnic studies does not have a solid understanding of the distinction between indigenous groups and racial minorities and typically fails to see the ways in which the colonizer–indigenous relationship is central to understanding other racial projects. At the same time, Indian studies as a field has focused so intently on what sets indigenous nations apart from racial minorities that we have failed to fully account for our common experiences as racial minorities. Indians are part of a racial system that goes beyond the binary racial relationship with whites and beyond the colonial relationship; we are part of a dynamic constellation, an entire system of race, and every node in that system affects Native people to some degree. We understand, for example, that white racializations of *Indian* people affect everything from the government-to-government relationship to the way Indian kids are socialized in educational systems. But Indians are part of and participate in a national conversation about race, and we need to understand more fully how racial formations and indigeneity are tied together, too. How do ideas about whiteness, Indianness, and blackness, for example, shape tribal identities? How were shifting attitudes toward Indians in the 1920s tied to the classification of Chicanos as white in the census of 1930 (Foley 2002)? How have Japanese- and Anglo-American myths of racial equality in Hawai'i undermined indigenous Hawaiian sovereignty efforts (Trask 2000)?

Stories from my experiences in Indian communities in Louisiana exemplify the complex historical relations between black, white, and Indian peoples, but this pattern of antiblack racism is evident in many Indian communities in the southeastern United States, as other scholars have documented extensively. James Merrell, for example, makes the starkly illustrative statement in an article from 1984 that "as recently as 1981, informants on the reservation called avoidance of and contempt for blacks 'a Catawba tradition'" (1984, 374). Similarly, Arica Coleman discusses the Rappahannock identity of Mildred Loving, one of the plaintiffs in *Loving v. Virginia*, the famous court case that struck down Virginia's antimiscegenation laws. While widely perceived as an African American woman, in an interview in 2004 Loving denied having any African ancestry, arguing that "the Rappahannocks never had anything to do with blacks" (Coleman 2006, 75). Helen Rountree discusses the ways in which Virginia's racial purity laws, beginning immediately after the Civil War, became "a veritable cornerstone" of Indian self-identity in Virginia because of the ways it distinguished the legal rights of Indians with no African ancestry from those with African ancestry.[3] The Mississippi Choctaws, a tribe notable for its high degree of language and cultural conservatism, historically refused to associate with blacks (Thompson and Peterson 1975, 180). The Lumbees, a tribe whose status as such is called into question by some who think they are mulattoes masquerading as Indians, have historically exhibited some of the same behavior, refusing to send their children to black schools when they were not allowed to enroll in white schools under Jim Crow (Blu 2001, 62–65). Each of the so-called Five Civilized Tribes of Oklahoma has in varying degrees excluded people from tribal enrollment because of their African ancestry, leading some of the remaining tribal members with African ancestry to hide their heritage behind particularly loud antiblack rhetoric.[4] The list goes on, but these examples should suffice to establish the broad, deeply set pattern of antiblack racism among southern Indians that reaches beyond the borders of any individual tribe or state. In fact, the pattern reaches beyond the southeastern United States and beyond indigenous communities, to be sure, but I will limit the conversation here to my area of expertise to make the arguments most effectively. I state this at the outset to help frame the discussion that follows and to shield tribes I am discussing specifically from being singled out for any special contempt they have not earned. I hope the fact that we are all in this narrative together provides some consolation to the fact that I am discussing here matters that many would rather bury. This is our common heritage as colonized subjects of a racist nation, and this is my attempt to contribute to our decolonization.

Research in Louisiana Indian Communities

I am a Native American studies scholar rather than an anthropologist or a historian, and the research for this project grew out of my interdisciplinary dissertation in American studies. While certainly informed by anthropological methods, theories, and methodologies, my research was never a strictly anthropological endeavor. My primary sources were oral history interviews and archival research focusing on the federal recognition process, though more traditional fieldwork during ten months in Louisiana also provided valuable context and points of discussion that would not have been available to me through formal interviews or archival research alone.

Rather than immersing myself in one tribal community, I worked with three tribal communities within an hour's drive of each other because I wanted to be able to examine their experiences with the federal recognition process from a comparative perspective. The dissertation focuses on the Tunica-Biloxi Tribe, federally recognized in 1981, the Jena Band of Choctaw Indians, federally recognized in 1995, and the Clifton-Choctaws, currently petitioning for federal recognition. Within these tribes and several others in the region, I interviewed tribal leaders almost exclusively—more than thirty people who had been involved in the tribal governments or tribal enterprises in some central way over the previous decades—people who I thought would be able to give me the most information about the federal recognition process. The resulting product might be called an intellectual history of recognition activism in Louisiana. This particular design has its limitations, but it provided insights into patterns of racial thinking that would not likely have been as visible with another research plan.

While the stories of every tribal community in Louisiana could supply ample material for discussion on this topic, I will focus on the Clifton-Choctaws presently because they epitomize the dilemma under study. The Clifton-Choctaws are a state-recognized tribe in the process of petitioning for federal recognition. Some local tribes and tribal members support the Clifton-Choctaws' bid for recognition while others oppose it. A substantial part of the opposition to recognition stems from the fact that some of the members of the community have African ancestry, which makes them automatically black, regardless of any other ancestry under legal and popular U.S. racial codes. As a result, the issue becomes central to Clifton-Choctaw identity construction.

When I visited the community between 1998 and 2000, the tribal member serving as the federal recognition liaison and unofficial office manager looked to be of Native, African, and European descent, as did her son and several other family members. Her name was Maria Dixon, and she occupied a position of visibility and power, a diplomatic position that in many ways made her the face of the tribe.[5] I assumed her presence in that position meant the Clifton-Choctaws were uninterested in downplaying their African ancestry, despite reports to the contrary from outsiders.

During my first interview with her I asked Dixon about the Clifton-Choctaws' relations with surrounding black and white communities. She said the Clifton-Choctaws have good relations with some blacks, such as the state representative from Alexandria, but that typically distrust flavors the relationship. She quickly added that distrust also typifies Clifton-Choctaw attitudes toward whites. They have good relations with some, bad with others, she said, citing conflicts with the sheriff's office and the school board as examples of the latter. She asserted that perceptions depended on the individuals involved in the relationship, given that many Clifton people distrust outsiders in general, regardless of their race. There is an element of truth in her statement about distrust of all outsiders, but after about ten seconds of silence, another truth burst out from its place just beneath the surface. "But on the whole," Dixon told me, "they trust whites more than they trust blacks."[6]

Setting aside for the moment her use of the word *they* rather than *we*, it is clear that Dixon was abundantly aware of the antiblack racism among her fellow community members but was trying, no doubt for a number of reasons both personal and political, to convey that reality in an understated way. Other leaders tiptoed around the subject of antiblack racism, too, distancing themselves from it, feeling me out, without necessarily performing an overt display of contempt for blacks. Consider, for example, the words of a Clifton man in his seventies, a man who might pass for white in many places. In his youth, he recalled, "they'd call you Redbone, they'd call you mulatto, they'd call you everything but probably what you are. So, we always, it was a fight with us when they'd call us all these other names, 'cause we always had been taught that we was from Indian people." The narrative implies that the inaccuracy of the labels mulatto and Redbone was at issue; antipathy hides in the subtext, where it is obvious that the blackness of the labels caused the offense. The element of Indian identity that depended on not only a lack of black ancestry but also antipathy toward blacks, it seemed to me, was a holdover from the older generations, a fading tradition, verging on becoming covert even in this older man's statement about his childhood. I recognized that it was a part of community history, but I categorically separated it from the modern community. I later realized it was a mistake to tie these attitudes to specific generations and assume declining acceptance of these traditions merely because of Dixon's central, visible position in the community.

After I had been away from the community for three years, a series of incidents made me realize I had been underestimating the importance of antiblack racism and the extent of community denials of black ancestry. In December 2003, as part of the collaborative process mandated by indigenous methodologies, I resent a draft of the Clifton-Choctaw chapter from my dissertation to Dixon so tribal members could read and comment on it before it was finalized. Dixon had left her position shortly after I sent the original draft, and apparently no one had seen it the first time around. The new recognition coordinator was a white woman, the wife of a tribal member who was eager to read the chapter. I sent off two copies and waited for the marked-up copy to be returned to me. I waited and waited, but nothing came. I called a couple of times in the intervening two months and left messages but never heard back. Finally, one day I reached her by phone and asked her what she and others thought of the draft. I was anxious because community approval represents a hurdle at least as significant as academic approval and infinitely more challenging and fraught with danger. More than mere courtesy, collaboration makes for more rigorous academic work because it makes scholars accountable to the expertise and authority of community members as lifelong participant-observers. The new coordinator was hesitant, and I could sense that a significant critique was about to emerge. She told me that "all this information" was new to her and that she was shocked by it. I asked her what information specifically was so shocking. She started talking in a tone that let me know she was choosing her words carefully. "You know, the stuff about the [pause] . . . *muhlahtas*."

She was referring to my discussions of blackness in the community's ancestry, to the fact that many of the ancestors of community members were identified as mulattoes in the census of 1910, to the history of intermarriage with the nearby Cane River Creoles of Color, to the fact that I had described the community as mixed Indian, black, and white. She said her husband was angry about this characterization, but that he acknowledged that the perception of his people as mulattoes had been present for a number of years. She guessed that many other community members would be similarly angry, but only about the issue of mixing with blacks—mixing with whites was completely acceptable.

As it turns out, she was right. When I next visited the Clifton-Choctaw community, she was no longer working for the tribe, so I talked with the new tribal recognition coordinator. I brought two copies of my completed dissertation on this trip: one to give to the tribal chair and one to the tribal council. While I had made some minor adjustments in phrasing to indicate that some of the community had African ancestry and some potentially did not, I did not remove discussions of blackness altogether. I talked with the new coordinator, who was a tribal member, and told her about the concerns of her predecessor. She concurred that it certainly would go over poorly with many tribal members, and it did not sit well with her, either. She said that blacks had always been excluded from the community and that if she had any say in the matter the tribe would uphold that tradition. She told me that Dixon had always, in fact, been marginal to the community because of her blackness, a troubling statement that opened a window onto Dixon's experiences of belonging in her community.

I had a conversation with the tribal chair about the issue later that week, and she spoke in the more diplomatic tones I had heard from other officials, though she, like others, expressed concern that I had suggested that the community had black ancestry and black cultural influences. Perplexed, I told her I thought it was commonly acknowledged that some members of the Clifton-Choctaw community had black ancestry, in particular through its ties to the Cane River Creoles of Color. Her eyes brightened in recognition and what appeared to be relief, and she said, "Oh, well, yes, the Cane River Creoles, we do share ancestry with them." In local terms, the Cane River Creoles, who have African, French, and Native ancestry, were distinguished from blacks by their large percentage of European ancestry, their history as free people of color and slaveholders themselves (which carries connotations about both race and class), their francophone traditions, and their celebrity as bearers of a unique tradition that sets Louisiana apart from the rest of the United States. In central Louisiana, they were "a race apart from blacks," certainly in their own minds and to a significant degree in local custom as well.[7] These were not the blacks that many Clifton-Choctaws were loath to be affiliated with. French and Latin American style racial gradations, which are multifaceted rather than binary, are still in operation in the area to the extent that the terms *black* and *Creole of Color* connote different sets of people and different levels of prejudice. This clarifies to some extent the protestations by Clifton-Choctaws against the suggestion that they had black ancestry.

Though the tribal chair acknowledged her community's connections with the Cane River Creoles of Color, she insisted that whatever racial ancestry the community had, they had been largely isolated from mainstream black and white influences and intermarriage for many years. That is, while there was intermarriage with Creoles of Color and white outsiders at various points, the community had been largely insular, marrying among themselves for the better part of 150 years. Certainly there was white influence and (less so, she points out) black influence in the community, but on some level she believes a discussion of black influences in particular diminishes the community's distinctive Indian identity. In terms of the perceptions of the community and of the federal recognition process, which is at its heart about perceptions, she may be right.

Regulating Racial Categories

The origin of antiblack racism among southern Indians rests in Anglo-American racism and colonialism, two phenomena that are so closely related that they might be better accounted for if we understand them as behavior resulting from an ideology centered in white supremacy—an ideology in which white people and their ancestors are understood to be morally, intellectually, politically, and spiritually superior to nonwhites and therefore entitled to various forms of privilege, power, and property.[8] This ideology was forced on southern Indian communities gradually but surely through the twin hammers of military conquest and assimilationism. A number of scholars have documented southern Indians' adoption of Anglo systems of racial thinking as one component of a multifaceted response to U.S. aggression; in mirroring the peculiar notions of civility held by southern Anglos around race and gender, tribes hoped to protect themselves against conquest based on constructions of Indian savagery (Saunt 2005, 1999; Miles 2004; Perdue, 1979, 1999; Littlefield, 1977). Claudio Saunt suggests that as a result, race became "a central element in the lives of southeastern Indians, not just as a marker of difference between natives and white newcomers but as a divisive and destructive force within Indian communities themselves" (2005, 4). Though there was conflict within the tribes over the issues of slavery and blackness, southeastern tribes increasingly adopted Anglo-American racializations of African-descended people over the course of the nineteenth century.

For much of the twentieth century, segregation policies were the arena in which the boundaries of race and privilege were officially policed, and because of this history in educational policy specifically Indians in the South learned to define themselves in ways that distanced them from blacks as much as possible. While there were simultaneous impulses toward isolationism from whites, when southern Indians, of African ancestry or not, wanted access to education they fought to have their children enrolled in white schools and refused to send them to black schools. Rather than challenging the existence of the color line, most tried to position themselves on the right side of it. By saying they would not go to school with blacks, an act of self-defense taken with the intention of ameliorating racial discrimination against Indian people and maintaining a distinct Indian identity, Indians were complicit in the segregation and oppression of blacks.[9] Consequently, antiblack racism seeped deeper still into the construction of Indian identity. The Clifton-Choctaws, like other southern Indians, continue to grapple with this legacy today.

More recently, federal Indian policy that determines whether previously nonfederal tribes should qualify for federal recognition has been a much clearer venue for the regulation of the boundaries of Indian identity, and by extension in this case of black, white, and Creole of Color identities as well. Blackness and its absence come into the federal recognition discussion in several ways. The first is the significance of previous recognition from governments, surrounding communities, and social scientists.[10] Because of

Anglo-American conceptions of race and the one-drop rule, anyone with visible or known African ancestry ("one drop" of African "blood") was considered black or colored for most purposes. An Indian community with even a small degree of black ancestry is much less likely historically to have been acknowledged as an Indian community by governments, social scientists, and surrounding populations than a community with greater degrees of white ancestry.[11]

The census is a good example of this bias in historical records. The census of 1910 for Rapides Parish, for example, lists many of the families in the Clifton community as mulattoes.[12] The special Indian Schedule for Rapides Parish in 1910 lists none of the seven family surnames represented in the Clifton community in recent years. The census enumerators in 1910 were instructed to use the Indian Schedules "principally for the enumeration of Indians living on reservations or in tribal relations, and also by the enumerators in certain counties containing a considerable number of Indians" (United States Census Bureau 2002, 55). They were given further instructions on deciding how to group mixed communities: "Detached Indians living either in white or negro families outside of reservations should be enumerated on the general population schedule as members of the families in which they are found; but detached whites or negroes living in Indian families should be enumerated on this special Indian schedule as members of the Indian families in which they are found. In other words, every family composed mainly of Indians should be reported entirely on this special schedule, and every family composed mainly of persons not Indians should be reported entirely on the general population schedule" (United States Census Bureau 2002, 56).

This presents a problem for the Clifton community. People of mixed black, white, and Indian ancestry were classified as mulattoes by the census, undifferentiated from people of solely white and black ancestry. The surrounding population did acknowledge Indian ancestry in the Clifton community when they called them Redbones, a derogatory term that connotes Indian, black, and white ancestry, but the official census record did not have a category to reflect that distinction, which would allow people to conclude that the record stated they were solely black and white instead of Indian.[13]

The census enumerator's decision also reflected the broader American understanding that the presence or absence of Indian ancestry did not usually alter a designation as mulatto, a term that could mean any mix of black and nonblack ancestry in the United States. The presence of African ancestry among any of the Clifton families may very well have closed the enumerator's eyes to the possibility that this might be an Indian community as much as anything else, particularly if any links to the Cane River Creoles were known to the enumerator.[14] Moreover, Jack Forbes's research on Virginia census records at the very least suggests that one needs to be cautious in assigning African ancestry to people listed in historical records as mulatto. Certainly people of visible African ancestry were classified as such, but so were people of undetermined racial ancestry. A designation as mulatto is not in itself confirmation of African ancestry and certainly is not confirmation of a lack of Indian ancestry (Forbes 1993). The only firm conclusion one can draw is that the enumerators believed the people they listed as mulatto should not be considered white.

Similarly, in terms of previous federal acknowledgment of Indian communities, the Bureau of Indian Affairs of the 1930s was extremely disinclined to serve communities with black ancestry because of the one-drop rule. Bureau officials expressed concern that they might be called on to serve Louisiana Indians who were "mixed with negroes" like other "so-called Indians in Louisiana particularly in Terrebonne Parish [in reference to the Houma tribe], such people being of various racial mixtures."[15] Bureau records indicate that black ancestry among *some* Louisiana Indian groups made officials less inclined to serve *any* of the Louisiana tribes, but they did briefly serve those who could demonstrate that they had not mixed with blacks, such as the Jena Choctaws and the Coushattas. Thus, tribes with black ancestry petitioning for federal recognition are at a disadvantage in this aspect as well.

Perhaps the most difficult rejection to deal with is that which comes from other Indians. While several Tunica-Biloxi tribal leaders have expressed support for Clifton-Choctaw tribal status, some of the neighboring and now federally recognized Jena Choctaws have been fairly critical of the Clifton-Choctaws' claims to tribal status. Individuals within the Jena Band respond to the Clifton-Choctaws in different ways, though, so any impression that they uniformly reject Clifton-Choctaws because of African ancestry in the community would flatten and compress the range of opinions other Indian people have about Clifton.

One Jena Choctaw leader argues that there certainly are Indian individuals in the Clifton-Choctaw community, but that the presence of Indian ancestry in some of the members does not make them a tribe. After attending a festival sponsored by the Louisiana Inter-Tribal Council in Clifton in the late 1990s, she noted that "one of the new leaders or council members or something, he looked just like a perfect old Choctaw Indian man would look like, you know, just Indian. I mean, he's Indian." She feels the same way about other state-recognized tribes, acknowledging that some members clearly have Indian ancestry but withholding support for their federal recognition. If the community as a whole could demonstrate more social, cultural, and, frankly, racial markers of Indian identity, they would seem more like a cohesive Indian community to her, one that could be classified as a tribe.

A Jena Choctaw elder adds that it is unfair to withhold recognition from the "real" Indians at places like Clifton and Houma, but by the same token it would be unfair to recognize non-Indians with them. Her definition of what constitutes a real Indian is not terribly complex—she believes anyone who can trace their genealogy back to any documented Indian can be a real Indian. Any relation is real, she says, and that ancestry cannot be cut off or erased. While she was a full blood, her tribe's minimum blood quantum is one-eighth, and she believed that would change soon since most of the young people were marrying whites at the time. The Clifton-Choctaws may meet her standards for tribal recognition if they can document that they all have at least one Indian ancestor.

Another Jena Choctaw leader believes the Clifton-Choctaws have no Indian ancestry at all and should have their state recognition revoked. His opinion relies on—and contributed to—a genealogical argument that erupted in 1988 between the Clifton-Choctaws and Mary Carter, a specialist in Indian genealogy who worked for both Jena and Clifton.[16] Carter concluded, after researching Clifton genealogy for six months, that the Clifton-Choctaws were not Indians but "really" blacks with some Indian ancestry. Apparently after arguing with the spouse of the Clifton tribal chair in 1988, Carter went to the newspapers with her "revelation," leading to articles that publicly declared them non-Indian poseurs. One Jena Choctaw leader described the articles as being horrible. The articles were supposed to say that the Clifton-Choctaws were primarily mixed black and white with only a little Indian ancestry, but that finding, the Jena Choctaw leader contends, ended up being distorted to say that they were not Indian at all.[17]

During another formal interview with Maria Dixon, I asked her about accusations made in those articles that the Cliftons were really black and not Indian at all. She bristled: "Mary Carter came up with that, who also worked for the tribe. As a matter of fact, she's the one that started training me to do genealogy. And she and [a former recognition coordinator] got in it about something, I don't really know. And next thing we knew, she did have two articles in the paper about it. . . . I would put it this way. We have documented our Indian ancestry. Now, whether—and I'm not going to say there's no black blood in the tribe, because quite a few people in the community are triracial. But the majority are—I mean, it all goes back to Native Americans. We have been able to document that. And I really don't think there's a tribe in Louisiana that can say that they did not have maybe a drop of black blood or Caucasian or anything else within them."

Members of the Clifton-Choctaw community who appear to have black ancestry, people such as Dixon, bear a unique burden in being discriminated against within the tribe, within their families. Doubts about tribal authenticity that are linked to accusations of blackness are placed on their shoulders or, more accurately, on their faces. This situation presents an ethical and scholarly dilemma: how do I encourage Clifton-Choctaws to embrace or at least acknowledge black ancestry in their community when there is a strong sentiment in the community to deny it altogether? I contend that it would help their recognition case if they dealt with their black ancestry directly; skirting around it gives the impression they are trying to hide the truth, never a productive stance in the acknowledgment process. It would also help ease their sense of shame over the issue and take some of the burden off phenotypically black tribal members. What is my responsibility as a Louisiana Choctaw researcher to this other Louisiana Choctaw community, of which I am not a member but with whom I share Choctaw heritage? How do I implement the supportive, collaborative model of indigenous methodologies without undermining my personal responsibilities as a racial activist? If the Clifton-Choctaws know that talking about African ancestry in the community has caused them problems in the past, I am putting myself in a position of betraying their trust and saying that I know better than they do about how and when to talk about these things.

Cornel Pewewardy, in grappling with his own role as an indigenous person within the academy, similarly concludes that "sometimes we (as Indigenous scholars) have to redefine our roles as scholars in academe to become involved as facilitators *and* informants in the process of tribal community empowerment. To take on the role of facilitator is to deny my own activism. I must recognize that my own liberation and emancipation in relationship with my tribal community are at stake, and that continued marginalization and subjugation are the perils" (Pewewardy 2004, 14). It is in that spirit of activism for the liberation of my people, of Indian people, from white supremacy that I move forward with this discussion.

In *Ties that Bind: The Story of an Afro-Cherokee Family in Slavery and Freedom*, Tiya Miles notes that various individuals, black and Indian, discouraged her from discussing the history of Cherokee slaveholding and of Cherokees as colonized and colonizing subjects. The desire to "disremember" these painful shared histories among communities of color is entangled with contemporary desires and anxieties about imagined histories of "natural affinity" or "natural animosity" among communities of color, the ways we construct race and righteousness, the ways we draw connections or construct boundaries. But there is a story to tell, even if it is "not a story to pass on," not a story anyone wants to remember or address publicly.[18] However, as Miles wrote, drawing on the theoretical underpinnings of Toni Morrison's *Beloved*, "The void that remains when we refuse to speak of the past is in fact a presence, a presence both haunting and destructive."[19] When we examine these histories, we gain knowledge that opens ways to work through the theoretical and emotional conflicts inherent in the subject. If I thought this conversation had no implications across Indian Country, I would not address it in this public forum, but we need healing and redemption around this issue. And we need decolonization.

We are dynamic people, and we have the power to change and adapt our strategies as new information comes to light. When we understand that the ideology of white supremacy performs multiple tasks, diverting multiple resources away from oppressed groups and toward whites through multiple kinds of behavior, we can see more clearly that antiblack racism, when performed by Indians, confirms a racial formation that places whites at the top of a racial hierarchy.[20] Such an ideology hardly seems to be in the best interests of Indians, especially when we connect it to the "cultural bomb" described by Ngugi wa Thiong'o as the most devastating weapon of the colonial project. Its effect, he writes, "is to annihilate a people's belief in their names, in their languages, in their environment, in their heritage of struggle, in their unity, in their capacities and ultimately in themselves."[21] Rather than pathologizing Indians, we need to recognize the source of Indian antiblack racism within a broader colonial project and acknowledge its hidden impact not only on Indian resources, but also on Indian senses of self.

In terms of the scholarly dilemma, the double meaning in the title of Linda Tuhiwai Smith's foundational book, *Decolonizing Methodologies*, clarifies and justifies the role of scholarly activism in a case such as this (1999). First, it speaks of creating methodologies that do not perpetuate colonial practices of exploitation and assimilation, that is, methodologies that have been decolonized. Second, it is about pursuing decolonization as a goal that can be achieved through methodologies designed for the task, that is, it is about decolonizing indigenous peoples through specific methodologies. The second definition motivates my decision to have this conversation in this essay: a desire to decolonize minds and illustrate the ways in which antiblack racism supports a white supremacist racial formation.[22] White supremacy clearly does not support indigenous people. Its pathology is well known, but, in the absence of a more inclusive understanding of how race works, we do not always see whom it infects and how. Racial theory and racial histories help us rethink indigenous studies, indigenous methodologies, and the collaborative process to better serve indigenous communities. Decolonizing can be dangerous, but that moment of danger is also a moment of opportunity.

Notes

1. Linda Tuhiwai Smith is often credited with developing this field as an area of focused study through her book *Decolonizing Methodologies: Research and Indigenous Peoples* (1999). Her work draws on and builds upon many traditional critiques of the relationship of the academy to subaltern groups, including the work of scholars in postcolonial studies and Native American studies as well as the writings of feminist women of color, feminist anthropologists, and postmodernists. Generally, see Vine Deloria, Jr., *Custer Died for Your Sins: An Indian Manifesto*, (1988, 78–100); Lila Abu-Lughod, "Writing Against Culture" (1991, 137–62); Edward Said, *Orientalism* (1978); Ngugi wa Thiong'o, *Decolonising the Mind* (1986); Frantz Fanon, *The Wretched of the Earth* (2004); Nannerl O. Keohane, Michelle Z. Rosaldo, and Barbara C. Gelpi, eds., *Feminist Theory* (1982).

2. Deloria critiques the "conceptual prison" created for Indians by anthropologists through notions of authenticity in his foundational work of 1969 (1988). Paige Raibmon offers a useful history of the development of the concept of authenticity and its impact on indigenous peoples in *Authentic Indians: Episodes of Encounter from the Late-Nineteenth-Century Northwest Coast* (2005). Abu-Lughod argues the merits of "ethnography of the particular" as a way of avoiding the flattening tendency of cultural theory (1991).

3. Any Indian person in Virginia who had more than one-quarter African blood (later one-sixteenth) would be classified as colored and have access to fewer rights and resources than those classified as Indians, people who had more than one-quarter Indian blood (later one-sixteenth) (Rountree 1990, 200, 211).

4. On Cherokees, see Sturm (1998) and Miles (2004). On Creeks, see Saunt (2005). Generally, see Miles and Holland (2006); Brooks (2002).

5. "Maria Dixon" is a pseudonym.

6. A close reading of this statement would note her use of the word *they* to refer to the Clifton community, when it would seem more appropriate for her to use *we*. This seems like evidence of discomfort in including herself in that opinion by saying "we trust whites more than we trust blacks." But it also seems to be a long-standing reflex to distance the community "on the whole" from blacks and blackness even though she is unwilling to ally herself with such thinking.

7. (Mills 1977, xiv). Lalita Tademy, a Cane River Creole herself, wrote a bestselling novel and Oprah's Book Club selection about her people, giving perhaps the most visible moment in recent Cane River history (Tademy 2002).

8. While typically the term *white supremacy* conjures images of Klan robes and neo-Nazi skinheads, the term as it is used in contemporary ethnic studies also refers to the everyday ideology of white racial superiority and domination carried even by people who do not consider themselves racist and even by people of color. For a general discussion of white racial ideology and material advantages in the United States, see Rothenberg (2002) and Lipsitz (1998).

9. Neil Foley draws heavily on Toni Morrison's ideas about southern European immigrants becoming white in the United States by demonstrating their hatred of blacks as he grapples with similar racial formation issues in Mexican-American integration activism in Texas in the 1930s (2002, 49–59).

10. Susan Greenbaum adeptly and precisely addresses this matter, though others have addressed it elsewhere (Greenbaum 1991; Paschal 1991; Starna 1996; Campisi 1991; Clifford 1988). A number of significant contributions can be found in Miles and Holland (2006) and in Brooks (2002).

11. Circe Sturm discusses this issue (Sturm 1998).

12. The Census of 1910, Rapides Parish, Louisiana, lists many Clifton, Tyler, and Smith families as mulatto. This is not a complete, diagnostic genealogical connection, but obviously these are the ancestors of at least some of the modern Clifton families.

13. See also Williams (1979).

14. United States Census Bureau 2002, 56: "Proportions of Indian and other blood.—If the Indian is a full-blood, write 'full' in column 36, and leave columns 37 and 38 blank. If the Indian is of mixed blood, write in column 36, 37, and 38 the fractions which show the proportions of Indian and other blood, as (column 36, Indian) $3/4$, (column 37, white) $1/4$, and (column 38, negro) 0. For Indians of mixed blood all three columns should be filled, and the sum, in each case, should equal 1, as $1/2$, 0, $1/2$; $3/4$, $1/4$, 0; $3/4$, $1/8$, $1/8$; etc. Wherever possible, the statement that an Indian is of full blood should be verified by inquiry of the older men of the tribe, as an Indian is sometimes of mixed blood without knowing it."

15. A. C. Hector to W. Carson Ryan, Jr., 12 September 1934, file 68776-1931-800, part I, National Archives Record Group 75.

16. "Mary Carter" is a pseudonym.

17. "La. Tribe Fights to Prove Its Heritage," *Times-Picayune*, 14 August 1988, C8.

18. Miles (2004, xv), citing Morrison (1987, 274–75).

19. Miles (2004, xvi). Miles and many others witnessed the calamity and pain of this ghostly presence at a conference on black–Indian relations she organized at Dartmouth in 1998 called "'Eating Out of the Same Pot': Relating Black and Native (Hi)stories." Several pieces have been written about the dramatic conflicts that surfaced throughout: Phillips (2002); Saunt (2005, 6–9); Tiya Miles, "Preface: Eating Out of the Same Pot?," in Miles and Holland (2006); Warrior, "Afterword," in Miles and Holland (2006).

20. George Lipsitz suggests the value of this formulation in his work (1998).

21. Thiong'o (1986, 3), cited in Silva (2004, 2).

22. Following Omi and Winant's definition of racial formation as "the sociohistorical process by which racial categories are created, inhabited, transformed, and destroyed," and a racial project as "simultaneously an interpretation, representation, or explanation of racial dynamics, and an effort to reorganize and redistribute resources along particular racial lines" (1994, 55–56).

EDGAR ESQUIT

Nationalist Contradictions

Pan-Mayanism, Representations of the Past,

and the Reproduction of Inequalities in Guatemala

For over three decades the Maya peoples of Guatemala have been transforming the ways in which they struggle against continuing colonial power relations in the country. Local processes of protest are now accompanied by protests with a national character that challenge not only the state, but also other dominant ideologies, like patriarchy, Protestant and Catholic visions, and certain popular constructions of history and identity. Now, new discussions about the Maya's national position occur between different actors and across opposing spaces. According to these analysts' different conceptions, the so-called pan-Mayanist or Mayan movement is engaged in a complex process of defining demands, discourses, ideological constructions, diverse forms of political struggle, new relationships of power, and the construction of other identities (Warren 1998; Fischer 2001; Cojtí Cuxil 1991; Bastos and Camus 2003). As this movement progresses, contradictions have emerged in relation to demands, representativeness, the conformation of intellectual elites, and ways of imagining the past.

In this essay I delineate relevant aspects of the Maya political movement, principally the reconstruction of history and its link to the present. The Maya political movement is primarily guided by an intelligentsia that produces and adopts a series of organizing and discursive ideological definitions and strategies about the struggle in which it is engaged. These leaders, linked to debates on human rights, religion, education, languages, Maya rights, and racism, belong to different organizations that get reorganized during each crisis the movement suffers. They generate a series of ideas and images about the Maya past with the double aim of pinning down the idea of the Maya people (Maya unity) and challenging the exclusionary makeup of the Guatemalan nation-state.

The general questions guiding the essay can be stated as follows: In what way does this emerging sector of educated Maya delimit a new narrative about the past? How is this narrative linked to the definition of new identities and the formation of unexpected power relations? Being a Maya and a researcher, I am personally involved in this process of constructing imaginaries (*imaginarios*) about the past.

We understand the notion of Maya as both a construct that evolved as the Maya movement developed and as a tool for defining the ethnic identity of those who up to now have been called indigenous, Indians, or aboriginals (*naturales*). This definition acknowledges the contradictions and political differences that Maya individuals encounter as they appropriate other identities. The Mayanists, as they are defined in this essay, are the people and institutions that openly promote Maya political rights and recover a culturalist definition of their own past. They do so with the purpose of assigning meaning and giving historical support to the notion of Maya peoples and multiculturalism.

Finally, since I will be speaking about the colonial forms of power relations in Guatemala, I consider how some of the Maya movement's intellectuals have characterized the concept of colonialism. Some of them define colonialism in relation to the Guatemalan state and ladinos, affirming that only one community, the ladino, currently controls the state.[1] They assert that ladinos instrumentalize the state to control and limit the development of subordinate indigenous nations. According to these intellectuals, Guatemala is a colonial state that manifests an internal colonialism in which one national group oppresses others within the same environment (Cojtí Cuxil 1989, 140–41).

Demetrio Rodríguez posits that colonialism, by definition, starts from the political domination, economic exploitation, and cultural and linguistic assimilation of one people over another and involves diverse historical conditions like invasion, conquest, or annexation (Rodríguez 2004, 46). Following the same line of thought, Demetrio Cojtí proposes that colonialism is a doctrine that legitimizes one people's domination over another and employs various arguments to justify Maya subordination (Cojtí Cuxil 1995, 148). These notions attempt to explain the political relations between indigenous peoples and ladinos in Guatemala, understanding the latter as almost homogeneous entities.

Colonial relations, however, are highly complex and must be observed at different moments and in specific spaces. Colonialism traverses relations between social sectors, genders, classes, regions and localities, institutions, and diverse organizations. In this case, one can talk about the colonial shape of power relations in Guatemala, where class relations are strongly tied to society's ethnic makeup, establishing a racial hierarchy that acts as the basis for exchange among social groups.[2]

Imagining New Histories

In their article "The Maya Workshop of Hieroglyphic Writing" Linda Schele and Nikolai Grube describe a series of activities related to teaching and learning the Mayas' ancient writing that they and other epigraphists developed together with a group of Maya activists and intellectuals (1999). The authors note that some Maya intellectuals requested that they carry out different workshops from 1987 to 1995. The workshops took place in the city of Antigua and in archeological sites like Tikal, Copán, and Iximché as well as in certain municipalities and smaller localities like San Andrés Semetabaj in the department of Sololá. Attendees at these activities included Mayas linked with organizations dedicated to strengthening and studying indigenous languages, professionals in linguistic fields, and people with less formal academic and professional training in these fields.

According to the authors, the Mayas who participated in these events showed a great deal of interest in the writings' meanings and were very creative when comparing the interpretations the specialists proposed with those that were recognized in their mother tongues. The participants were keenly interested in studying the glyphs in order to understand ancient Maya history and particularly Maya cultural development. Schele and Grube propose that the workshop on the classical period's story of creation was one of the most meaningful because it related directly to religious, social, ritual, and agricultural practices of the modern Maya. According to the authors, the participants' reactions and conversations over the following year suggest that the information extracted from the epigraphic texts created strong ties between contemporary experience and the ancient pre-Colombian past (Schele and Grube 1999).

In addition to the workshops in Guatemala, Schele and Grube developed a workshop in Mérida, Mexico, attended by a sizable number of Yukateco speakers. During the final event, held at the ruins of Chichén-Itzá, a participant named Kokom affirmed that on his previous visits to the ruins he had not taken the glyphs and their meanings into account. Yet on this occasion he had noticed that his last name was written in the glyphs. The authors think it is important that the Yucatekan and Guatemalan Maya meet in the future to share their knowledge. This and other experiences led different Guatemalan organizations to use the glyphs in new ways to support sharing their newfound knowledge and newly recognized history. By participating in similar workshops, other Maya took this newfound knowledge to their communities of origin, such as Chimaltenango, Cobán, Palín, and Tecpán, and shared it with community members. The authors propose that this represented the transfer and dissemination of a system of teaching and writing into Maya hands.

Kay Warren wrote an article about a weeklong workshop developed in 1992 by a group of Kaqchikel linguists. The participants studied the book *Annals of the Kaqchikels*, a work written by Kaqchikel authorities (*principales*) during the colonial era (Warren 1999). Warren explains that the participating linguists had taken part in other community education projects and had developed a series of activities and, later, published extracts of the book, which were used as material in informal educational programs. Warren argues that Maya culturalists see these ancient texts as both vital resources for learning about the past and fundamental guides for contemporary projects.

According to Warren, the participants believed the study of the ancient texts could reveal that Kaqchikels have a unique origin. However, some of the participants thought this revision was not necessarily an argument against official history, but a search for the truths that have not been completely understood. Citing another participant in the workshop, Warren highlights new perspectives on the ancient texts. Some Maya activists, she says, think this book describes official Maya history. In other words, they see the book as a retelling of Maya origins, cosmology (*cosmogonía*), and experiences with the European invasion as well as of the genealogical continuity of one of Guatemala's most important peoples.

Warren's text proposes that the culturalists argue heatedly among themselves as they try to strip Maya cosmovision of its contact with European religions, other ideologies, and intentional manipulations. The new readings of certain parts of the text are counterposed to traditional ones made by national and foreign scholars in relation to, for example, the arrival of the Spanish and the ensuing armed struggle. In their eagerness to imagine continuity in Maya descent, culture, and languages, Maya activists face the challenge of confronting official histories that talk about conquest and assimilation (Warren 1999).

The texts I have cited show some of the activities Mayanists are engaging in to recover and define another representation of their past. This interest, however, is not recent. The effort to develop a new perspective on the Maya past and present likely has its origins in these individuals' first attempts to study their mother tongues. In the mid-twentieth century Adrián Inés Chávez, an eminent K'iche intellectual, organized congresses of Maya educators to discuss topics related to languages. Since then, Chávez has posited the need to establish truly indigenous symbols to write K'iche, while emphasizing linguistic and cultural unity (Fischer 1990, 90). In 1979, he translated and published the Pop Wuj (Popol Vuh) into graphics that laid out a new alphabet exclusively for this language (Chávez 2001).

In the 1980s and 1990s Maya intellectuals began shaping a new content and meaning of Maya history by organizing activities such as meetings, workshops, and seminars as well as by editing bibliographic and didactic material. They produced a number of important texts on this issue, for example, those by Víctor Racancoj (1994), Raxche' Demetrio Rodríguez (1995), Demetrio Cojtí Cuxil (1991, 1995), and Víctor Montejo (1997). Important Maya leaders and investors founded a press that reprinted books by national and foreign authors, among them Robert Carmack, Carlos Guzmán Böckler and Jean-Loup Herbert, and Robert M. Hill, that analyze the history of the Maya.[3] Currently, various institutions are also editing popular texts, including children's stories that evoke the Maya past. Many people are putting a great deal of effort into building new ways of representing and analyzing Maya history.

These representations can be synthesized as the construction of a historical base, which recognizes the principles that unite the actions and knowledge of the ancient Maya with those that nourish the contemporary Maya. By examining these sorts of ancient texts as well as works by archeologists, anthropologists, linguists, and historians, Mayanists try to rebuild a version of their past that specifies the particularity or essentiality of Maya culture. They also attempt to reconstruct the history of resistance and leadership that they believe can have an important role in thinking about and imagining resistance today.

Mayanists look to contribute to a definition of Maya unity with this new historical narrative. Through these efforts they affirm that we Maya share common ancestors who bequeathed us a common culture and languages of origin that we need to protect. We Maya participate in a specific way of looking at the world and at ourselves, recognizing that all Maya intellectuals have shared a similar adversity since 1524—an adversity Maya intellectuals have defined as internal colonialism.[4]

The new historical narrative feeding the pan-Mayanist movement's political struggle has defined dates and periods of historic succession, tracing the greatness and catastrophes lived and suffered by the Maya people. Now, we could say that as a people we probably have a date of birth (some five thousand years ago) and of growth, something that until just a few decades ago was not defined in the historical narratives that our parents, grandparents, elders in general, and the leaders and community guides presented to us. In different ways this new historic Mayanist imaginary is expressed as the real Maya history that reveals a past hidden or distorted by official history. These discourses form the notion of the Maya people and are tied to the speeches about multiculturalism that are generated by Mayanist intellectuals and their organizations as well as by the state.

This way of evoking the past represents an important break in the Maya imaginary and in the ways they are recreating themselves to build and confront their own present and that of Guatemala. This narrative generates pride among those familiar with it, primarily Mayanists. Maya individuals, for example, can make reference to their millenarian past when they present their demands to the government, just as they can cite their history of greatness when they appear in public, attend universities, or talk on national and international stages.

Maya educators who are directing schools known as Maya schools are teaching children this new way of understanding the past. Here, the ancient Maya are not seen as a civilization of great inventors who disappeared before the arrival of the Spanish, as the state schools taught and continue to teach. Instead, teachers instruct students that they are the grandchildren of Maya ancestors who created a great civilization, as evidenced in architecture, mathematical advances, and hieroglyphic writing, in the artistic creations found in our sacred centers and in our ancient books, as well as in our restored political and religious ceremonies. In addition, some community histories and histories of municipalities with a Maya majority incorporate this way of viewing the past.

Nationalist Contradictions 201

Educated Maya and Narratives about the Past

It is primarily one sector of educated Maya who construct and evoke this new narrative. From Chávez in the middle of the twentieth century to Montejo at the start of the twenty-first century, what characterizes these historical narrators is their professional formation.[5] In this case, the new imaginary or historical representation is generated not only from communities' oral tradition, but also (and more extensively) from other knowledges acquired as a result of close contact with schools, organizations, and other worlds, from Western or ladino to North American.

Since the 1960s, a sector of the Maya from different communities entered secondary schools and university (Bastos and Camus 2003). In subsequent decades, in spite of the repression this population suffered in the 1970s and 1980s, some continued this trajectory, adding to the number of Maya who have graduated from secondary school and university. These well-educated Maya assumed other identities that partly contrasted with those of uneducated (*iletrados*) Maya, men and women who cultivate the earth and maintain a subsistence economy.[6] Those identities also contrast with those of the ladinos with whom they had lived in their communities as well as with those of colleagues in schools and workplaces (Sincal Coyote 2004).

This tradition of education since the 1960s was most evident among the Kaqchikels and K'iche, but similar processes can be observed in other ethnic groups. An exemplary case is that of the Comalapa municipality, located in the central department of Chimaltenango, where the majority of the inhabitants are Kaqchikels. From the beginning of the twentieth century a small group of distinguished families characterized by their status as intermediaries, their economic resources, and their capacity for political negotiation, began to implement a series of transformations at the productive level, in political participation, and in the educational formation of some of their young members. In the 1920s a small group of Maya teachers from this community graduated from the country's normal schools. They returned to their community, where they served as primary school teachers in a school founded by prominent families specifically for indigenous people. From the 1970s until the present, the number of professionals emerging from this municipality has increased significantly. They distinguished themselves in several important professions. Many graduated as primary school teachers and others as accountants, engineers, doctors, lawyers, linguists, soldiers, priests, and administrators. Many lived through processes of cultural change and economic ascent that transformed their ways of relating to one another and to the people in their communities who are involved in agricultural, artisanal, and commercial activities. Most of these professionals continue differentiating themselves from ladinos, but at the same time they value highly their professional identities and their ties with urban centers like the department capital, Chimaltenango, or the country's capital, Guatemala City. They also recognize the importance of their linguistic, ideological, and nationalist connections.

These well-educated Maya now define themselves as Kaqchikels, Mayas, Chimaltecos, inhabitants of the capital, and as Guatemalan. Their identification with liberal state ideology is prominent when they speak about citizenship, democracy, the legal system, their political participation, and human rights. They have so capitalized on their time and knowledge that they can now reject so-called traditional forms of cooperation and ties with other groups and peoples in Comalapa. The remaining Comalapans, agriculturalists and merchants, can simultaneously reject or legitimize these new professional identities, thoughts, and practices according to the specific circumstances.

Starting in the 1970s people from this community with a lower level of education began participating in different organizational bodies, such as Protestant and Catholic churches, political parties, and guerrilla groups—although certainly some professionals did likewise. Through this participation, these less-educated Maya discovered other ways of living and understanding their communities' social reality and thereby devised their own ways of transforming the lives of Comalapans and of the Maya in general. Other Comalapans have recently occupied important posts in the government, including the National Congress and some ministries.

Some national leaders who support Mayanism are from Comalapa and are members of this professional sector.[7] Together with activists and intellectuals from other Guatemalan communities, principally Kaqchikels and K'iche, these leaders foster the novel discourse about the Maya past. Nevertheless, at present most of these Comalapans can simultaneously resort to discourses and political practices inherently tied to the liberal state's ideology. On the basis of these facts (paraphrasing Dipesh Chakrabarty), I must still insist on asking, Who speaks in the name of our Maya ancestors (Chakrabarty 1999)? The answer is obviously not simple because it requires understanding other important facts.

Heretofore the analysis of Guatemala's pre-Hispanic and colonial history has been in the hands of Creoles, ladinos, and foreigners, commentators who have constructed different images about the Maya and their past.[8] At other moments, the state has used this historiography and archeology to delineate a national history that is taught in schools and transmitted through official discourses. That history has been expressed in racist and colonial terms. It fosters a vision of the Maya and of indigenous people in general as backward, childlike (*mozos*), uncivilized peasants subject to integration and incapable of realizing, to use a contemporary concept, development without outside intervention.[9]

Despite these tendencies, people in the communities continue to narrate their own histories, which are also categorized disdainfully by liberal and racist Guatemalan ideology. In any case, Maya narratives delineate and construct images about recent and remote ancestors. In diverse ways these histories have given life to past indigenous communities, to their identities and ways of organizing as well as to the conditions of resistance produced at different moments and in distinct eras (Florescano 2001). In many of these stories the ancestors remembered are nameless and the dates of events are not precisely defined because the stories simultaneously relate to the daily life of listeners and narrators.[10] Many Maya people in communities and villages have never stopped sharing and listening to these remembrances. Nevertheless, these narratives do not comprise the dominant history. Even though they form part of the social and ideological reproduction of the Maya, they do not resonate nationally. Instead, other voices are taken to be the true ones, primarily Creole and ladino narratives that up to now have told us how our past truly happened.

For the past two decades well-educated Maya have been telling their own stories, talking about the Maya past through the use of westernized images and narrative styles. As a rule, these new stories questioned the literary constructions of national and foreign academics and of official discourses. For some people, such self-expression means that the Maya are starting to take their turn at speaking about their past, and consequently the history they are telling now represents the truth for them. Now, well-educated Maya are the narrators and are often legitimated as such and welcomed by different sectors. Carmack, for example, affirms that great civilizations like the K'iche are destined to influence the modern world and that this great culture's time has come inside Guatemala and must be welcomed (Carmack 2001; see also Warren 1998; Fischer 2001; Cojtí Cuxil 1991; Bastos and Camus 2003; Fischer and Brown 1999). These assertions raise many questions: Who receives us?

In what space are we welcome, and why are we appreciated now (or not until now)? Finally, if this is the Maya's time, what importance can a critique have for imagining new ways to giving meaning to the past?

Elites, Narratives about the Past, and Fragility

Even though it has been said that Mayanists' new versions of the past challenge official history, the reality is not that simple. The contemporary Guatemalan state also speaks about Guatemala's history, about the history of the Maya as a people, and about interculturalism. This represents an apparent acceptance of Mayanist discourse and demands from the four peoples (Maya, Garífuna, Xinka, and ladino), their multiculturalism and diversity.[11] The state has thereby supposedly accepted educated Mayas' version of history and rights.

Mayanists and the State Construction of Multiculturalism

In the past two decades Maya leaders have created a series of organizations like the Consejo de Organizaciones Mayas en Guatemala and the Coordinación de Organizaciones del Pueblo Maya de Guatemala. Using these associations as platforms, the Maya leaders wrote documents and negotiated, protested, and elaborated discourses about history, cultural diversity, rights, and identity. Through this process, they created ties with the government and the state, setting the terms of their relationships.

The discussion and signing in 1995 of the Identity and Rights of the Indigenous Peoples Accord between the Unión Revolucionaria Nacional Guatemalteca (URNG) and the government is considered one of the key moments in the consolidation of these relations. Mayanists took part in this process, and their proposals were incorporated into the document's formal definitions. In this way, the Guatemalan nation's multiethnic, pluricultural, and multilingual character was formally recognized. This accord embraced Mayanists' concept of a people, a concept that alludes to and is based upon their new notions of history.[12]

Currently, the government has promulgated some secondary laws that give legal support to Maya rights, spirituality, languages, and education. There are government entities designed to support the Maya peoples' effort, such as the Fondo Indígena (Indigenous Fund), the Academia de las Lenguas Mayas de Guatemala (Academy of Maya Languages of Guatemala), and the Defensoría de la Mujer Indígena (Indigenous Women's Defense Office). School texts sponsored by the Ministry of Education include new lessons about the Maya's millenarian history, and children in public schools even learn Maya numeration. From the moment the multicultural discourse gained legitimacy, the state began defining ethnic difference in Guatemala and recognized Maya organizations and their leaders as interlocutors and representatives of the Guatemalan Maya.

Many would interpret this new situation to mean that the state's recognition of Guatemala's cultural diversity implies that the nation is now a democratic, plural body.[13] Alternatively, one might see the state's recognition as a Mayanist victory in the Maya's ideological and political struggle to influence dominant history and thought. This victory, however, was not so straightforward because it also represented the state's influence in the political definition of multiculturalism, identity, and rights. Even though the state purports to support Mayanist claims, this recognition also restricts Mayanists' capacity to establish their own parameters and discourses of the past and of their identity, their rights, and the elaboration of proposals (Bastos and Hernández 2005). This suggests that the Guatemalan state and governing elites are able to nourish themselves with Mayanist ideology and discourse to again impose and redefine their own legitimacy at the local as much as the international level. Brackette Williams has defined this process as transformist hegemony; in other words, a process through which the state appropriates certain resources defined by subaltern groups, leaving these peoples once again at the margins of the national process (1989).

An interesting example in this regard is that of a group of Kaqchikels from the western department of Sololá who, in early 2005, protested against the establishment of a mining company in the Guatemalan highlands. They claimed that nature ("Mother Earth," they said) was being damaged and that the government had not consulted indigenous peoples or communities regarding the company's new installations; some groups invoked Convention 169 of the International Labor Organization on the rights of indigenous peoples within existing states. The protests were violent, and the government used the police and the army to repress the population opposed to the mine's operations. The Mayas in the region succeeded in achieving strong political cohesion around the so-called indigenous municipality and managed to sustain an important discourse and practice regarding the "traditional" conservation of their natural resources. Because of their protests, they were repressed.[14]

We can see here, as Rachel Sieder posits, that the recomposition of the state and of Latin American multiculturalism tie into other processes, such as neoliberalism and subsequent subaltern challenges to these policies. Tensions emerge between the state and Maya groups when state actors seek to exploit natural resources located in territories historically occupied by the Maya, territories they wish to continue using according to their local interests. Sieder proposes that the public policies implemented by Latin American governments contributed to the reorganization of the state but did not necessarily reduce existing inequalities. This establishes that a model of a multicultural society must not only address the rights of ethnic groups but also confront patterns of development established by neoliberalism or capitalism (Sieder 2004).

The intervention of Maya peoples is central in defining a new model of the nation. Their ideological constructions of the past overlap with current notions and images of a multicultural Guatemala. Here one has to analyze how the state legitimizes itself through Mayanist discourses of the past and of Maya culture but at the same time uses force and violence, also legitimized, against those supposedly represented in the plural nation to impose the realities and new logics of the global economy.

The newly deployed historical discourse about Mayanness and multiculturalism influences official acts, including the teaching of national history and the discursive definition of the rights of the peoples who live together in Guatemala. Nevertheless, images of our past greatness and discourses about a multicultural country have little impact on other processes, including the definition of coexistence, development, the establishment of rights and obligations, and citizenship. The question therefore is, What is the place of a people, of their culture and their rights, in the definition and negotiation of the country's democracy and economy? Within liberal, capitalist logic, the question is of little importance and might even be understood as imprudent. Yet it is highly relevant if one thinks of the colonial manner in which power, democratization, and cultural and social diversity are exercised in Guatemala.

How are the discourses about the Maya past and about multiculturalism that are formulated by Mayanist intellectuals used? And what status are they granted? Rather than constituting a simple opposition to official history, Mayanist history can itself constitute the basis for developing new discursive perspectives that the state then replicates. Mayanists can believe they have achieved their objectives when the government begins to print books reproducing their new history and recreated symbols. The ministers and vice ministers of education who encourage the publication and use of these new texts may even be Mayas themselves, yet the majority of the Maya continue to be seen as backward and ignorant when the state supposedly brings them progress and development that they oppose.

Unfortunately for the Mayanists, they still do not have enough power to control the reconstructions and ideologies that their movement has generated and that are now reshaping the state and government. Their incipient participation as government functionaries still does not represent a significant force, yet their ideological creations about the past and the present are molding the narratives that strengthen new images of the multicultural nation. These narratives also construct other forms of legitimacy and state power that do little to eliminate privileges or equalize the concentration of resources and power.

In light of the preceding discussion, we are now in a better position to determine who speaks in the name of the Maya past. Now that they are well educated and have the power to do so, Maya elites effectively discuss their past. Nevertheless, the power achieved by some Mayanist leaders coexists with other conditions and contexts that may generate contradictions. On the one hand, Mayanists do not have the capacity to control how others use their discourses and images. On the other hand, some Mayanists are satisfied when they hear government functionaries talking about Guatemala's cultural wealth. Many Mayanists speak in the name of all Maya and their past, but their new discourses of the glorious Maya past run counter to the reality that many Maya individuals and communities still face a power that responds to their concerns with violence and continues to exclude them from the nation.

Mayanist Elites: Redefining Identities and Power Relations

One can ask how Mayanists, or at least some Mayanists, live these new histories. In other words, how are they using these new discourses to nurture their social life, their identity, and their political activity? The intellectuals of the Maya movement are primarily educated men and women who are highly visible at the local and national levels. In some central highland communities, principally in the department of Chimaltenango, they are present in sizable numbers. Even though many do not live in their communities of origin, but in cities like Chimaltenango or the capital, at certain moments they run into and greet each other in their local communities. Likewise, when they converge on places like Guatemala City, they also distinguish their fellow Maya who come from specific towns, regions, and linguistic groups. They also cross paths with Maya who profess Mayanist ideology only moderately or not at all but who are also educated or hold positions in the professions and who are familiar with ladino and Western spaces and perspectives.[15]

The story of a Maya political leader from the department of Chimaltenango, a man who was prominent at the local and national levels, is instructive in this context. In the mid-twentieth century the man was an important promoter of Acción Católica in his municipality and one of the most widely known catechists. His allegiance to this organization led him to participate in the local branch of a major national political party, as a result of which he rose to the post of mayor in his home municipality during the second half of the twentieth century. In the 1970s his party nominated him to fill a seat in the federal parliament, making him one of the first Maya deputies to sit in Guatemala's Congress.[16] Although little was heard about his political activities at the national level during the 1980s, his name was associated with Mayanist organizations in the 1990s and up to the present. At one point, he was a member of the Consejo de Ancianos del Fondo de Desarrollo Indígena de Guatemala (Council of Elders of the Indigenous Development Fund of Guatemala), a government entity founded at the demand of and led by Mayanists. He was also an active member of organizations that encourage Maya spirituality.

Though the man lived his last years outside of his municipality, his remains were transferred there after his death. The day of his funeral, his friends and relatives, myself included, attended a Mass celebrated in the community church; several of these people held important positions in the national political arena, either at the governmental level or in popular or Mayanist organizations. During the Eucharist ceremony the priest spoke of how this was an uncommon and even special ceremony given the dignity and trajectory of the deceased. Once the religious service ended, we left for the cemetery, where a customary prayer was said. Afterward, a close K'iche relative of the deceased climbed onto a podium and spoke in his native tongue about how the deceased was now reunited with Maya elders (*abuelos*). The speech was translated into Spanish. Some said that the deceased had probably heard these same words about respect for the ancestors spoken to him by his mother in K'iche when he was a child. The same relative read a text about the deceased's life, highlighting his participation in the Congress and in organizations that fought for and defended Maya rights. Most of those attending the wake returned to the house, where a vigil was held and coffee and bread were served. At the vigil someone circulated a photograph of the deceased, explaining that it had been taken in the Congress during his tenure in that legislative body.

Several conclusions can be arrived at from this anecdote. On the one hand, even though the dead man's ancestors were not explicitly labeled as Maya, such labeling was implicit in the discourse. When Maya peasants remember their dead, they generally affirm that the deceased's soul now rests in peace to be resuscitated by God when the world ends. The speeches at the wake likewise made references to the ancestors using allusions to Mayanist discourses about elders. On the other hand, many people who attended the wake were promoters of Mayanism, and by translating the K'iche speeches into Spanish they were positioning Mayanist values and symbols at center stage and thereby using Spanish in an instrumental way.

What I want to highlight here is the relationship between Maya historical discourse, the new identities of the professionals and leaders who promote this discourse, and their linkage with the state through policies regarding Maya rights and multiculturalism. What is happening among these elites? The description of the funeral highlights how Maya professionals can link different events or facts by articulating them with their new historical discourse and with their connections to state policy on rights and culture. We can see that in this case Mayanists are not deploying a discourse about history and culture in an isolated way, so as to define their nationalism, difference, and pride only in relation to their glorious past, as they might do in other speeches and texts. In cases like this, for Maya historical discourses to succeed they must interconnect with other narratives about contemporary Mayas' ability to enter the state apparatus, become professional, and engage other worlds assumed to be closed to most Maya. They must also connect with arguments and proclamations about their own capacity to represent and defend the rights of the rest of the Maya people. Evidently in operation here is a complex process of attempted legitimation in which new power relations are being constructed.

To understand all of this, I want to continue exploring the historical effects of Western modernity, liberal ideology, capitalism, government policies regarding education and integration, and racism in the lives of Mayanists and the rest of the Maya people. It is important to analyze both the particular ways in which political and economic elites are constituted historically and the links they establish with systems of inequality.

Greg Grandin and Irma Alicia Nimatuj entered into this discussion with their analyses of historical processes lived by the Quetzaltec elites in the nineteenth century and the twentieth. Grandin proposes that K'iche leaders of this area reconfigured their communal relations and maintained their social and cultural authority by forming alliances with the colonial and republican states. Amidst the political and economic changes of the eighteenth century and the nineteenth, K'iche elites transformed Quetzaltenango into a commercial, multiethnic city. Ethnic leaders (*principales*) used Creole elites to sustain their domination over K'iche cultural processes, strengthening their political power and access to capital. With the support of indigenous principales, Creoles maintained the city's caste divisions and thereby controlled the population and the possibility of multiethnic alliances. These nineteenth-century elites pursued similar alliances with the Guatemalan president Rafael Carrera to protect their privileges.

These alliances, in combination with late nineteenth-century liberal ideology and capitalist economy, led K'iche elites to develop alternative understandings of ethnicity and nationalism. The elites built a conception of ethnicity that was intimately tied to ideas of progress encouraged by liberal intellectuals. They thought that indigenous people's regeneration would necessarily lead to civil and political equality. These ideological constructions ultimately justified K'iche elites' positions of authority as well as those of ladinos at the local and national level. Privileged K'iche looked to reproduce an ethnic identity based on their common origin and on the maintenance of cultural markers primarily grounded in women's roles (Grandin 2000).

Nimatuj, in turn, observes that these elites were not homogenous and responded in different ways to historical processes and concrete social contexts. Similarly, she shows that this Quetzaltec sector, characterized by their commercial economic power, shared and continue to share diverse contexts with the rest of the Guatemalan Maya. They thereby reproduce a patriarchal system that subordinates Maya women. Like the rest of the country's Maya, they confront the racism dividing Guatemalan society and share general Maya cultural patterns like dress, collective memory, languages, and diverse wisdoms (Velásquez Nimatuj 2002).

At the beginning of the twentieth century and in a way similar to the K'iche elites in Quetzaltenango, indigenous elites from different Chimaltenango municipalities simultaneously acted as intermediaries, speaking on behalf of Chimaltenango's indigenous peoples and their rights, while also competing with local ladino elites even as they shared some privileges with those elites, such as the right to vote and exemptions from forced labor and taxes. Indigenous elites' competition with ladinos led them to not only discuss and demand citizenship rights, but also to take action. They founded schools for indigenous people and educated a small group of youth who in certain ways and at certain moments could compete with ladinos.

At the present time ladinos in many of this department's communities no longer have decisive political power, and it is Maya who lead local politics. But as we have seen, the Maya are also gaining prominence within the governmental apparatus at the national level. In diverse ways they often act as intermediaries speaking in the name of all Maya, doing so by building a linear discourse about the past, demanding rights, and establishing development programs for the Maya.

Many of these indigenous elites have been successful because they understood and entered the world of national politics and familiarized themselves with the practices and customs of ladino elites. Much of this awareness was the result of education and adaptation. Even though the indigenous elites still endure what they view as virulent racism, they do not experience it in the same way or under the same conditions as other Maya. Education has been central to the elites in achieving recognition and relative acceptance in some nonindigenous circles; once educated, they are still indigenous, but "civilized." Likewise, the Mayanist version of their past has acquired moderate acceptance by certain intellectuals, politicians, and businessmen because it entails a rational, as opposed to a mythical, way of comprehending the past, while at the same time serving to minimize the violence used against Maya protests.[17]

These processes empower Mayanists (and also other professional Maya who do not follow this ideology) in the eyes of some ladino and Creole sectors and also of community and village-based Maya. Maya students and professionals enjoy greater prestige where they live or originate from, not only because of their knowledge, but also because of the ties and networks they presumably have developed with ladinos, organizations, and institutions at the national level. An important differentiation thus arises between sectors of the Maya, one that cannot be analyzed simply in terms of a description of social stratification within localities or municipalities, but must consider processes like power relations, the development of ideologies, and the historical constitution and reproduction of elites.

During the nineteenth century and the twentieth, some ladinos and Creoles reproduced their power, prestige, and legitimacy by claiming to be civilized and modern. Similarly, in the twenty-first century Mayanists and some non-Mayanists are constructing their prestige and legitimacy on the basis of education, professionalization, and links to the government apparatus. New to this contemporary construction, however, is the identification with a People that has a glorious and millenarian history, one that is imagined by these selfsame actors.[18]

Apparently, Mayanists' discursive control over the past and their demands regarding rights ultimately have produced results for these individuals. Nevertheless, this discursive control is diluted by the control and power relations established by Guatemala's oligarchy and political class. As Claudio Lomnitz-Adler proposed in 1995 in the Mexican case, intellectuals' discourses often serve to generate closer relationships between the intellectuals and dominant groups and in this way continue to perpetuate state ideologies (Lomnitz-Adler 1995). Much the same can be said about contemporary Mayanists' historical narratives.

Alternative Histories and the Present

How can we Maya benefit from this power to locate not only our past but also our present? In what way does the Maya people's alternative history, as developed by Mayanists, generate the possibility of imagining a different nation and nationalism? There are many answers to these questions because these new historical narratives also question the forms of exclusion historically reproduced by the state and the dominant sectors. We can see nevertheless that Mayanist history partly constructs itself by taking official history as a model when it establishes or seeks to represent the unity of the four peoples living in this territory.

When Mayanists elaborate a historical narrative delineating the Maya people's cultural inheritance and their existential basis, while at the same time constructing an imaginary about the four peoples of Guatemala, they are helping to build the myth of the multicultural nation. This myth, as we have seen, is easily appropriated, manipulated, and redefined, both in the discourses of governing elites and in the auxiliary laws they have proposed and approved. From this historical definition of the four peoples, it is possible to build linear and diaphanous narratives about identity, equality, and cultural inheritance—that is to say, about Guatemalan multiculturalism. These narratives underestimate the differences, contradictions, power relations, and economic inequality prevalent in the country.

Some Maya, for example, can now speak about multiculturalism and globalization processes like free trade treaties as inescapable realities in which we must necessarily involve ourselves. These Maya hold that multiculturalism offers a formula for confronting globalization, implying that so long as we maintain our identity as a people and remain creative, we will be able to navigate free trade successfully and offer the world important goods and products.[19] This Mayanist reasoning is centered in market logics and leaves history and the present agenda of the oligarchy almost unquestioned. In this case, the Maya, too, can participate in the colonial form taken by Guatemalan and global power relations.

Under such conditions it is crucial to bring different Maya historical experiences into the discussion, for they are central to the definition of multiculturalism's ideological and material foundations. Different sectors of the Maya (and Guatemalan) people have long developed, according to their own life situations, a variety of relations with their social and natural surroundings. Just like well-educated Maya, peasants, women, merchants, and others have had contact with the national society, the global economy and politics, the culture and knowledge preserved by other societies, and diverse religious forms. The Maya have not been isolated from Guatemala's politics, economy, and liberal and nationalist ideologies, or from the ladino and Western worlds. It is unlikely they have lived in a homogeneous way. Their diverse historical circumstances have given rise to diverse viewpoints, interests, and identities. Among the Maya, one can therefore discern many forms of memory and thought. In short, we Maya must pay close attention to the relationship between memory and identity in order to recognize that our own images about history are not uniform and instead reflect the complexity of our lives and relations (Norval 2001).

We must therefore focus our reflections on how these memories can support the construction of the present and control of the future. It is important to posit, as Partha Chatterjee says, that the form of remembering the past and the power to represent oneself is nothing other than political power (Chatterjee 1995). We Maya can imagine a multicultural society by taking into account these multiple historical conditions. Also central to constructing a multicultural society is an understanding of the ways in which Guatemalans have historically linked themselves and been linked to their environment, keeping in mind their experiences, positions, and relations of power.

All of this can help us reflect more deeply about the many ways in which we can construct our alternative histories, perhaps seek out a variety of styles of development and understand and construct a multicultural nation. Santiago Bastos and Domingo Hernández, for example, highlight an interesting case detailing the process of state control and the Maya struggle for autonomy (Bastos and Hernández Ixcoy 2005). They analyze some of the attempts to advance the recognition and indemnification of the victims of armed conflict. They argue that the social and political experiences of people involved in the process have prompted them to rethink how they imagined and spoke about the past and about Maya needs and rights.

According to Bastos and Hernández, the people and organizations involved in this task have assumed the category of Maya as part of an ideological construction tied to the indemnification, using it as an ethnic category that also helps explain the past and the violence suffered. In this case, the process of recovering the Maya's long-term history is also linked with more recent memories of political violence endured by Maya peasants, women, and students. In this way, peoples' own actions, that is, their struggles and the paths they chose to take, mark them not as victims but as individuals and as Maya who have struggled in the face of repression and exclusion. All these factors form part of the Maya experience and the memory they are constructing.

These efforts are fundamental, and their recognition through ethnographic description is central to the discovery of other explanations related to the interactions of different political actors (Hale 2002). These academic analyses are important contributions as long as they do not fall into a simple celebration of Maya resistance. By taking a more critical perspective we can see the contradictions generated in the different arenas where Maya launch their struggles and the ensuing consequences. By focusing on these multiple arenas, we can understand how political resistance and memory often challenge the control and power of dominant groups and of their common sense, even as they can sometimes reinforce the established order and neutralize the strength of Maya organizations and communities (Hale 2002).

Epilogue

Nobody could argue that the Guatemalan Maya movement has not been an important force in the transformation of Guatemalan society. Over the past two decades a national discussion of indigenous peoples' cultural and political rights has opened multiple opportunities for struggle for people in different regions and localities. Many Maya women, for example, now make their voices heard in diverse contexts, emphasizing their suffering, desires, and struggles and challenging patriarchal domination in their homes, localities, and country (Chirix 2003). Similarly, Maya spirituality represents an important challenge to the Protestant and Catholic churches as well as to society in general through the public presentation of religious rituals prohibited until the 1990s. Mayanists have brought to light many issues and problems, including racism, an outdated educational system from the elementary to the postsecondary level, political and social exclusion, and unequal landholding patterns.

My essay does not talk in terms of betrayal. Rather, it has dealt with social processes that deserve recognition and careful analysis so as to further clarify the relation between hegemonic processes and indigenous resistance in Guatemala (Scott 2002). I have attempted to represent and analyze the relationship between the narratives about the past constructed by Mayanist intellectuals and the vested interests present in the state that are also involved in defining Guatemalan multiculturalism. We have been able to observe that the ties established, the discourses and ideologies promoted and implemented, are often contradictory because they both represent and unfold within Guatemala's complex social reality. Elite and nonelite Maya have also been fundamental participants in the construction of the Guatemala of the past two decades. They participate not only because they have been and continue to be the most important labor force in the country's economy, but also because they model the Guatemalan state with their ideological constructions and political interests. They remain linked to nationalist ideologies—ideologies whose form dominant groups adopted and used to build their hegemony—but they also constitute an important social force in the transformation of our society.

This work is a critical approximation by the Maya themselves to the social processes we live. Our experiences in these diverse environments provide evidence both of what our struggles have achieved and of the mistakes we have made. We Maya will not give too much away if we see our intellectual activity and creations in a more *problematic* way and not as diaphanous, as we would like our reality or our past to be.[20] This may be too much to ask, given how we Mayanists make strategic use of essentialist notions about the continuity of our past and present.[21] Yet we must also listen to our many voices, which, though contradictory, influence the processes we live.

Maya peasants, businessmen, women, Catholics, and youth have many historical experiences and talk in many ways, and their discourses and practices tie into the ideologies they employ. With their multiple identities, interests, and dreams, they inevitably, together with elites, take part in the contradictions our current nationalisms generate.

Notes

1. In the Guatemalan context, *ladino* refers to most non-Indians, including Guatemalans of European or mixed descent (translator's note).

2. In citing Quijano, Walter Mignolo (2004) explains how one should understand the concept of the coloniality of power and talks about the historical establishment of a racial division of labor in America. A racial hierarchy that overdetermined social relations and ideologies and influenced ideas of equality and liberty was put in place. At the beginning of the nineteenth century and with the onset of independence, he argues, instead of being overcome, colonialism was rearticulated. Following Greg Grandin's (2000) ideas, we can also say that even though all the Maya of Guatemala are not oppressed for being Maya, they suffer domination as Maya.

3. Carmack (2001), Gúzman Böckler and Herbert (1998), and Hill (2001). The first two books were first edited in the 1960s and the last in 1992.

4. See Edgar Esquit (2004) for a more in-depth critical study of this topic in relation to recent narratives about the past by Maya activists.

5. Montejo (2004) is a recent text about Maya history.

6. In some municipalities these identities also contrasted with Maya merchants, most of whom have a low level of educational training.

7. Many other professionals from Comalapa or the region have few or no ties with the Maya movement and its discourse.

8. Creoles (*criollos*) refers to elite Guatemalans of European descent (translator's note). For example, see Batres Jáuregui (1989), Martínez Peláez (1973), and Carmack (2001).

9. But the political, cultural, and economic exclusion of the Maya within the nation does not occur only at the discursive level. There are concrete, material practices that establish exclusion, implying that the state's historic narrative contributes to the construction of colonial forms within Guatemala's power relations.

10. In the K'iche language, for example, *najtir*, meaning "ancient," is used only to talk about an ancestor's past and culture. In the Mam language, *ojtxe* refers to the remote past. García Ruiz (1992).

11. Mayanists have created the image of Guatemala as made up of four peoples—the Maya, Garífuna, Xinca, and ladino—each with its respective history.

12. MINUGUA (2001).

13. See Donna Lee Van Cott's (2000) discussion about constitutional multiculturalism. Santiago Bastos deals critically with this issue in the notion of cosmetic multiculturalism, which refers to the creation of new state policies that adopt laws

and discourses attempting to always include indigenous people (Conference at the Colegio de Michoacán, 2003).

14. Some people have suggested that political members of the leftist party Unión Revolucionaria Nacional Guatemalteca (URNG) manipulated the Maya in these events. Though it is clear that the URNG has influence in the Indigenous Municipality of Sololá and other departmental organizations, we cannot disregard the interests and agency of the region's Kaqchikels.

15. Uneducated Maya are also not isolated from liberal Guatemalan politics, economics, and ideology or from the ladino and Western world. The problem is not whether the Maya are tied to national and global processes or not; rather, it is important to understand the forms and conditions in which such connections happen and, extrapolating from there, peoples' experiences, positions, and relations of power.

16. Two former Maya congresspeople were the K'iche Augusto Sac Racancoj, a lawyer, and Pablo Pastor, a professor. They obtained their posts in the 1940s only because of the space the Revolution of 1944 opened. Velásquez Nimatuj (2002).

17. Nevertheless, there are ladinos who question the way in which Mayanism recovers the past through essentialist and fundamentalist arguments. See Morales (1998). Some provincial ladinos also question Mayanism, but their main arguments originate within official history. They affirm that indigenous peoples no longer have the right to call themselves Maya because the Maya empire disappeared with the Spanish conquest and subsequent communities were no longer pure but mixed. Moreover, these provincial ladinos believe the adhesion of indigenous peoples to the ancient Maya is a strategy of some opportunistic individuals. Hale (2002).

18. This comparison is not overly ahistorical because the nation is still constructed on exclusion, even though the national and global social, political, and economic contexts have varied.

19. For Walter Mignolo (2004) globalization is a rearticulation of the coloniality of power, similar to what happened in the nineteenth century with the foundation of nations in America. Many Mayanists who have adopted a perspective that includes the concept of internal colonialism hardly question globalization processes and the contexts in which they are produced.

20. I use the term *problematic* to denote the complexity of our social life and to argue about the many paths our struggles can take if we pay attention to our many realities.

21. In discussing cultural continuity, Fischer and Watanabe (2004) affirm that we frequently do not realize the different ways it can happen, such as through the recreation of the present or through profiling the legacy of our ancestors as unchanging. According to the authors, Mayanists would have opted for the first way. The authors' conclusion may be quite correct; nevertheless, we also have to point out that the recreation of the present is mediated by power relations, social contexts, and new identities.

FLORENCIA E. MALLON

Conclusion

When Noenoe Silva and Stéfano Varese attempted, at the close of our conference in Madison, to summarize our discussions as a frame for our last plenary session, they highlighted both the promises and the difficulties in taking the kind of international and comparative perspective we have attempted in this book. In this brief conclusion I revisit some of the general themes and challenges associated with such a perspective. I cannot presume to represent here the richness of the perceptions and conclusions contained in each essay. Instead, I highlight three general points that emerge from the overall conversation, reiterating the desire—present in the work of all the contributors to this book as well as of all those present at the conference—that we can contribute in some way to a deeper and more productive dialogue among Native peoples and between Native and other forms of knowledge.

At the core of the project envisioned by the authors represented in this book is the understanding of Native histories and narratives in international and comparative context. As the recent history of indigenous movements has demonstrated, international collaboration has fostered new possibilities for indigenous mobilization and empowerment. At the same time, the process of examining Native histories and narratives in comparative and international perspective extends and deepens our understanding of each one. Both the similarities and the differences we find among them sharpen our appreciation of how, and for what purpose, these narratives are elaborated and constructed. Finally, our comparisons of North and South America as well as of the continental Americas with the Pacific world help remind us how deeply geography itself, and through it the relationships among distinct indigenous peoples and traditions, has been affected by colonialism.

A second theme that arises from the essays collected here is that decolonization begins at home. Taken together, the authors demonstrate the multiple ways in which Native narrative and history can be rendered, from local community history or personal story to discussions of indigenous rights on an international level. That each provides a different but necessary perspective on Native histories is an important lesson that we all relearn, again and again, as we labor to decolonize indigenous narratives with the very same tools we have inherited from colonialism. And as we continue to strive toward this goal, we see the importance, also represented in this book, of the work that has been done by generations of activist-intellectuals, both Native and non-Native. In the context of collaboration and solidarity, the authors suggest, it is also possible to speak about and analyze internal divisions and differences in productive and inclusive ways.

A third and final salient theme here is that indigenous theorizing and translation—understood as the interpretation, reinterpretation, and improvement of ideas and concepts in their transition from one language or epistemology to another—transform our understanding of national and global processes and histories. Indigenous histories themselves have never really been local, except in the eyes of the colonizers. Rather, they have from the very beginning participated and been embedded in, transformed by, and resistant to globalization. At the same time, with the powerful revitalization worldwide of indigenous identity-based politics and in the new globalized context that has emerged after the fall of the Berlin Wall, the long and critical engagement of Native peoples with world histories and processes can more easily and clearly come into view. Our goal is that the multiple experiences and perspectives offered here can contribute to a deeper, more grounded debate over our common, global, and hopefully ever more decolonized future. As became clear from the plenary session at our conference, the work of decolonization will not be done until Native narratives and epistemologies not only occupy a prominent position within the circle where knowledge is produced, but also constitute a central part of the knowledge that everyone seeks out.

REFERENCES

Primary Sources: Websites, Unpublished Papers, Legislation, Newspaper Articles, Historical Published Sources

Los Acuerdos de San Andrés. 2003. Bilingual edition Spanish–Tzotzil. Tuxtla Gutiérrez, Chiapas: Gobierno del Estado.

Akaka, D. K. 2009. "Akaka Bill. Native Hawaiian Government Reorganization Act Reintroduced in Senate and House." Press release, 4 February.

———. 2005. "Hawaii Congressional Delegation Introduces Native Hawaiian Government Reorganization Act." Press release, 25 January.

———. 2001a. "Native Hawaiian Federal Recognition Bill Introduced." Press release, January 22.

———. 2001b. "Statement of Senator Daniel K. Akaka on Revisions to the Native Hawaiian Federal Recognition Bill." 16 April. http://www.senate.gov/~akaka/speeches (accessed 11 August 2009).

———. 2000. "Native Hawaiian Recognition Bill Introduced." Press release, 20 July.

Apology Resolution to acknowledge the 100th anniversary of the January 17, 1893 overthrow of the Kingdom of Hawaii, and to offer an apology to Native Hawaiians on behalf of the United States for the overthrow of the Kingdom of Hawaii. Resolution No. 19, known as the Apology Resolution, 103d Congress, 23 November 1993; U.S. Public Law 103-150.

Barrientos, D. 1998. "Informe sobre el D.L. 2.885 y de la Ley No 19.253. Referencia al Régimen jurídico aplicable a las tierras insulares." Paper.

DePledge, D. 2003. "Lawmakers Agree to Revise Hawaiian Recognition Bill. *Honolulu Advertiser*, 14 May. http://www.the.honoluluadvertiser.com (accessed 11 August 2009).

Documento de la Marina. 1926. *Memorias, Balances, Inventarios y Registro de Propiedades*.

Enomoto, K. 2009. "Akaka Bill May Have a Shot at Law: Opposition Continues, But Sympathetic New President Could Be Key." *Maui News*, 1 March. http://www.mauinews.com/page (accessed 11 August 2009).

Gómez, R. 2004. *Informe final sobre Catastro de tenencia, dominio y transferencias de Inmuebles en Isla de Pascua*. Isla de Pascua. Bienes Nacionales. Unpublished document.

Gómez Vargas, J. H. 2006. "Consultoría Internacional para el asesoramiento en la elaboración del Estatuto Especial para Isla de Pascua. Informe primera visita." Unpublished document.

Guatemala: Memory of Silence. 2003. Report of the Commission for Historical Clarification. http://www.shr.aaas.org/guatemala.

Informe de la Comisión Verdad Histórica y Nuevo Trato de los Pueblos Indígenas. Santiago: Gobierno de Chile.

Joint-Senate Resolution to Provide for Annexing the Hawaiian Islands to the United States. 1898. Resolution No. 55, known as the Newlands Resolution, 2nd Session, 55th Congress, 7 July 1898; 30 Sta. at L. 750; 2 Supp. R. S. 895.

Kingdom of Hawaiʻi—International Treaties. Http://www.hawaiiankingdom.org/treaties.shtml.

Libro de Registros de propiedades llevado por la Armada de Chile, Isla de Pascua. 1962.

Ministerio de Marina: Oficios de la Dirección General de la Armada. 1902.

Namuo, C. 2004. "Misinformation Abounds on Revisions to Akaka bill." *Honolulu Advertiser*, 2 May. Http://www.thehonoluluadvertiser.com/article (accessed 8 August 2009).

Omandam, P. 2003. "Native Hawaiians Will Not Benefit by Bill, Say Some Sovereignty Groups." *Honolulu Star-Bulletin*, 25 February.

———. 1998. "Report: Annexation Could Be Declared Invalid." *Honolulu Star-Bulletin*. 11 August.

Revista de Marina: Publicación Bimestral de la Armada de Chile. 1983. Año XCVIII. May–June.

Taller Tzotzil. 1982. *Kʼalal ichʼay mosoal/Cuando dejamos de ser aplastados: La Revolución en Chiapas*. 2 vols. San Cristóbal: Editorial Tiempo. Tzotzil of Zinacantán and Spanish.

———. 1983. *Liʼi jaʼ sventa tzobol chijʼabtej ta komon/Organización comunitaria del trabajo*. Tzotzil of San Andrés and Spanish.

———. 1985. *Jaʼ kʼu xʼelan ta jpojbatik ta ilbajinel yuʼun jkaxlanetik / Cómo escapamos del control de los ladinos*. Tzotzil of Zinacantán and Spanish.

———. 1986. *Abtel ta Pinka*. Tzotzil of Chamula. Republished in 1990 in a bilingual Tzotzil-Spanish edition.

———. 1988a. *Loʼil yuʼun Kuskat: Skʼop mol Marian Koyaso Panchin*. Tzotzil of Chamula.

———. 1988b. *Buchʼu lasmeltzan Jobel? / ¿Quién hizo San Cristóbal?* Tzotzil of Chamula and Spanish.

———. 1990a. *Kipaltik: Loʼil sventa kʼuchaʼal la jmankutik jpinkakutik / La historia de cómo compramos nuestra finca, por los socios de la Unión "Tierra Tzotzil."* Tzotzil of San Andrés and Spanish.

———. 1990b. *Ta jlok'ta chobtik ta k'u'il / Bordando milpas*. Tzotzil of Chamula and Spanish.

———. 1990c. *Slo'il cha'vo' kumpareil / Los dos compadres*. Tzotzil of Zinacantán and Spanish.

———. 1993. *Historia de un pueblo evangelista: Triunfo Agrarista*. Ricardo Pérez.

———. 1996. *Jchi'iltak ta slumal Kalifornia / Chamulas en California*. Tzotzil of Chamula and Spanish.

———. 1995. "Los primeros meses de los zapatistas: Una crónica tzotzil en siete escenas by Marián Peres Tzu (Xalik Kusman)." J. Rus (Trans.). *Ojarasca*, numbers 40–41, January–February 1995, 13–16.

———. 2000. "Conversaciones ininterrumpidas: Las voces indígenas del mercado de San Cristóbal." Marián Peres Tzu (Xalik Kusman). Translated by J. Rus. J. P. Viqueira and W. Sonnleitner, eds., *Democracia en tierras indígenas: Las elecciones en los Altos de Chiapas (1991–1998)*, 259–67. Mexico City: CIESAS/Colegio de México/Instituto Electoral Federal.

Toro, P. P. 1892. "Informes de la comisión nombrada para estudiar la colonización (Juan Fernandez y Pascua)." *Memoria del Ministerio de Culto i Colonización*, 188–216. 15 November.

United Nations General Assembly Resolution 1514. 1960. "Declaration on the Granting of Independence to Colonial Countries."

United States Congress. 1900. "The Act of Congress Organizing Hawaii into a Territory, An Act to provide a government for the Territory of Hawaii, April 30." *Rice v. Cayetano Governor of Hawaii* (98-818) 528 U.S. 495 (2000) 146 F.3d 1075, reversed.

Viotti, V. 2003a. "Conservatives Blamed for Stalling Akaka Bill." *Honolulu Advertiser*, 29 August.

———. 2003b. "Inouye: Maybe 2004 for Akaka Bill." *Honolulu Advertiser*, 30 August.

Secondary Sources

Abu-Lughod, L. 1991. "Writing against Culture." *Recapturing Anthropology: Working in the Present*, ed. Richard G. Fox, 137–62. Santa Fe: School of American Research.

Albert, B. 1995. "O ouro canibal e a queda do céu: uma crítica xamânica da economia política da naturaleza." *Série Antropologica*, no. 174, 1–33. Departamento de Antropología, Universidade de Brasília.

Albó, X. 1998. "Expresión indígena, diglosia y medios de comunicación." *Sobre las huellas de la voz: Sociolingüística de la oralidad y la escritura en su relación con la educación*, ed. Luis Enrique López and Ingrid Jung, 126–55. Cochabamba: Morata, PROEIB Andes, DSE.

Albó, X., and Anaya, A. 2003. *Niños alegres, libres, expresivos: La audacia de la educación intercultural bilingüe en Bolivia*. La Paz: UNICEF, CIPCA.

Alfred, T. 2004. "Warrior Scholarship: Seeing the University as a Ground of Contention." *Indigenizing the Academy: Transforming Scholarship and Empowering Communities*, ed. D. A. Mihesuah and A. C. Wilson, 88–99. Lincoln: University of Nebraska Press.

Allen, C. 2002. *Blood Narrative: Indigenous Identity in American Indian and Maori Literary and Activist Texts*. Durham: Duke University Press.

Anonymous. 2000. "Sxabwes' 'El ombligo': El juego didáctico de las matemáticas." *Cayu'ce* 4, 42–43. Popayán, Colombia.

Anonymous. 1988. "Informe sobre la situación de derechos humanos de los grupos étnicos aborígenes en Chile." *Revista Chilena de Derechos Humanos* 16 (May), 83–91. Santiago: Academia de Humanismo Cristiano.

Andueza Guzmán, P. 2005. "La tierra en Rapanui como desafío jurídico intercultural." Paper presented at the VI International Conference on Rapa Nui and the Pacific, in Reñaca, Chile.

Anzaldúa, G. 1987. *Borderlands/La Frontera: The New Mestiza*. San Francisco: Aunt Lutte Books.

Arias, J. 1984. *Historia de la colonia de "Los Chorros," Chenalhó*. Tuxtla Gutiérrez, Chiapas: Gobierno del Estado.

Arnold, D., and J. de Dios Yapita. 2000. *El rincón de las cabezas: Luchas textuales, educación y tierras en los Andes*. La Paz: UMSA, ILCA.

Arratia, M. 2001. *Wata Muyuy: Ciclos de vida en culturas agrocéntricas y tiempos de la escuela. Una aproximación sobre gestión educativa e interculturalidad en un distrito quechua de Bolivia*. Buenos Aires: UNESCO.

Asad, T. 1986. "The Concept of Cultural Translation in British Social Anthropology." *Writing Culture: The Poetics and Politics of Ethnography*, ed. James Clifford and George E. Marcus, 141–64. Berkeley: University of California Press.

Aubry, A. 2005. "La experiencia de Chiapas y la democracia intelectual, testimonio de una práctica alternativa de las ciencias sociales." *Contrahistoria* 4 (March–August), 103–7.

———. 1988. *El rescate del 'libro robado': La producción histórica del Taller Tzotzil del INAREMAC*. San Cristóbal: INAREMAC.

Aubry, A., and A. Inda. 2003. *Los llamados de la memoria: Chiapas 1995–2001*. Tuxtla Gutiérrez, Chiapas: CONECULTA.

———. 1998. "Who Are the Paramilitaries in Chiapas?" *North American Congress on Latin America* 31:5 (March–April), 8–9.

Barsh, R. L. 1986. "Indigenous Peoples: An Emerging Object of International Law," *American Journal of International Law* 80, 369–85.

Bastos, S., and M. Camus. 2003. *Entre el Mecapal y el Cielo: Desarrollo del Movimiento Maya en Guatemala. Cholsamaj, Guatemala: Facultad Latinoamericana de Ciencias Sociales (FLACSO)–Sede Guatemala.

Bastos, S., and D. Hernández Ixcoy. 2005. *Resarcimiento y Reconstitución del Pueblo Maya en Guatemala: Entre la acción autónoma y el reconocimiento estatal.* Guatemala: n.p.

Batres Jáuregui, A. 1989. *Los indios, su historia y su civilización.* Guatemala: Tipografía Nacional.

Benjamin, T. 2000. "A Time of Reconquest: History, the Maya Revival, and the Zapatista Rebellion in Chiapas." *American Historical Review* 105:2, 417–50.

Bishop, R. 1994. "Initiating Empowering Research?" *New Zealand Journal of Educational Studies* 29:1, 175–88.

Blu, K. 2001 (1980). *The Lumbee Problem: The Making of an American Indian People.* Lincoln: University of Nebraska Press.

Bobrow-Strain, A. 2007. *Intimate Enemies: Landowners, Territory, and Violence in Chiapas.* Durham: Duke University Press.

Bolaños, G., A. Ramos, J. Rappaport, and C. Miñana. 2004. *¿Qué pasaría si la escuela . . . ? Treinta años de construcción educativa.* Popayán, Colombia: Programa de Educación Bilingüe e Intercultural, Consejo Regional Indígena del Cauca.

Bricker, V. R. 1981. *The Indian Christ, the Indian King.* Austin: University of Texas Press.

Brooks, J. F., ed. 2002. *Confounding the Color Line: The Indian–Black Experience in North America.* Lincoln: University of Nebraska Press.

Burguete, A., and J. Montero Solano. N.d. "Morir en la impunidad: Violencia política en regiones indígenas de Chiapas, Cronología 1974–1988." Manuscript. San Cristóbal, Chiapas, Mexico.

Burstein, J., Á. Past, and R. Wasserstrom. 1979. *En sus propias palabras: Cuatro vidas tzotziles.* San Cristóbal: Editorial Fray Bartolomé de Las Casas.

Bushnell, D., and N. Macaulay. 1988. *Latin America in the Nineteenth Century.* Oxford: Oxford University Press.

Campisi, J. 1991. *The Mashpee Indians: Tribe on Trial.* Syracuse: Syracuse University Press.

Carmack, R. 2001. *Kik'ulmatajem le k'iche'aab' Evolución del Reino k'iche'.* Guatemala: Editorial Cholsamaj.

Castro-Gómez, S. 2003. "Apogeo y decadencia de la teoría tradicional: Una visión desde los intersticios." *Estudios culturales latinoamericanos: Retos desde y sobre la región andina,* ed. C. Walsh, 59–72. Quito: UASB, Abya Yala.

———. 2000. "Teoría tradicional y teoría crítica de la cultura." *La reestructuración de las ciencias sociales en América Latina,* ed. S. Castro-Gómez, 93–107. Bogotá: Pensar.

Chakrabarty, D. 2000. *Provincializing Europe: Postcolonial Thought and Historical Difference*. Princeton: Princeton University Press.

———. 1999. "La poscolonialidad y el artilugio de la historia: ¿Quién habla en nombre de los pasados 'indios'?" *Pasados Poscoloniales*, ed. S. Dube, 441–71. Mexico City: El Colegio de México.

Chandler, N. D. 1996. "The Economy of Desedimentation: W. E. B. Du Bois and the Discourses of the Negro." *Callaloo* 19:1, 78–93.

Chanteaux, M. 1999. *Las andanzas de Miguel: La biografía del padre expulsado de Chenalhó*. San Cristóbal: Editorial Fray Bartolomé de Las Casas.

Chatterjee, P. 1995. "Alternative Histories, Alternative Nations: Nationalism and Modern Historiography in Bengal." *Making Alternative Histories: The Practice of Archaeology and History in Non-Western Western Settings*, ed. P. R. Schmidt and T. C. Patterson, 229–54. Santa Fe: School of American Research Press.

———. 1986. *Nationalist Thought and the Colonial World. A Derivative Discourse?* Tokyo: Zed Books / United Nations University.

Chávez, A. I., ed. 2001. *Pop Wuj*. Guatemala: TIMACH.

Chirix, E. 2003. *Alas y raíces: Afectividad de las mujeres mayas rik'in ruxik' y ruxe'il ronojel qajowab'al ri mayab' taq ixoqi'*. Kaqla', Guatemala: n.p.

Chocué Guasaquillo, A. A. 2000. "Nuestra doble conciencia." *C'ayu'ce* 4, 14–15.

Choque, C. 1982. *Criterios para la normalización en la escritura de la lengua quechua en Bolivia*. Sucre: P.EIB.

Chow, R. 1995. *Primitive Passions: Visuality, Sexuality, Ethnography, and Contemporary Chinese Cinema*. New York: Columbia University Press.

Clifford, J. 1988. "Identity in Mashpee." *The Predicament of Culture: Twentieth-Century Ethnography, Literature, and Art*, ed. J. Clifford, 277–346. Cambridge: Harvard University Press.

Clifford, J., and G. Marcus, eds. 1986. *Writing Culture: The Poetics and Politics of Ethnography*. Berkeley: University of California Press.

Cobo, J. M. 1987. *Study of the Problem of Discrimination against Indigenous Populations. Volume 5: Conclusions, Proposals and Recommendations*. UN Doc. E/CN.4/Sub.2/1983/21/dd8. New York: United Nations.

Cojtí Cuxil, D. 1996. "The Politics of Maya Revindication." *Maya Cultural Activism in Guatemala*, ed. E. F. Fischer and R. McKenna Brown, 19–50. Austin: University of Texas Press / Institute of Latin American Studies.

———. 1995. *Ub'aniik ri una'ooj uchomab'aal ri maya' tinamit: Configuración del pensamiento político del pueblo maya*. Guatemala: n.p.

———. 1991. *Configuración del pensamiento político del Pueblo Maya*. Guatemala: Asociación de Escritores Mayances.

———. 1989. "Problemas de la 'identidad nacional' guatemalteca." COCADI, *Cultura Maya y Políticas de Desarrollo*. B'okob', Guatemala: n.p.

Coleman, A. L. 2006. "'Tell the Court I Love My [Indian] Wife': Interrogating Race and Self-Identity in *Loving v. Virginia.*" *Souls* 8:1, 67–80.

Collier, G. A. 1994. *Basta! Land and the Zapatista Rebellion in Chiapas.* Oakland: Food First Books.

———. 1991. "Mesoamerican Anthropology: Between Production and Hegemony." *Latin American Research Review* 26:2, 203–10.

Condori, G. 2003. "Experiencias comunicacionales de la Asociación de Radioemisoras Aimaras de La Paz." *Los andes desde los andes: Aymaranakana, qhichwanakana yatxatawipa, lup'iwipa,* ed. E. Ticona, 81–121. La Paz: Yachaywasi.

El Consejo de Jefes de Rapa Nui. Te Mau Hatu'O Rapa Nui. 1988. Santiago: Editorial Emisión.

Coronil, F. 2004. "¿Globalización liberal o imperialismo global? Cinco piezas para armar el rompecabezas del presente." *Comentario Internacional,* no. 5, 103–32. Quito: UASB.

Cristino, C., et al. 1984. *Isla de Pascua: Proceso, Alcances y Efectos de la Aculturación.* Santiago de Chile: Universidad de Chile.

Cruikshank, J. 2002. "Oral History, Narrative Strategies, and Native American Historiography: Perspectives from the Yukon Territory, Canada." *Clearing a Path: Theorizing the Past in Native American Studies,* ed. N. Shoemaker, 3–27. New York: Routledge.

Delgado Pop, A. 2000. "¿Qué es ser indígena a las puertas del nuevo milenio?" *Identidad: rostros sin máscaras. Reflexiones sobre cosmovisión, género y etnicidad,* ed. M. McLeod and M. L. Cabrera, 15–24. Guatemala: Oxfam-Australia.

Deloria Jr., V. 1988 (1969). *Custer Died for Your Sins: An Indian Manifesto.* Norman: University of Oklahoma Press.

Deloria Jr., V., and C. Lytle. 1984. *The Nations Within: The Past and Future of American Indian Sovereignty.* New York: Pantheon.

Dirlik, A., V. Bahl, and P. Gran, eds. 2000. *History after the Three Worlds: Post-Eurocentric Historiographies.* Lanham, Md.: Rowman and Littlefield.

Dresser, D. 1991. *Neopopulist Solutions to Neoliberal Problems: Mexico's National Solidarity Program.* La Jolla, Calif.: Center for U.S.–Mexican Studies.

Du Bois, W. E. B. 1989 (1903). *The Souls of Black Folk.* New York: Bantam.

Eber, C., and B. Rosenbaum. 1993. "'That We May Serve beneath Your Flowery Hands and Feet:' Women Weavers in Highland Chiapas, Mexico." *Crafts in Global Markets,* ed. J. Nash, 154–80. Albany: SUNY Press.

Eber, C., and J. M. Tanski. 2001. "Obstacles Facing Women's Grassroots Development Strategies in Mexico." *Review of Radical Political Economics* 33, 441–60.

Escobar, A. 2000. "El lugar de la naturaleza y la naturaleza del lugar: ¿globalización o postdesarrollo?" *La colonialidad del saber: Eurocentrismo y ciencias sociales, perspectivas latinoamericanas,* ed. E. Lander, 113–43. Buenos Aires: CLACSO.

———. 1999. *El final del salvaje: Naturaleza, cultura y política en la antropología contemporánea*. Bogotá: CEREC, ICAN.

Esquit, E. 2004. "Las Rutas que nos Ofrecen el Pasado y el Presente: Activismo Político, Historia y Pueblo Maya." *Memorias del Mestizaje*, ed. D. A. Euraque, J. L. Gould, and C. Hale, 167–92. Guatemala: CIRMA.

Fanon, F. 2004. *The Wretched of the Earth*. New York: Grove, 2004.

Fenton, S., and P. Moon. 2002. "The Translation of the Treaty of Waitangi: A Case of Disempowerment." *Translation and Power*, ed. M. Tymoczko and E. Gentzler, 25–44. Amherst: University of Massachusetts Press.

Fernández Osco, M. 2000. *La ley del ayllu: Práctica de jach'a justicia y jisk'a justicia (justicia mayor y justicia menor) en comunidades aymaras*. La Paz: PIEB.

Field, L. 1999. "Complicities and Collaborations: Anthropologists and the 'Unacknowledged Tribes' of California." *Current Anthropology* 40(2), 193–209.

Fischer, E. 2001. *Cultural Logics and Global Economies*. Austin: University of Texas Press.

Fischer, E., and M. Brown, eds. 1999. *Rujotayixik ri maya' b'anob'al. Activismo Cultural Maya*. Guatemala: Editorial Cholsamaj.

Fishman, J. 1995. *Sociología del lenguaje*. 4th edn. Madrid: Cátedra.

Florescano, E. 2001. "Memoria indígena: Un nuevo enfoque sobre la construcción del pasado." *Trayectorias, Revista de Ciencias Sociales*, no. 4/5, 133–41. Mexico City: Universidad Autónoma de Nuevo León.

Foley, N. 2002. "Becoming Hispanic: Mexican-Americans and Whiteness." *White Privilege: Essential Reading on the Other Side of Racism*, ed. P. S. Rothenberg, 49–59. New York: Worth.

Forbes, J. 1993. *Africans and Native Americans: The Language of Race and the Evolution of Red-Black Peoples*. 2d edn. Urbana: University of Illinois Press.

Freire, P. 1969. *La educación como práctica de la libertad*. Montevideo: Tierra Nueva.

Garcés, F. 2006. "Herramientas para pensar la globalización, el capitalismo y la cultura sin morir en el intento." *Punto Cero: Revista de la carrera de communicación social*, no. 12: 43–58. Cochabamba: UCB.

———. 2005a. "Las políticas del conocimiento y la colonialidad lingüística y epistémica." *Pensamiento crítico y matriz (de)colonial: Reflexiones latinoamericanas*, ed. C. Walsh, 137–67. Quito: Abya Yala, UASB.

———. 2005b. *De la voz al papel: La escritura quechua del Periódico CONOSUR Ñawpaqman*. La Paz: CENDA, Plural.

Garcés, F., and S. Guzmán. 2006. "La 'escuela ayni' de Rumi Muqu." *Escuelas y proceses de cambins*, ed. Alejandra Ramírez, 35–44. Cochabamba: CESU.

———. 2003. *Educacionqa kawsayninchikmanta kawsayninchikpaq kanan tiyan. Elementos para diversificar el currículo de la Nación Quechua*. Cochabamba: CENAQ.

García, F. 2005. *Yachay. Concepciones sobre enseñanza y aprendizaje en una comunidad quechua*. La Paz: Plural, PINSEIB, PROEIB Andes.

García Ruiz, J. 1992. *Historias de nuestra historia*. Guatemala: IRIPAZ.

Garza, A. M., and S. Toledo. 2008. "Women, Agrarianism and Militancy: Chiapas in the 1980s." *Latin American Perspectives* 35:6, 61–78.

Gilroy, P. 1993. *The Black Atlantic: Modernity and Double Consciousness*. Cambridge: Harvard University Press.

González Casanova, P. 1965. "Internal Colonialism and National Development." *Studies in Comparative Development* 1:4, 27–37.

Goody, J. 1996 (1968). "Introducción." *Cultura escrita en sociedades tradicionales*, ed. J. Goody, 11–38. Barcelona: Gedisa.

Gottret, G. 1999. "Interculturalidad en el aula." *Interculturalidad y calidad de los aprendizajes en ámbitos escolares urbanos*, ed. N. Mengoa, 31–40. La Paz: Centro Boliviano de Investigación y Acción Educativas.

Grandin, G. 2000. *The Blood of Guatemala: A History of Race and Nation*. Durham: Duke University Press.

Greenbaum, S. "What's in a Label? Identity Problems of Southern Indian Tribes." *Journal of Ethnic Studies* 19:2 (summer 1991), 107–26.

Griswold, E. A. 1996. "State Hegemony Writ: International Law and Indigenous Rights." *Political and Legal Anthropology Review* 19:1, 91–104.

Guamán Poma de Ayala, F. 1993 (1615). *Nueva Coronica y Buen Gobierno*. Edited by F. Pease. Translated by J. Szeminski. Mexico City: Fondo de Cultura Económica.

Gugelberger, G. 1996. *The Real Thing: Testimonial Discourse and Latin America*. Durham: Duke University Press.

Guha, R., and G. C. Spivak, eds. 1998. *Selected Subaltern Studies*. New York: Oxford University Press.

Guzmán, S. 2005. "El quechua en las radios urbanas." Presentation given at the National Seminar Las lenguas andinas y su enseñanza en contextos urbanos. Cochabamba, 24–26 November 2005.

Guzmán Böckler, C., and J. Herbert. 1998. *Guatemala: Una interpretación histórico social*. Guatemala: Editorial Cholsamaj.

Hale, C. R. 2002. "Does Multiculturalism Menace? Governance, Cultural Rights and the Politics of Identity in Guatemala." *Journal of Latin American Studies* 34, 485–524.

Hale, C. R., and R. Millamán. 2006. "Cultural Agency and Political Struggle in the Era of the Indio Permitido." *Cultural Agency in the Americas*, ed. D. Sommer, 281–304. Durham: Duke University Press.

Harvey, N. 1998. *The Chiapas Rebellion: The Struggle for Land and Democracy*. Durham: Duke University Press.

Hasager, U., and J. Friedman. 1994. *Hawai'i Return to Nationhood*. Copenhagen: International Working Group for Indigenous Affairs, Document no. 75.

Heise, M., F. Tubino, and W. Ardito. 1994. *Interculturalidad: Un desafío*. Lima: Centro Amazónico de Antropología y Aplicación Práctica.

Hernández Castillo, R. A., ed. 2001. *The Other Word: Women and Violence in Chiapas before and after Acteal*. Copenhagen: International Work Group for Indigenous Affairs.

Herrero, J., and F. Sánchez de Lozada. 1979. *Diccionario quechua: Estructura semántica del quechua cochabambino contemporáneo*. Cochabamba: CEFCO.

Hill, R. 2001. *Los kaqchikeles de la época colonial*. Plumsock Mesoamerican Studies. Guatemala: Editorial Cholsamaj.

Howe, L. 2002. "The Story of America: A Tribalography." *Clearing a Path: Theorizing the Past in Native American Studies*, ed. N. Shoemaker, 29–48. New York: Routledge.

Hurtado de Mendoza, W. 2002. *Pragmática de la cultura y la lengua quechua*. Quito: Abya Yala.

James, D. 2000. *Doña María's Story: Life History, Memory, and Political Identity*. Durham: Duke University Press.

Jameson, F. 1991 (1984). *El posmodernismo o la lógica cultural del posmodernismo avanzado*. Barcelona: Paidós.

Jones, D. J. 1970. "Towards a Native Anthropology." *Human Organization* 29:4, 251–59.

Kameʻeleihiwa, L. 1992. *Native Land and Foreign Desires*. Honolulu: Bishop Museum Press.

Kauanui, J. K. 2008. "Colonialism in Equality: Hawaiian Sovereignty and the Question of US Civil Rights." *South Atlantic Quarterly* 107:4 (October), 635–50.

———. 2005a. "The Multiplicity of Hawaiian Sovereignty Claims and the Struggle for Meaningful Autonomy." *Comparative American Studies* 3:3, 283–99.

———. 2005b. "Precarious Positions: Native Hawaiians and Federal Recognition." *Contemporary Pacific* 17:1, 1–27.

———. 2002. "The Politics of Blood and Sovereignty in *Rice v. Cayetano*." *Political and Legal Anthropology Review* 25:1, 100–128.

Kent, N. 1993. *Hawaiʻi: Islands under the Influence*. 2d edn. Honolulu: University of Hawaiʻi Press.

Kirch, P. V. 2000. *On the Road of the Winds: An Archeological History of the Pacific Islands before European Contact*. Berkeley: University of California Press.

Kotschi, T., W. Oesterreicher, and K. Zimmermann, eds. 1996. *El español hablado y la cultura oral en España e Hispanoamérica*. Madrid: Iberoamericana.

Kristeva, J. 1982. *Semiótica I*. Madrid: Espiral.

Laclau, E., and C. Mouffe. 1985. *Hegemony and Socialist Strategy: Towards a Radical Democratic Politics*. London: Verso.

Laime, T. 1998. *Qhichwata allinta qillqanapaq p'anqa. Manual de ortografía quechua*. La Paz: CEIPLIM.

Lakoff, G., and M. Jonson. 1995 (1980). *Metáforas de la vida cotidiana*. Madrid: Cátedra.

Lam, M. C. 2000. *At the Edge of the State: Indigenous Peoples and Self-Determination*. Ardsley, N.Y.: Transnational.

———. 1992. "Making Room for Peoples at the United Nations: Thoughts Provoked by Indigenous Claims to Self-Determination." *Cornell International Law Journal* 25:3, 603-22.

Lame, M. Q. 2004 (1939). *Los pensamientos del indio que se educó dentro de las selvas colombianas*. Cali and Popayán, Colombia: Editorial Universidad del Valle/Editoral Universidad del Cauca.

Lander, E. 2002a. "La utopía del mercado total y el poder imperial." *Revista venezolana de Economía y Ciencias Sociales* 8:2, 51-79.

———. 2002b. "Los derechos de propiedad intelectual en la geopolítica del saber de la sociedad global." *Indisciplinar las ciencias sociales: Geopolíticas del conocimiento y colonialidad del poder, Perspectivas desde lo andino*, ed. C. Walsh, F. Schiwy, and S. Castro-Gómez, 73-102. Quito: UASB, Abya Yala.

Laughlin, R. M. 1993. "En la vanguardia: Sna Jtz'ibajom." *Situación actual y perspectivas de las literaturas en lenguas indígenas*, ed. C. Montemayor 155-72. Mexico City: CONECULTA.

Legorreta, C. 1998. *Religión, política y guerrilla en Las Cañadas de la Selva Lacandona*. Mexico City: Cal y Arena.

Leyva Solano, X. 2003. "Regional, Communal, and Organizational Transformations in Las Cañadas." *Mayan Lives, Mayan Utopias: The Indigenous People of Chiapas and the Zapatista Movement*, ed. J. Rus, R. A. Hernández Castillo, and S. L. Mattiace, 161-84. Lanham, Md.: Rowman and Littlefield.

Lienhard, M. 1992. *La voz y su huella: Escritura y conflicto étnico-cultural en América Latina 1492-1988*. 3d edn. Lima: Horizonte.

Lipsitz, G. 1998. *American Studies in a Moment of Danger*. Minneapolis: University of Minnesota Press.

———. 2006 (1998). *The Possessive Investment in Whiteness: How White People Profit from Identity Politics*. Philadelphia: Temple University Press.

Littlefield, D. F. 1977. *Africans and Seminoles: From Removal to Emancipation*. Westport, Conn.: Greenwood Press.

Lomnitz-Adler, C. 1995. *Las salidas del Laberinto*. Mexico City: Editorial Planeta.

Loomba, A., S. Kaul, M. Bunzl, A. Burton, and J. Esty, eds. 2005. *Postcolonial Studies and Beyond*. Durham: Duke University Press.

López, L. E. 1999. "El lenguaje en el desarrollo de los conocimientos en ámbitos escolares urbanos con diversidad cultural." *Interculturalidad y calidad de los aprendizajes en ámbitos escolares urbanos*, ed. N. Mengoa, 47-70. La Paz: Centro Boliviano de Investigación y Acción Educativas.

———. 1996. "No más danzas de ratones grises: Sobre interculturalidad, democracia y educación." *Educación e interculturalidad en los Andes y la Amazonía*, ed. J. Godenzzi Alegre, 23–80. Serie Estudios y Debates Regionales Andinos, 93. Cusco: Centro de Estudios Regionales Bartolomé de Las Casas.

———. 1995. *La educación en áreas indígenas de América Latina: Apreciaciones comparativas desde la educación bilingüe intercultural.* Guatemala City: Centro de Estudios de la Cultura Maya.

López, L. E., and W. Küper. 2004. *La educación intercultural bilingüe en América Latina.* La Paz, Cochabamba: PINSEIB, PROEIB Andes.

Loveman, B. 2001 (1979). *Chile: The Legacy of Hispanic Capitalism.* Oxford: Oxford University Press.

Luykx, A. 1998. "La diferencia funcional de códigos y el futuro de las lenguas minoritarias." *Sobre las huellas de la voz: Sociolingüística de la oralidad y la escritura en su relación con la educación*, ed. L. E. López and I. Jung, 192–212. Madrid, Cochabamba, Bonn: Morata, PROEIB Andes, DSE.

———. 2001. "Diversity in the New World Order: State Language Policies and the Internationalization of Quechua." Abstract of paper presented at the Second Spencer Early Career Institute in Anthropology and Education: Globalization and Education, 10–13 May. Chicago.

McCall, G. 1976. "Reaction to Disaster: Continuity and Change in Rapanui Social Organization." Ph.D. diss., Australian National University.

Makihara, M. 1999. "Bilingualism, Social Change, and the Politics of Ethnicity on Rapanui (Easter Island), Chile." Ph.D. diss., Yale University.

Mannheim, B. 1991. *The Language of the Inka since the European Invasion.* Austin: University of Texas Press.

Marcone, J. 1997. *La oralidad escrita: Sobre la reivindicación y la re-inscripción del discurso oral.* Lima: PUC-P.

Marcus, G. 1995. "Ethnography in/of the World System: The Emergence of Multi-Sited Ethnography." *Annual Review of Anthropology*, 24, 95–117.

Marcus, G., and M. Fischer. 1986. *Anthropology as a Cultural Critique: An Experimental Moment in the Human Sciences.* Chicago: University of Chicago Press.

Marimán, Pablo, Sergio Caniuqueo, José Millalén, and Rodrigo Levil. 2006. ¡... Escucha, winka...! Cuatro ensayos de Historia Nacional Mapuche y un epílogo sobre el futuro. Santiago, Chile: LOM Ediciones.

Martínez Peláez, S. 1973. *La Patria del Criollo.* Costa Rica: EDUCA.

Menchú, R. 1984. *I, Rigoberta Menchú.* Edited by Elisabeth Burgos. London: Verso.

Mengoa, N. 1999. "Diversidad y procesos pedagógicos: Lineamientos para una propuesta de educación intercultural en escuelas urbano-populares de la región andina en Bolivia." *Interculturalidad y calidad de los aprendizajes en ámbitos escolares urbanos*, ed. N. Mengoa, 11–20. La Paz: Centro Boliviano de Investigación y Acción Educativas.

Merrell, J. H. 1984. "The Racial Education of the Catawba Indians." *Journal of Southern History* 50:3, 363–84.

Merry, S. 2000. *Colonizing Hawai'i: The Cultural Power of Law*. Princeton: Princeton University Press.

Métraux, A. 1971 (1940). *Ethnology of Easter Island*. Honolulu: Bishop Museum Press.

Mignolo, W. 2004. "Capitalismo y geopolítica del conocimiento." *Modernidades Coloniales*, ed. S. Dube, I. Banergee Dube, and W. Mignolo. Mexico City: El Colegio de México.

———. 2002. "El potencial epistemológico de la historia oral: Algunas contribuciones de Silvia Rivera Cusicanqui." *Estudios y otras prácticas intelectuales latinoamericanas en cultura y poder*, ed. D. Mato, 201–11. Caracas: CLACSO, FACES.

———. 2001. "Introducción." *Capitalismo y geopolítica del conocimiento: El eurocentrismo y la filosofía de la liberación en el debate intelectual contemporáneo*, 9–53. Buenos Aires: Signo.

———. 2000. *Local Histories / Global Designs. Coloniality, Subaltern Knowledges and Border Thinking*. Princeton: Princeton University Press.

———. 1999. "Globalización, procesos civilizatorios y la reubicación de lenguas y culturas." *Pensar (en) los intersticios: Teoría y práctica de la crítica poscolonial*, ed. S. Castro-Gómez, O. Guardiola-Rivera, and C. Millán de Benavides, 55–74. Bogotá: Pensar.

Mihesuah, D. A. 2004. "Should American Indian History Remain a Field of Study?" *Indigenizing the Academy: Transforming Scholarship and Empowering Communities*, ed. D. A. Mihesuah and A. C. Wilson, 143–59. Lincoln: University of Nebraska Press.

Mihesuah, D. A., ed. 1998. *Natives and Academics: Researching and Writing about American Indians*. Lincoln: University of Nebraska Press.

Mihesuah, D. A., and A. C. Wilson, eds. 2004. *Indigenizing the Academy: Transforming Scholarship and Empowering Communities*. Lincoln: University of Nebraska Press.

Miles, T. 2004. *The Ties that Bind: The Story of an Afro-Cherokee Family in Slavery and Freedom*. Berkeley: University of California Press.

Miles, T., and S. P. Holland, eds. 2006. *Crossing Waters, Crossing Worlds: The African Diaspora in Indian Country*. Durham: Duke University Press.

Mills, G. B. 1977. *The Forgotten People: Cane River's Creoles of Color*. Baton Rouge: Louisiana State University Press.

MINUGUA. 2001. *Proceso de negociación de la Paz en Guatemala*. Guatemala: MINUGUA.

Montejo, V. 2005. *Maya Intellectual Renaissance: Identity, Representation and Leadership*. Austin: University of Texas Press.

———. 2004. "Angering the Ancestors: Transnationalism and Economic Transformation of Maya Communities in Western Guatemala." *Pluralizing Ethnography: Comparison and Representation in Maya Cultures, Histories, and Identities*, ed. J. Watanabe and E. Fischer, 231–56. Santa Fe: School of American Research Press.

———. 2002. "The Multiplicity of Maya Voices: Maya Leadership and the Politics of Self-Representation." *Indigenous Movements, Self-Representation, and the State in Latin America*, ed. K. B. Warren and J. Jackson, 123–48. Austin: University of Texas Press.

———. 1999. *Voices from Exile: Violence and Survival in Modern Maya History*. Norman: University of Oklahoma Press.

———. 1997. "Panmayanismo: La pluriformidad de la cultura maya y el proceso de autorepresentación de los mayas." *Mesoamérica*, no. 33, 93–123. Antigua, Guatemala: CIRMA, PMS.

———. 1987. *Testimony: The Death of a Guatemalan Village*. Willimantic, Conn.: Curbstone Press.

Morales, M. R. 1998. *La articulación de las diferencias*. Guatemala: FLACSO-Guatemala.

Morales Bermúdez, J. 1992. "El Congreso Indígena de Chiapas: Un testimonio." *Anuario 1991*, 242–370. Instituto Chiapaneco de la Cultura, Tuxtla Gutiérrez.

Morrison, T. 1988. *Beloved*. New York: Plume.

Muelas Hurtado, B. 1995. "Relación espacio-tiempo en el pensamiento guambiano." *Proyecciones Lingüísticas* 1:1, 31–40.

Muyulema, A. 2001. "De la cuestión indígena a lo indígena como cuestionamiento: Hacia una crítica del latinoamericanismo, el indigenismo y el mestiz(o)aje." *Convergencia de tiempos: Estudios subalternos/contextos latinoamericanos. Estado, cultura y subalternidad*, ed. I. Rodríguez, 327–63. Amsterdam: Editions Rodopi.

Nannerl, O. K., M. Z. Rosaldo, and B. C. Gelpi, eds. 1982. *Feminist Theory: A Critique of Ideology*. Chicago: University of Chicago Press.

Nash, J. 1993. *Crafts in Global Markets: Changes in Artisan Production in Middle America*. Albany: State University of New York Press.

Newcomb, S. 2008. *Pagans in the Promised Land: Decoding the Doctrine of Christian Discovery*. Golden, Colo.: Fulcrum.

Norval, A. 2001. "Reconstructing National Identity and Renegotiating Memory: The Work of the TRC." *States of Imagination: Ethnographic Explorations of the Postcolonial State*, ed. T. Blom Hansen and F. Stepputat, 182–202. Durham: Duke University Press.

Olson, D. 1998 (1994). *El mundo sobre el papel: El impacto de la escritura y la lectura en la estructura del conocimiento*. Barcelona: Gedisa.

Omi, M., and H. Winant. 1994. *Racial Formation in the United States from the 1960s to the 1990s*. 2d edn. New York: Routledge.

Ong, W. 1992. "Writing Is a Technology that Restructures Thought." *The Linguis-*

tics of Literacy, ed. P. Downing, S. Lima, and M. Noonan, 293-319. Philadelphia: John Benjamins.

———. 1999 (1982). *Oralidad y escritura: Tecnologías de la palabra*. Mexico City: FCE.

Osorio, J. K. 2002. *Dismembering Lahui: A History of the Hawaiian Nation to 1887*. Honolulu: University of Hawai'i Press.

Pachacuti Yamqui Salcamaygua, J. 1993 (1613). *Relacion de antiguiedades deste reyno del Piru*. Estudio etnohistórico y lingüístico de Pierre Duviols y César Itier. Lima, Cuzco: IFEA, CBC.

Pancho Aquite, A., et al. 2004. *Educación superior indígena en Colombia: Una apuesta de futuro y esperanza*. Cali, Colombia: IESALC-UNESCO.

Pari, A. 2005. "Epistemología del conocimiento científico andino: yachaymanta yachay." *Qinasay, Revista de Educación Intercultural Bilingüe* 3:3, 67-81. Cochabamba: PROEIB Andes.

Paschal, R. 1991. "The Imprimatur of Recognition: American Indian Tribes and the Federal Acknowledgment Process." *Washington Law Review* 66 (1991), 209-28.

Past, Á. 2005. "Notes on the Creators." *Incantations by Mayan Women*, ed. Á. Past, X. Okotz, and X. Ernándes, 257-84. San Cristóbal: Taller Leñateros.

———. 1989 (1980). *Bon, tintes naturales*. San Cristóbal: Taller Leñateros.

Paz, S. 2005. "Propuesta base para pensar las autonomías indígenas en Bolivia." Paper given in the Seminar Territorios indígenas, interculturalidad, participación y autonomías. Cochabamba, 3-4 March.

Paz Paredes, L., R. Cobo, and A. Bartra. 1996. "Dos siglos de cafeticultura en México a muchas voces." *Ojarasca*, no. 46, 26-49.

Perdue, T. 1999. *Cherokee Women: Gender and Culture Change, 1700-1835*. Lincoln: University of Nebraska Press.

———. 1979. *Slavery and the Evolution of Cherokee Society, 1540-1866*. Knoxville: University of Tennessee Press.

Peres Tzu, M. 2002. "A Tzotzil Chronicle." *The Mexico Reader*, ed. G. Joseph and T. Henderson, 655-69. Durham: Duke University Press.

Pérez, Calvo, J. 1993. *Pragmática y gramática del quechua cuzqueño*. Cuzco: CBC.

Pewewardy, C. 2004. "So You Think You Hired an 'Indian' Faculty Member?: The Ethnic Fraud Paradox in Higher Education." *Indigenizing the Academy: Transforming Scholarship and Empowering Native Communities*, ed. D. A. Mihesuah and A. C. Wilson, 200-217. Lincoln: University of Nebraska Press.

Phillips, V. J. 2002. "Epilogue: Seeing Each Other through the White Man's Eyes." *Confounding the Color Line: The Indian-Black Experience in North America*, ed. J. Brooks, 371-85. Lincoln: University of Nebraska Press.

Plaza, P. 1995. *Qhichwata qillqanapaq*. La Paz: MDH, UNST-P.

Portelli, A. 1997. *The Battle of Valle Giulia: Oral History and the Art of Dialogue*, Madison: University of Wisconsin Press.

———. 1991. *The Death of Luigi Trastulli and Other Stories: Form and Meaning in Oral History.* Albany: State University of New York Press.

———. 1989. "Historia y memoria: La muerte de Luigi Trastulli." *Historia y fuente oral*, no. 1, 15–32. Barcelona: Universidad de Barcelona.

Porteous, D. 1981. *The Modernization of Easter Island.* Victoria, British Columbia: University of Victoria Press.

Postero, N. 2005. "Movimientos indígenas bolivianos: Articulaciones y fragmentaciones en búsqueda de multiculturalismo." *Movimientos Indígenas y Estado en Bolivia*, ed. L. E. López and P. Regalsky, 53–96. La Paz: PROEIB Andes, CENDA, Plural.

Pozas, R. 1962. *Juan, the Chamula.* Berkeley: University of California Press.

———. 1952. "El trabajo en las plantaciones de café y el cambio socio-cultural del indio." *Revista Mexicana de Estudios Antropológicos* 12:1, 31–48.

Prakash, G., ed. 1995. *After Colonialism: Imperial Histories and Postcolonial Displacements.* Princeton: Princeton University Press.

Qayum, S. 2002. "Nationalism, Internal Colonialism and the Spatial Imagination: The Geographic Society of La Paz in Turn-of-the-Century Bolivia." *Studies in the Formation of the Nation-State in Latin America*, ed. J. Dunkerley, 275–98. London: Institute of Latin American Studies, University of London.

Quijano, A. 2000. "Colonialidad del poder y clasificación social." *Journal of World-Systems Research* 6:2, 342–86.

Quiroz, A. 1998. *Chichwa simipirwa.* Qullasuyu, Bolivia: MECyD, UNICEF.

Racancoj, V. 1994. *Socioeconomía maya precolonial.* Guatemala: Editorial Cholsamaj.

Raibmon, P. 2005. *Authentic Indians: Episodes of Encounter from the Late-Nineteenth-Century Northwest Coast.* Durham: Duke University Press.

Rajpopi' ri Mayab' Amaq' COMG. 1995. *Ru junamil ri Mayab' Amaq' pa Rubi'inib'al Runuk'ik ri Saqk'aslemal. Construyendo un futuro para nuestro pasado.* Guatemala: Editorial Cholsamaj.

Ramos, A., and Cabildo Indígena de Mosoco. 1993. *Ec ne'hwe's': Constitución política de Colombia en nasa yuwe.* Bogotá: CCELA-UniAndes.

Rappaport, J. 2008. "Beyond Participant Observation: Collaborative Ethnography as Theoretical Innovation." *Collaborative Anthropologies* 1, 1–31.

———. 2005. "Los nasa de frontera y la política de la identidad en el Cauca Indígena." *Retornando la mirada: Una investigación colaborativa interétnica sobre el Cauca a la entrada del milenio*, ed. J. Rappaport, 31–56. Popayán, Colombia: Editorial Universidad del Cauca.

———. 2004. "Imaginando una nación pluralista: Intelectuales y la jurisdicción especial indígena." *Revista Colombiana de Antropología* 39, 105–38.

———. 1998. *The Politics of Memory: Native Historical Interpretation in the Colombian Andes.* Durham: Duke University Press.

Regalsky, P. 2003. *Etnicidad y clase: El Estado boliviano y las estrategias andinas de manejo de su espacio*. La Paz: CENDA, CEIDIS, Plural.

Reuque Paillalef, R. I. 2002a. *When a Flower Is Reborn: The Life and Times of a Mapuche Feminist*. Edited and translated by F. E. Mallon. Durham: Duke University Press.

———. 2002b. *Una flor que renace: Autobiografía de una dirigente Mapuche*. Santiago, Chile: DIBAM.

Rivera, S. 2004 (1987). "El potencial epistemológico y teórico de la historia oral: De la lógica instrumental a la descolonización de la historia." *Peri-feria*, no. 4, 16–26. Neiva: Editorial Universidad Surcolombiana.

Rivera Cusicanqui, S., and R. Barragán. 1997. "Presentación." *Debates Post Coloniales: Una Introducción a los Estudios de la Subalternidad*, ed. S. Rivera Cusicanqui and R. Barragán, 11–19. La Paz, Bolivia: Editorial *historias*/Ediciones Aruwiyiri/SEPHIS.

Rochna-Ramírez, S. 1996. *La propiedad de la tierra en Isla de Pascua*. Santiago: CONADI.

Rodríguez, D. R. 2004. "Racismo y discriminación: Conceptualización y sus manifestaciones." *Genocidio, la máxima expresión del racismo*. Guatemala: CALDH.

Rodríguez, D. R., et al. 1995. *Nab'ey taq tzij pa ruwi' ri maya' k'aslemal. Introducción a la cultura maya*. Guatemala: Editorial Cholsamaj.

Rojas Curieux, T. 2000. "Transportar la cosa hablada a otra lengua: La experiencia de la traducción de la Constitución de la República a lenguas indígenas." *Concepciones de la Conquista: Aproximaciones interdisciplinarias*, ed. F. Castañeda and M. Vollet, 361–88. Bogotá: Ediciones UniAndes.

Romero, R. 1994. *Ch'iki: Concepción y desarrollo de la inteligencia en niños quechuas pre-escolares de la comunidad de Titicachi*. La Paz: CEE, PEIB.

Rothenberg, P. S., ed. 2002. *White Privilege: Essential Readings on the Other Side of Racism*. New York: Worth.

Rountree, H. C. 1990. *Pocahontas's People: The Powhatan Indians of Virginia through Four Centuries*. Norman: University of Oklahoma Press.

Routledge, K. 1998 (1919). *The Mystery of Easter Island*. Kempton, Australia: Adventurers Unlimited Press.

Rus, D. 1990. *La Crisis y la mujer indígena: El caso de Chamula, Chiapas*. San Cristóbal: INAREMAC.

Rus, D., and J. Rus. 2004. "Los últimos diez años en las comunidades de Los Altos en el contexto de los últimos treinta." Paper presented to the symposium Chiapas, 10 años después. San Cristóbal, 23–27 August.

Rus, J. 2005. "The Struggle against Indigenous Caciques in Highland Chiapas, 1965–1993." *Cacique and Caudillo in 20th Century Mexico*, ed. A. Knight and W. Pansters, 169–200. London: Institute for Latin American Studies.

———. 2004. "Rereading Tzotzil Ethnography: Recent Scholarship from Chiapas,

Mexico." *Pluralizing Ethnography: Comparison and Representation in Maya Cultures, Histories and Identities*, ed. J. Watanabe and E. Fischer, 199–230. Santa Fe: School of American Research.

———. 1995. "Local Adaptation to Global Change: The Reordering of Native Society in Highland Chiapas, 1974–1994." *European Review of Latin American and Caribbean Studies* 58, 82–91.

———. 1989. "The 'Caste War' of 1869 from the Indians' Perspective: A Challenge for Ethno History." *Memorias del Segundo Coloquio Internacional de Mayistas* 2, 1033–47. Mexico City: Centro de Estudios Mayas, UNAM.

———. 1983. "Whose Caste War? Indians, Ladinos, and the 'Caste War' of 1869." *Spaniards and Indians in Southeastern Mesoamerica*, ed. M. MacLeod and R. W. Wasserstrom, 127–68. Lincoln: University of Nebraska Press.

Rus, J., ed. 1999. *If Truth Be Told: A Forum on David Stoll's "Rigoberta Menchú and the Story of All Poor Guatemalans."* Special issue of *Latin American Perspectives* 26:6.

Rus, J., and G. A. Collier. 2003. "A Generation of Crisis in the Chiapas Highlands: The Tzotzils of Chamula and Zinacantán, 1974–2000." *Mayan Lives, Mayan Utopias: The Indigenous People of Chiapas and the Zapatista Movement*, ed. J. Rus, R. A. Hernández Castillo, and S. L. Mattiace, 33–61. Lanham, Md.: Rowman and Littlefield.

Rus, J., R. A. Hernández Castillo, and S. L. Mattiace, eds. 2003. *Mayan Lives, Mayan Utopias: The Indigenous People of Chiapas and the Zapatista Movement*. Lanham, Md.: Rowman and Littlefield.

Rus, J., and G. Morquecho. 2008. "El movimiento indígena de San Cristóbal, Chiapas, Mexico." Paper presented to the conference Enduring Reform, Responses to Civil Society-Based Reform. Porto Alegre, Brazil, 22–24 November.

Rus, J., and J. D. Vigil. 2007. "Rapid Urbanization and Migrant Indigenous Youth in San Cristóbal, Chiapas." *Gangs in the Global City*, ed. John Hagedorn, 152–83. Urbana: University of Illinois Press.

Said, E. W. 1978. *Orientalism*. New York: Pantheon.

Santos, B. 2003. "Desigualdad, exclusión y globalización: Hacia la construcción multicultural de la igualdad y la diferencia." *La caída del Angelus Novus: Ensayos para una nueva teoría social y una nueva práctica política*, ed. B. Santos, 125–65. Bogotá: ILSA, Universidad Nacional de Colombia.

Saunt, C. 2005. *Black, White, and Indian: Race and the Unmaking of an American Family*. Oxford: Oxford University Press.

———. 1999. *A New Order of Things: Property, Power, and the Transformation of the Creek Indians, 1733–1816*. Cambridge: Cambridge University Press.

Schele, L., and N. Grube. 1999. "El Taller maya de escritura jeroglífica." *Rujotayixik ri maya' b'anob'al. Activismo Cultural maya*, ed. E. Fischer and M. Brown, 175–86. Guatemala: Editorial Cholsamaj.

Scott, J. 2002. "Prólogo." *Aspectos cotidianos de la Formación del Estado*, ed. G. Joseph and D. Nugent, 17–23. Mexico City: Editorial Era.

Sichra, I. 2003. *La vitalidad del quechua: Lengua y sociedad en dos provincias de Cochabamba*. La Paz: PROEIB Andes, Plural.

Sieder, R. 2004. *Del indigenismo institucional integracionista a la gestión pluralista de las políticas públicas*. London: Institute for the Study of the Americas, University of London.

Silva, N. K. 2007. "Indigenous Hawaiian Political Thought." Presentation on New Research Project, Wesleyan University, April.

———. 2004. *Aloha Betrayed: Native Hawaiian Resistance to American Colonialism*. Durham: Duke University Press.

———. 1998. "Kanaka Maoli Resistance to Annexation." *'oiwi: a native hawaiian journal*. Inaugural issue (December), 40–80.

Silva Galdames, O. 1995. *Breve historia contemporánea de Chile*. Mexico City: Fondo de Cultura Económica.

Sincal Coyote, E. 2004. "Elites e identidades: La diferenciación social del sector profesional indígena de Patzún, Chimaltenango." Thesis, Universidad de San Carlos de Guatemala.

Sociedad Bíblica de México. 1997. *Xch'ul C'op Jtotic Dios*. Mexico City: Sociedad Bíblica de México, S.A.

Spaulding, T. M. 1923. *The Crown Lands of Hawaii*. Honolulu: University of Hawai'i Press.

Spivak, G. C. 1988. "Can the Subaltern Speak?" *Marxism and the Interpretation of Culture*, ed. C. Nelson and L. Grossberg, 271–313. Urbana: University of Illinois Press.

Starna, W. 1996. "'We'll All Be Together Again': The Federal Acknowledgment of the Wampanoag Tribe of Gay Head." *Northeast Anthropology* 51, 3–12.

Stavenhagen, R. 1965. "Classes, Colonialism, and Acculturation." *Studies in Comparative Development* 1:6, 53–77.

Stoll, D. 1999. *Rigoberta Menchú and the Story of All Poor Guatemalans*. Boulder: Westview Press.

Street, B. 1984. *Literacy in Theory and Practice*. Cambridge: Cambridge University Press.

Sturm, C. 1998. "Blood Politics, Racial Classification, and Cherokee National Identity: The Trials and Tribulations of the Cherokee Freedmen." *American Indian Quarterly* 22:1–2 (winter/spring 1998), 230–58.

Subercaseaux, B. 1997. *Historia de las ideas y de la cultura en Chile*. Vol. 2: *Fin de siglo: La época de Balmaceda*. Santiago: Editorial Universitaria.

Tademy, T. 2002. *Cane River: A Novel*. New York: Warner.

Thiong'o, Ngugi wa. 1986. *Decolonising the Mind: The Politics of Language in African Literature*. Portsmouth, N.H.: Heinemann.

Thompson, B., and J. H. Peterson, Jr. 1975. "Mississippi Choctaw Identity: Genesis and Change." *The New Ethnicity: Perspectives from Ethnology*, ed. J. W. Bennett, 179–96. St. Paul: West Publishing.

Toledo, S. 2002. *Fincas, poder, y cultura en Simojovel, Chiapas*. Mexico City: Universidad Nacional Autónoma de México/Universidad Autónoma de Chiapas.

Toledo Llancaqueo, V., and S. Fuenzalida Bascuñan. 2005. "Reforma al artículo 17 de la ley indígena y política de suelos (DL 3.516): Análisis preliminar de sus efectos jurídicos e impactos territoriales." Notes for an analytical workshop. Colegio de Antropólogos de Chile. Santiago, 19 May.

Trask, H. 2000. "Settlers of Color and 'Immigrant' Hegemony: 'Locals' in Hawai'i." *Amerasia Journal* 26:2, 1–24.

———. 1993. *From a Native Daughter: Colonialism and Sovereignty in Hawai'i*. Monroe, Maine: Common Courage Press.

Trask, M. 1994. "The Politics of Oppression." *Hawai'i Return to Nationhood*. IWGIA Document 75, ed. Ulla Hasager and Jonathan Friedman, 68–87. Copenhagen: IWGIA.

Tuhiwai Smith, L. 1999. *Decolonizing Methodologies: Research and Indigenous Peoples*. Dunedin, New Zealand: University of Otago Press; and London: Zed Books.

United States Census Bureau. 2002. *Measuring America: The Decennial Censuses from 1790 to 2000*.

Uyehara, M. 1977. *The Ceded Land Trusts: Their Use and Misuse*. Honolulu: Hawaiiana Almanac.

Vallejos, F. 1995. *Tata Fermin yachaq. Inti k'anchay jina yachayniyki qhipakuchkan*. Cochabamba: CENDA.

Van Cott, D. L. 2000. *The Friendly Liquidation of the Past: The Politics of Diversity in Latin America*. Pittsburgh: University of Pittsburgh Press.

Vasco Uribe, L. G. 2002. *Entre selva y páramo: Viviendo y pensando la lucha indígena*. Bogotá: Instituto Colombiano de Antropología e Historia.

Vasco Uribe, G., A. Dagua Hurtado, and M. Aranda. 1993. "En el segundo día, la Gente Grande (Numisak) sembró la autoridad y las plantas y, con su jugo, bebió el sentido." *Encrucijadas de Colombia amerindia*, ed. F. Correa, 9–48. Bogotá: Instituto Colombiano de Antropología.

Velásquez Nimatuj, I. A. 2002. *La pequeña Burguesía Indígena Comercial de Guatemala*. Guatemala: SERJUS.

Vergara, V. 1939. *La Isla de Pascua: Dominación y dominio*. Santiago: Publicaciones de la Academia Chilena de Historia.

Viluche, J. 2001. "¿Por qué una organización social como CRIC asume un proceso de investigación y construcción de la educación alternativa?" Manuscript. Popayán, Colombia.

Wallace, R. 1997. *International Law*. London: Sweet and Maxwell.

Warren, K.B. 1999. "La lectura de la historia una forma de Resistencia: Intelectuales públicos mayas en Guatemala." *Rujotayixik ri maya' b'anob'al. Activismo Cultural maya*, ed. E. Fischer and M. Brown, 133–54. Guatemala: Editorial Cholsamaj.

———. 1998. *Indigenous Movements and Their Critics: Pan-Maya Activism in Guatemala*. Princeton: Princeton University Press.

Warrior, R. 2006. "Afterword." *Crossing Waters, Crossing Worlds: The African Diaspora in Indian Country*, ed. T. Miles and S. P. Holland, 321–25. Durham: Duke University Press.

Watanabe, J., and E. Fischer, eds. 2004. *Pluralizing Ethnography*. Santa Fe: School of American Research Press.

Wilkins, D. E. 1997. *American Indian Sovereignty and the U.S. Supreme Court: The Masking of Justice*. Austin: University of Texas Press.

Williams, B. 1989. "A Class Act: Anthropology and Race to Nation across Ethnic Terrain." *Annual Review of Anthropology*, no. 18, 401–44.

Williams, W. L. 1979. "Patterns in the History of the Remaining Southeastern Indians, 1840–1975." *Southeastern Indians since the Removal Era*, 193–210. Athens: University of Georgia Press.

Wilson, A. C. 2004. "Reclaiming Our Humanity: Decolonization and the Recovery of Indigenous Knowledge." *Indigenizing the Academy: Transforming Scholarship and Empowering Communities*, ed. D. A. Mihesuah and A. C. Wilson, 69–87. Lincoln: University of Nebraska Press.

———. 1998a. "American Indian History or Non-Indian Perceptions of American History." *Natives and Academics: Researching and Writing about American Indians*, ed. D. A. Mihesuah, 23–26. Lincoln: University of Nebraska Press.

———. 1998b. "Grandmother to Granddaughter: Generations of Oral History in a Dakota Family." *Natives and Academics: Researching and Writing about American Indians*, ed. D. A. Mihesuah, 27–36. Lincoln: University of Nebraska Press.

Womack, J. 1999. *Rebellion in Chiapas: An Historical Reader*. New York: Free Press.

Yupanqui, T. C. 1992 (1570). *Instrucción al licenciado Lope García de Castro*. Edited by Liliana Regalado de Hurtado. Lima: PUC-P.

Zavala, V. 2002. *Desencuentros con la escritura: Escuela y comunidad en los andes peruanos*. Lima: Red para el Desarrollo de las Ciencias Sociales en el Perú.

Žižek, S. 1993. "Multiculturalismo, o la lógica cultural del capitalismo multinacional." *Estudios culturales: Reflexiones sobre el multiculturalismo*, ed. F. Jameson and S. Žižek, 137–88. Buenos Aires: Paidós.

CONTRIBUTORS

RIET DELSING is an independent researcher. She received her Ph.D. in anthropology from the University of California at Santa Cruz in 2009. She conducts research in the history and place of Rapa Nui in the narratives of the Chilean nation-state.

EDGAR ARTURO ESQUIT CHOY is a Kaqchikel Maya historian and researcher at the Instituto de Estudios Interétnicos in Guatemala. He is the author of *Otros Poderes, Nuevos Desafíos: Relaciones Interétnicas en Tecpan y Su Entorno Departamental, 1871–1935* (2002) and the coauthor, with Víctor Gálvez Borrell, of *The Mayan Movement Today: Issues of Indigenous Culture and Development in Guatemala* (1997).

FERNANDO GARCÉS V. received his M.A. in social sciences from FLACSO-Quito (Ecuador) and is currently a Ph.D. candidate in Latin American cultural studies at the Universidad Andina Simón Bolívar (Quito). In addition to working in bilingual and intercultural education in both Ecuador and Bolivia, he coordinates the educational program at the Centro de Comunicación y Desarrollo Andino in Cochabamba, Bolivia, where he has also worked with the bilingual newspaper *Conosur Ñawpagman*. He has published several articles on Quichua and Quechua linguistics and sociolinguistics and on the relationship between writing and orality in Quechua.

J. KEHAULANI KAUANUI is an associate professor of anthropology and American studies at Wesleyan University. Her first book, *Hawaiian Blood: Colonialism and the Politics of Sovereignty and Indigeneity*, was published in the Narrating Native Histories series by Duke University Press in 2008. In 2008 she helped found the Native American and Indigenous Studies Association and was elected to its council the same year. In addition to coediting three special issues of journals and publishing widely in professional journals, she is working on two new book projects, one on gender, sexual politics, and indigeneity in Hawaiian identities and the other on Hawaii and New England colonialism.

BRIAN KLOPOTEK is an associate professor of ethnic studies at the University of Oregon. He is the author of *Recognition Odysseys: Indigeneity, Race, and Federal Tribal Recognition Policy in Three Louisiana Indian Communities*, in the Narrating Native Histories (Duke University Press, 2011). He has also published an article on Indian masculinity and is working, with Brenda Child, on a forthcoming edited book on Indian education.

FLORENCIA E. MALLON is the Julieta Kirkwood Professor and chair of the History Department at the University of Wisconsin, Madison. She is the author of *The Defense of Community in Peru's Central Highlands: Peasant Struggle and Capitalist Transition, 1860–1940* (Princeton, 1983); *Peasant and Nation: The Making of Postcolonial Mexico and Peru* (Berkeley, 1995), for which she received the Bryce Wood Award for the Best Book in Latin American Studies from the Latin American Studies Association; and *Courage Tastes of Blood: The Mapuche Indigenous Community of Nicolás Ailío and the Chilean State, 1906–2000* (Duke University Press, 2005), which was awarded the Bolton-Johnson Prize for the Best Book in Latin American History by the Conference on Latin American History. She is also the editor and translator of Rosa Isolde Reuque Paillalef, *When a Flower Is Reborn: The Life and Times of a Mapuche Feminist* (Duke University Press, 2002). She is one of the founding editors of the series Narrating Native Histories.

ABELARDO RAMOS PACHO is a Nasa linguist and activist with the Consejo Regional Indígena del Cauca in Colombia. He received his M.A. in ethnolinguistics from the Universidad de los Andes in Bogotá in 1987. He works in the Intercultural Bilingual Program of the Consejo Regional Indígena del Cauca. He is the coauthor, with Graciela Bolaños, Joanne Rappaport, and Carlos Miñana, of *¿Qué pasará si la escuela...? Treinta años de construcción educativa* (2004), and the author of numerous articles on translation, ethnolinguistics, and the Nasa Yuwe language.

JOANNE RAPPAPORT is a professor of anthropology and Spanish and Portuguese at Georgetown University. She has published three books in English: *Cumbe Reborn: An Andean Ethnography of History* (University of Chicago Press, 1994); *Intercultural Utopias: Public Intellectuals, Cultural Experimentation, and Ethnic Pluralism in Colombia* (Duke University Press, 2005); and *The Politics of Memory: Native Historical Interpretation in the Colombian Andes* (Cambridge University Press, 1990; Duke University Press, 1998). *Intercultural Utopias*, the product of collaborative research with indigenous activists from the Consejo Regional Indígena del Cauca, is a study of indigenous intellectuals and cultural planners in Colombia.

JAN RUS and **DIANE L. RUS** have worked in the Tzotzil-Maya speaking region of highland Chiapas since the early 1970s. In 1985 they became coordinators of the Taller Tzotzil and helped local communities organize discussion groups and publish native language books on such themes as the historical struggle for the land, labor contracting and coffee plantations, women's artisan cooperatives, the rise of urban indigenous *colonias*, and the beginning of undocumented migration to the United States. Diane is the coauthor and editor of *Bordando Milpas* (1990), the life history of a Chamula weaver, and Jan is coeditor of *Mayan Lives, Mayan Utopias: The In-*

digenous People of Chiapas and the Zapatista Rebellion (2003), and the author of the forthcoming "Still We Are Here: Historical Ethnography of the Mayas of Highland Chiapas, 1867–1994." Together, they are the coauthors of a number of articles on migration and economic change and the editors of a forthcoming bilingual compilation of Tzotzil Maya oral histories.

INDEX

Abercrombie, Neil, 42, 53n15
Abu-Lughod, Lila, 193n2
Abya Yala (mature and fertile earth), 85, 119n3
Academia de las Lenguas Mayas de Guatemala (Academy of Maya Languages of Guatemala), 205–6
Academia de Lenguas Mayas de Guatemala, 173n9
academic/activist collaboration, 5, 9. *See also* collaboration and historical writing
Acción Católica (Guatemala), 209
Acteal massacre (Chiapas, Mexico, 1997), 154–55, 174n17
activism, activists: academics and, 5, 9, 124, 131, 137, 140; antiracist, 176; assassinated in Chiapas, 164, 167; Mapuche intellectuals as, 9–10
"Agreement of Wills" ("Cession" and "Proclamation"; Rapa Nui, 1888), 56–57, 68, 73, 75n2, 76n11
agriculture, 80, 111–12, 164–65
AICO (Indigenous Authorities of Colombia), 142n8
Akaka, Daniel Kahikina, 27–28
Akaka bill, 27–29, 35–43, 48–50, 52n10, 52–53n14
Albarracín, Roberto, 118
Albert, Bruce, 128
Albó, X., 93
Alfabeto Único para el Idioma Quechua (Unified Alphabet for the Quechua Language), 120n16

Alfred, Taiaiake, 15
Allen, C., 142n5
American Indian Law Alliance, 44, 53n19
American Indian Religious Freedom Act (U.S., 1996), 50n1
Americas, the, and the Pacific, 6–7, 24, 219
Añaskitu, 120n14
Anaya, A., 93
Andean Communication and Development Center, 89, 110–12, 120n7, 120n14, 121n23
Annals of the Kaqchikels, 199–200
anthropology, 2, 122, 129. *See also* collaboration and historical writing; ethnography
antimiscegenation laws, 181, 193n3
Anzaldúa, Gloria, 17
Apology Resolution (U.S., 1993), 36, 52n13
Archipelago of Juan Fernández, 70, 72–73
ariki (chief or king), 56–57, 75n3
Arnold, D., 121n25
Asad, Talal, 125–26
Atacama desert (Bolivia and Peru), 56
Atamu Tekena, king of Rapa Nui, 56–57, 60
Aubry, Andrés, 146, 148, 171n1, 174n17, 174n20
Australia, on indigenous rights, 45
authenticity, 193n2
authority, intellectual/cultural, 4

autonomy: in Colombia, 142n5; culture and, 128–30, 140–41; via decolonization, 7; via deoccupation, 7; internationalization effects on, 22; in Rapa Nui, 71–72, 74, 78n22; sovereignty and, 142n5
Avendaño, Amado, 171n1
Aylwin, Patricio, 63–64, 70
Aymara language, 93, 95
Aymara people (Bolivia, Peru, and Chile), 55–56, 86
Ayni School (Rumi Muqu, Bolivia), 106–7

Bachelet, Michelle, 71
Balmaceda, José Manuel, 56, 75n5
Basham, Leilani, 17
Bastos, Santiago, 215
Bayonet Constitution (Hawai'i, 1887), 31
Beloved (Morrison), 192
Bible translations, 9. *See also* SIL/WBT
bilingual education, 106–8, 172n2, 173–74n13. *See also* PEBI
biotechnology, 116
blue water doctrine, 33–35
Bolaños, Graciela, 130, 141, 143n15
Bolivia: agrarian reform in, 80; indigenous peasant movement in, 83–84; indigenous vein in, 86; War of the Pacific and, 55–56
Bolivian Revolution (1952), 81
Bordando Milpas (*Ta jlok'ta chobtik*; D. L. Rus), 12, 158–61, 164
Bureau of Indian Affairs, 189
Burstein, John, 171n1
Bush, George H. W., 164–65
Bush, George W., 37

Canada, on indigenous rights, 45
Cane River Creoles of Color (Louisiana), 185–87, 189, 194n7
Caniuqueo, Sergio, 19n12

capitalism: communal organization and, 114; indigenous knowledge and, 116–18; on private property, 57; transnational markets needed for global, 102
Carmack, Robert, 200, 204
Carmen, Andrea, 53n19
Carrasco (Cochabamba, Bolivia), 88–89
Carrasco, Patricio, 76n7
Carrera, Rafael, 211
Catholic Church (Chiapas, Mexico), 171n1, 173n9
Catholic Church (Rapa Nui), 59
Catholic Church (Tahiti), 56
Cauca, Colombia, 24; community councils (*cabildos*) in, 132, 142n9; CRIC in, 10, 81–82, 124–26, 130, 133–34, 137, 142n1, 142n8, 142n9, 143n14, 143n15; cultural heterogeneity or syncretism in, 129, 138. *See also* PEBI
CELALI, 172n2
CENDA (Andean Communication and Development Center; Bolivia), 89, 110–12, 120n7, 120n14, 121n23
census, U.S. (1910), 185, 188–89, 194n12
cession of sovereignty, 77n11
Chakrabarty, Dipesh, 2, 14, 203
Chamula (Chiapas, Mexico), 8, 10, 151–53, 156, 158, 161, 174n15. *See also* Taller Tzotzil
Chanteaux, Michel, 174n17
Chapare (Bolivia), 90
Chatterjee, Partha, 214
Chávez, Adrián Inés, 200, 202
Cherokees, 192
Chiapas, Mexico, 24; activists assassinated in, 164, 167; Catholic Church in, 171n1, 173n9; critical historical narrative in, 170; economic crisis in, 10, 147, 155, 157–58, 171n4; human rights abuses in, 167–68, 174nn17–18; landowners vs. debt-laborers in, 162–63; minimum wage in, 172n7; political

248 INDEX

and cultural changes in, 147–49, 164, 170; political and economic reform in, 80–81. See also Taller Tzotzil
Chicanos' classification as white, 181
Chichén-Itzá, (Yucatán, Mexico), 199
ch'iki (socially intelligent child), 121n24
Chile: constitution of, 72–73, 75; democracy in, 63–64, 68; imperialism of, 55–56; independence of, from Spain, 55; trading by, 56; victory of, in War of the Pacific, 6–7. See also Rapa Nui
Chilean civil war (1891), 58, 75n5
Chilean National Television (TVN), 54
Chimaltenango, Guatemala, 24, 202–3, 208, 211–12
Choctaws (Mississippi), 11, 181. See also Clifton-Choctaws
Chow, Rey, 125, 141
Civil Code (Chile), 60–61
Cleveland, Grover, 31–32
Clifton-Choctaws (Louisiana), 182–91, 194n6, 194n12
Clinton, William J., 36
Cobo, José Martinez, 43
coca, 90, 92, 96–97
Cochabamba, Bolivia, 24; drought in, 88; NGOs and development projects in, 88; peasant organizations in, 10, 119n4, 120n8; political militancy in, 81–82
CODEIPA (Development Commission; Rapa Nui), 64–66, 68
coffee market, 164–65
coffee workers, 149–51, 165
Cojtí Cuxil, Demetrio, 197, 200
Coleman, Arica, 181
collaboration: via *diálogo de saberes* (exchange of epistemologies), 8, 130; engagé, 9; *minga* (project of collective work for collective benefit), 8, 82–83, 131–32; overview of, 80–84; respect for difference and the integrity of cultures as underlying, 17; tension/negotiation in, 10, 17, 133; truth telling and, in research methodologies, 4
collaboration and historical writing, 219; of academics and activists, 5, 9, 124, 131, 137, 140; collaborative theorizing and, 130–33, 142nn7–8, 143n10; community control, interculturalism, cosmovision, and, 137–40; cotheorizing, 131–32; culture and political autonomy and, 128–30, 140–41; indigenous theory, and definition/overview of, 122–24, 127, 131, 142n2; interculturalism and, 126–27, 137–39, 141, 143n11; minority theorizing, 129; PEBI's history, 124, 133–37, 141, 143n11, 143n15; theorizing and definition of, 220; translating theory, 124–26
Colla people (Argentina, Bolivia, and Chile), 55–56
Colombia: academics in, 143n10; constitution of 1991 of, 83, 124–26, 128, 131–32; Free Trade Area of the Americas accepted by, 127; national integration in, 81; Native autonomy in, 142n5
colonialism: as central to indigenous peoples' history, 7; colonies defined under international law, 43; colonization vs. occupation and, 34; definition of, 197; internal colonialism, 12, 16, 18n4, 33, 43, 49, 197, 201, 218n19; language, law, and archives as instruments of, 3; racial hierarchy established via, 198, 217n2. See also decolonization
Comalapa (Chimaltenango, Guatemala), 202–3, 217n7
Comité Catholique Contre la Faim et Pour le Dévellopement (France), 171n1
Commerce Clause (U.S. Constitution), 39
Commission on Historic Truth and New Relationship with Indigenous Peoples (Rapa Nui), 68–69

INDEX 249

communal organization, 111–14, 117–18
community control, 137–38
CONADI (National Corporation for Indigenous Development; Chile), 63, 66, 70, 73, 77n16
conceptual prison, 180, 193n2
concientización (consciousness raising or empowerment), 144
Congreso Internacional de Mayistas (1989), 172n7, 172n9
Conosur Ñawpagman. See PCÑ
conquest, sovereignty via, 77n11
Consejo de Ancianos del Fondo de Desarrollo Indígena de Guatemala (Council of Elders of the Indigenous Development Fund of Guatemala), 209
Consejo de Organizaciones Mayas en Guatemala, 205
Consejo Regional Indígena del Cauca. See CRIC
Coordinación de Organizaciones del Pueblo Maya de Guatemala, 205
cosmovision, 137–39, 199
Coushattas (Louisiana), 189
Creoles (*criollos*; Guatemala), 203–4, 211–13, 217n8
CRIC (Consejo Regional Indígena del Cauca), 10, 81–82, 124–26, 130, 133–34, 137, 142n1, 142n8, 142n9, 143n14, 143n15. *See also* PEBI
Cruikshank, Julie, 14
CSUTCB (United Confederation of Bolivian Workers and Peasants), 89, 114
culture: colonizer vs. colonized, 1–2; continuity of, 218n21; minority forms of, 129; political autonomy and, 128–30, 140–41; revival of, 127
Çxayu'çe, 136, 143n13

debt-laborers, 162–63
Decades of Indigenous Peoples (UN; 1990–2000, 2000–2010), 22

Declaration on the Granting of Independence to Colonial Countries and Peoples—Resolution 1514 (UN, 1960), 33–34, 43–44, 51n5
Declaration on the Rights of Indigenous Peoples (UN; 2007), 22, 28, 43–48, 53n19
Declaration regarding Non-Self-Governing Peoples (UN, 1945), 43
decolonization, 25; to combat racism, 192–93; definition and scope of, 28; deoccupation vs., 23, 28–29; racial and evolutionary bases of colonial power and, 2; violence engendered by, 17
decolonizing methodologies, 6, 176, 219–20
Decolonizing Methodologies (Smith), 192–93, 193n1
Defensoría de la Mujer Indígena (Indigenous Women's Defense Office; Guatemala), 205–6
Deloria, Vine, Jr., 193n2
Delsing, Riet, 7, 23
democracy, 123, 126–27
Denetdale, Jennifer, 17
deoccupation: arguments for, 35, 46; decolonization vs., 23, 28–29; definition and scope of, 28; internal colonialism denied by, 49; international laws of occupation and, 34
Departmental Peasant Federation (Cochabamba, Bolivia), 89
Department of Hawaiian Home Lands, 36–37
Development Commission (CODEIPA; Rapa Nui), 64–66, 68
diálogo de saberes (exchange of epistemologies), 8, 130
Dindicué, Benjamín, 133–34
Dole, Sanford Ballard, 32
double consciousness (second-sight), 122–23, 141–42n1

Duarte, Carlota, 173n8
Du Bois, W. E. B., 122, 129, 141n1
Duquesne, Isabelle, 173–74n13

Easter Island. *See* Rapa Nui
East Timor, 34
Edmunds, Petero, 72
education: bilingual, 106–8, 127, 172n2; intercultural, 127; for Maya, 201–2, 206, 212, 216; social change and, 127. *See also* PEBI
Education Reform (Bolivia), 115, 121n25
EIB (Educación Intercultural Bilingüe project; Intercultural Bilingual Education; Bolivia), 107–8
Ejército Zapatista de Liberación Nacional (EZLN; Chiapas), 84, 167, 174n17
El Mizqueño, 88, 93
El Totoreño, 88, 93
enganche (contract labor), 149
Ernantes, Chep (José González Hernández), 148, 153, 173–74n13
Esquit, Edgar, 11–12, 176–77
ethnicity and progress, 211
ethnic movements, 122, 129–30
ethnic organizations, 124, 127–28, 137
ethnic studies, U.S., 180
ethnography: autoethnography vs., 141; of particular, 193n2; perspective and methodology in, 24–25, 125–26; as translation, 125–26. *See also* anthropology
Eurocentrism, 102
European Community, 171n1
exclusion, forms of, 85
Explora hotels, 65
EZLN (Ejército Zapatista de Liberación Nacional; Chiapas), 84, 167, 174n17

Fanon, Frantz, 163
feminist movement/research, 123–24

Fermín, Tata, 118–19
Field, L., 142n5
Fischer, E., 218n21
Five Civilized Tribes (Oklahoma), 181–82
Foley, Neil, 194n9
FOMMA (Fortaleza de la Mujer Maya), 173n8
Fondo Indígena (Indigenous Fund; Guatemala), 205–6
Fondo Nacional de Artesanías (FONART; Mexico), 159
Forbes, Jack, 189
forests, communal ownership of, 114
Fortaleza de la Mujer Maya (FOMMA), 173n8
free trade. *See* trade agreements
Free Trade Area of the Americas, 127
Freire, Paulo, 144
Frichner, Tonya Gonnella, 53n19
Friends of Easter Island (Chile), 78n19
frontier as painful or uncomfortable, 17

Garcés V., Fernando, 10–11, 81–83
gender and power relations, 12, 19n7. *See also* women, indigenous
Gilroy, Paul, 129
globalization, 82–83, 116, 176–77, 214, 218n19, 220
Gómez Vargas, J. H., 78n22
Grandin, Greg, 211, 217n2
Great Depression, 80
green revolution, 112, 117
Grube, Nikolai, 198–99
Guambiano History Committee (Colombia), 128
Guambiano peoples (Colombia), 81
Guatemala: colonialism in, and Maya movement, 197–98; four peoples of (Maya, Garífuna, Xinka, and ladino), 205, 213, 218n11; ladino control of, 197; mining in, 206; power relations of, 217n9. *See also* Maya

INDEX 251

Guatemalan civil war (1962–96), 176
Guzmán, Salvador, 153, 159, 164, 168–69
Guzmán, Soledad, 120n13
Guzmán Böckler, Carlos, 200

Hague Convention IV (1907), 34
Hale, Charles R., 16–17
Hanga Roa (Rapa Nui), 59–60, 62, 67–68
Harrison, Benjamin, 31
Hawai'i, 24, 43–45, 47–50; autonomy movement in, 7; capitalism and Christianity's effects on, 31; independence movement in, 27–28, 34–38; kingdom restoration movement in, 34–35, 51n7; land claims in, 32–33, 37–38, 41–42, 46, 53n14; Mahele land division (1848), 30–31, 46; occupied state of, 34–35; recognition of, as independent kingdom, 7, 23, 28–30, 39, 51n2; Republic of, 32, 52n13; secession vs. independence of, 46; self-government and self-determination by, 27, 33–37, 40, 46, 51n3; sovereignty claim of, under international law, 28–29, 34, 38–39; statehood of, 29, 33–36, 51n3, 52n13; territorial integrity of, 46; U.S. colonization and annexation of, 6, 23, 28–35, 46, 52n13; use-rights concessions by, 6; U.S. militarism in, 40–41; U.S. treaties with, 29–30; white foreign population in, 30–31. *See also* Kanaka Maoli; Native Hawaiian Government Reorganization Act; *State of Hawaii v. Office of Hawaiian Affairs*
Hawaiian Independence Action Alliance, 28
Hawai'i Institute for Human Rights, 28
Henderson, Timothy, *Mexico Reader*, 168
Herbert, Jean-Loup, 200
Hernández, Domingo, 215
Hernández, José González (Chep Ernantes), 148, 153, 173–74n13

Hill, Robert M., 200
Hill, Roberta, 6
Historia de un pueblo evangelista (R. Pérez), 174n13
historical writing. *See* collaboration and historical writing
HONI (Hui o Na Ike), 28
Honolulu Rifles, 31
Hotel Hanga Roa (Rapa Nui), 72
Hotus, Alberto, 77n14, 78n24
Hotus, Carolina, 71
Hui Aloha 'Aina and Hui Kalai 'Aina nationalist groups, 32
Hui Pu (Hawai'i), 28

I, Rigoberta (Menchú), 145
Ibañez, Pedro, 65
Identity and Rights of the Indigenous Peoples Accord (Guatemala, 1995), 205
ILO Convention 169 (International Labor Organization; 1989), 22, 206
INAREMAC (Instituto de Asesoría Antropológica para la Región Maya, A.C.), 159, 167–68, 171n1, 173–74n13, 174n17
Indian Gaming Regulatory Act (U.S., 1988), 53n14
Indian Reorganization Act (U.S., 1934), 52n10
Indians' antiblack racism (southern United States), 188; Anglo-American racist and colonialist origins of, 186–87; decolonization to combat, 192–93; Indian identity/denials of black ancestry and, 183–87, 189–91, 194n12; overview and background of, 179–82; racial formation and, 181, 192–93, 194n9, 195n22; regulating racial categories and, 186–93; research in Louisiana Indian communities, 182–86, 194n6; research methodologies for studying, 179–80, 184–85, 191–93,

193n1, 193n2; tradition of, 181–82, 184; Virginia antimiscegenation laws and, 181, 193n3; white supremacy and, 179, 186–87, 191–93, 194n8
Indian Schedules (population), 188
Indian studies, 180
Indian Trade and Intercourse Act (U.S.), 53n14
Indigenous Authorities of Colombia (AICO), 142n8
Indigenous Caucus (UN and OAS), 47
indigenous identity: definitions of, 12; double consciousness about, 142n1; Indian, and denials of black ancestry, 183–87, 189–91, 194n12; Rapanui, 23, 54–55, 67–68, 74–75
indigenous organizations, 83, 90, 119n3, 122–24, 127–31, 133, 162, 177. *See also under names of individual organizations*
"Indigenous Politics: From Native New England and Beyond," 53n19
indigenous rights: Convention 169 (International Labor Organization) on, 206; Declaration on the Rights of Indigenous Peoples, 22, 28, 43–48; under international law, vs. states' rights, 29; Native American rights and privileges extended to Kanaka Maoli, 27, 50–51n1; of peoples vs. people, 44, 48; preexisting human rights, 43; self-determination, 33–34, 43–48, 51n5; sovereignty and, 46–47; territorial integrity and, 46–47
indigenous sovereignty, 4
indigenous universities, 124, 142n2
indio permitido (permissible Indian), 16–17
INEA (Instituto Nacional de Educación Adulta), 152–53, 173n9
INI (Instituto Nacional Indigenista; Mexico), 152, 172n2, 172–73n7

inscription, 4
inside vs. outside, 4, 129–30
Instituto de Asesoría Antropológica para la Región Maya, A.C. *See* INAREMAC
Instituto de Estudios Indígenas of the Universidad Autónoma de Chiapas, 172n2
Instituto Nacional Indigenista (INI; Mexico), 152, 172n2, 172–73n7
integrationism, 2, 61–66
intellectual property rights, 116–17
interculturalism, 126–27, 137–39, 141, 143n11, 205
International Coffee Agreement, 164–65
International Forum of Indigenous Peoples (FIPAU), 69
International Indian Treaty Council, 53n19
intertextuality, 10–11, 83, 91–92

Jacobs Research Fund (Bellingham, Wash.), 171n1
Jaima, 93
Jena Choctaws (Louisiana), 182, 189–90
Johnson, M., 98
Jones, Delmos, 122
Joseph, Gilbert, *Mexico Reader*, 168
Juan, the Chamula (Pozas), 172n5

kainga (ancestral lands), 58, 60, 65, 73, 75n4
Kalakaua, king of Hawai'i, 31
Ka Lei Maile Ali'i Hawaiian Civic Club, 28
Kamehameha III, king of Hawai'i, 30
Kanaka Maoli (indigenous Hawaiians): Akaka bill's impact on, 42–43; assimilationist policies imposed on, 35; decolonization eligibility of, 34, 42–43; federal recognition for, 7, 28, 48; Hawaiians defined, 51n1; historical struggle of, 22–23; Hui Aloha

INDEX 253

Kanaka Maoli (*continued*)
'Aina and Hui Kalai 'Aina nationalist groups among, 32; international law strategies of, 28; *kupuna* (elders) and *kumu* (educators), 49; as a minority in Hawai'i, 49; Native American rights and privileges extended to, 27, 50–51n1; Native Hawaiian Government Reorganization Act, 27–29, 35–43, 48, 52–53n14; oppression and subordination of, by white supremacists, 35, 49; "Urgent Open Letter to U.S. President Barack Obama," 49–50; U.S. apology to, 36, 51–52n8, 52n13; voting by, 31, 33, 36, 51n3. *See also* Hawai'i
Ka Pakaukau, 28, 34
Kaqchikels, 177, 199–200, 202–3, 206, 218n14
Katarismo, 86
Kauanui, J. Kehaulani, 5, 7, 22–23, 80
K'iche language and people, 177, 200, 202–4, 209–12, 217n10, 218n16
Kimsa Pacha Ara Mboapi, 93
Kipaltik collective (Chiapas, Mexico), 159–66
Klopotek, Brian, 5–6, 11–12, 176–77
knowledge: coproduction of, 146; geopolitics of, 102–3, 108; indigenous, and capitalism, 116–18; *jawamanta yachay* (knowledge from abroad), 118; local vs. universal, 102–3; modern, as essentialist/binary, 102; neocolonial domination and, 116; peasant, technology's appropriation of, 112, 116–17; Quechua peasant vs. Western urban, 103–5; racial/evolutionary bases of colonial power as underlying construction of, 2; scientific, primacy of, 116–17. *See also* peasant knowledge
Koani Foundation, 28
Komes, Maruch (María Gómez), 12, 158–62, 164–66

Komike Tribunal, 28, 34
Kopenawa, Davi, 128
Ko Tu'u Aro Kote Mata Nui (Rapa Nui), 58
Ko Tu'u Hotu Iti Mata Iti (Rapa Nui), 58
Koyaso Panchin, Marian, 156–57
Kurus, Xalid. *See* Rus, Jan
Kurus, Tina. *See* Rus, Diane L.
Kusman, Xalik (Salvador Guzmán; Mariano Peres Tsu), 153, 159, 164, 168–69

labor, intellectual, 132
La Castalia, 172n2
ladinos (Hispanicized people; non-Indians), 12, 19n5, 197, 202–4, 211–13, 217n1
Lagos, Ricardo, 68
Lakoff, G., 98
Lâm, Maivân Clech, 46
Lame, Manuel Quintín, 139; *Los pensamientos del indio que se educó dentro de las selvas colombianas*, 143n14
language: diglottic, 91, 115, 120n10; neologisms in, 92, 115–16, 125; power and empowerment and, 3, 11, 13; subalternized indigenous, 86–87, 108. *See also* Quechua language and knowledge; Taller Tzotzil
La Prensa, 93
Latin America: class-based social and political movements in, 16, 80; indigenous intellectuals in, 15, 19n12; indigenous movements in, 15–16; indigenous peoples of, vs. United States, 80; national-popular states' emergence in, 80–81. *See also under names of specific indigenous movements*
Laughlin, Miriam, 173n8
Laughlin, Robert M., 172n2
Lenkersdorf, Carlos, 172n2
Lenkersdorf, Gudrun, 172n2

Levil, Rodrigo, 19n12
Ley Indígena (Indigenous Law; Chile, 1990), 63–66, 68, 74
Ley Pascua (Easter Law; Chile, 1966), 61–63, 67–68, 74
Ley Pinochet (Pinochet Law; Chile, 1979), 62–64, 74
Libro de registros de propiedades llevado por la Armada de Chile, Isla de Pascua (Chilean navy), 59–60
Lili'uokalani, queen of Hawai'i, 31–32, 52n13
literacidad, 119n1
Living Nation, 28
llawar (blood), 98, 101
Lomnitz-Adler, Claudio, 213
López Pérez, Antonio, 148
Los Acuerdos de San Andrés, 174n20
Los Chorros (Chenalhó, Chiapas, Mexico), 154, 157, 173n11
Los pensamientos del indio que se educó dentro de las selvas colombianas (Lame), 143n14
Louisiana, 24. *See also* Indians' antiblack racism
Louisiana Inter-Tribal Council (Clifton), 189–90
Loving v. Virginia, 181
Lumbees (North Carolina), 181
Luykx, A., 115

majï (labor), 132
maki (hand), 98, 100
Mam language, 217n10
MANA (Movement for Aloha No Ka 'Aina), 28
Mapuche (Chile), 9–10, 55
Marimán, Pablo, 19n12
Maya: ancestors remembered by, 204, 209–10; domination of, 217n2; education for, 201–2, 206, 212, 216; exclusion of, 208, 217n9; government support of, 205–6; in Guatemalan civil war, 176; historiography and archeology of, 203–4, 217n9; ladinos and, 12, 202, 204, 211–13; as merchants, 217n6; perceived as backward, 204, 208; political transitions challenged by, 84; repression of, 202; struggle for self-determination by, 176, 215; subsistence economy of, 202; unified vs. self-created official history of, 11; women, 211; women's weaving and embroidering cooperative, 12; Yucatekan and Guatemalan, 198–99
Maya movement, 196–217; alternative histories and present, 213–17, 218n20; colonialism in Guatemala and, 197–98; definition of Maya and Mayanists, 197; educated/professional vs. uneducated Maya, 202–3, 217n6; elite- and state-constructed multiculturalism and, 201, 205–8, 210, 213–16; elites' identification with liberal state ideology, 203; elites' redefining of identities and power relations, 196–97, 208–13, 218n21; elites' version of history, 202–5; guerrilla groups, 203; imagining new histories, 198–201; Maya continuity vs. conquest and assimilation, 199–200; Maya demand for rights, 211–13; Maya protests and repression and, 206, 212, 215, 218n14; Maya spirituality, 205, 209, 216; memories' role in, 214; overview and background of, 177, 196–98; patriarchy and, 196, 211, 215–16; political parties and, 203; professionals' role in, 203, 210, 217n7; Protestant and Catholic visions and, 196, 203, 216; workshops on ancient writing and, 198–99
McKinley, William, 32
Memorias, Balances, Inventarios y Registro de Propiedades (Chilean navy), 59

Menchú, Rigoberta: *I, Rigoberta*, 145
Merrell, James, 181
mestizos (Hispanicized people), 19n5, 126, 162, 167
Mexican Revolution (1910), 80–81, 148, 162, 164
Mexico: agrarian reform in, 80, 164–65; economic crisis in, 10, 144, 147, 155, 157–58, 171n4; Salinas's reforms in, 164–65
Mexico Reader (Joseph and Henderson), 168
Mignolo, Walter, 102, 217n2, 218n19
Mihesuah, Devon, 2, 15
Miles, Tiya, 195n19; *Ties that Bind: The Story of an Afro-Cherokee Family in Slavery and Freedom*, 192
Millalén, José, 19n12
Millamán, Rosamel, 16–17
Miñana, Carlos, 142n7
minga (project of collective work for collective benefit), 8, 82–83, 131–32
Ministry of Education (Guatemala), 206
Mizque (Cochabamba, Bolivia), 88–89, 106
Mizque Provincial Trade Union (Cochabamba, Bolivia), 89
Mobile Unit for Rural Patrolling (Bolivia), 92
Montejo, Víctor, 2, 19n6, 200, 202
Morales, Evo, 81–84, 120n8
Morrison, Toni, 194n9; *Beloved*, 192
Mosoco, Colombia, 125, 131–32
Movement toward Socialism (MAS; Bolivia), 89, 120n8
Movimiento Al Socialismo, 81–83
Moyapampa Union (Cochabamba, Bolivia), 89
Moyopampa Agricultural Union (Totora, Carrasco, Bolivia), 88
mulattoes, 181, 184–85, 188–89, 194n12
multiculturalism: in Guatemala, 201,
205–8, 210, 213–16; interculturalism vs., 126–27; neoliberalism and, 176, 207
Muyolema (also Muyulema), Armando, 15, 119n3

NAFTA (North American Free Trade Agreement), 116–17, 164–65
najtir (ancient), 217n10
Nā Pua No'eau (Center for Gifted and Talented Native Hawaiian Children), 37
Narrating Native Histories conference (University of Wisconsin, Madison, 2005), 1–5, 219
Narrating Native Histories series, 2–4
Nasa peoples (Colombia), 8, 81, 126
Nasa Yuwe language: alphabet and orthography for, 143n13; board game and, 136; translating the Colombian Constitution into, 125–26, 128, 131–32
National Corporation for Indigenous Development, 63, 66, 70, 73, 77n16
National Historic Preservation Act (U.S., 1966), 50n1
National Institute for Adult Education (Instituto Nacional de Educación Adulta; INEA), 152, 173n9
National Museum of the American Indian Act (U.S., 1989, amended 1996), 50n1
Native American Graves Protection and Repatriation Act (U.S., 1990), 50n1
Native American Languages Act (U.S., 1990), 50n1
Native American Programs Act (U.S., 1974), 50–51n1
Native Americans: Akaka bill's impact on, 52–53n14; antiblack sensibilities among, 11–12; federal classification and recognition of, 187–91, 194n12, 194n14; land held in trust for, 53n14;

tribal identities of, 181; whites and, 180–81. *See also* Choctaws; Indians' antiblack racism
Native and indigenous movements, 2, 4, 123, 128
Native Hawaiian Bar Association (NHBA), 42, 53n15
Native Hawaiian Education Act (U.S., 2004), 51n1
Native Hawaiian Government Reorganization Act (Akaka bill; U.S., 2009), 27–29, 35–43, 48–50, 52n10, 52–53n14
Native Hawaiian Health Care Act (U.S., 1988), 51n1
Native Hawaiian Interagency (U.S.), 42
Native intellectuals in the academy, 6, 13, 15
Native peoples' intellectual agency, 2–3
nature, 101, 121n21
Navajo Nation, 45
neoliberalism, 176, 207
Newlands Resolution (U.S., 1898), 32, 52n13
New Zealand, on indigenous rights, 45
NFIP—Hawai'i, 28
NHBA (Native Hawaiian Bar Association), 42, 53n15
Nimatuj, Irma Alicia, 211
North American Free Trade Agreement (NAFTA), 116–17, 164–65
North and South, 219; differences in indigenous intellectuals' place, 4, 15, 17, 19n12; historical differences between, 4, 15; North-centrism, 102
"not-yet" principle of historical evolution, 2

Obama, Barack, 37, 49
objectivity in writing, 95, 121n19
occupation, 34, 76n11
Office of Hawaiian Affairs, 36–37, 51–52n8, 52n13

'Ohana Koa, 28
ojtxe (remote past), 217n10
Omi, M., 195n22
one-drop rule, 11–12, 189
oral history/tradition, 13–14. *See also* Quechua yachay
orality vs. textuality, 3, 10, 94–95, 139
Organic Act (U.S., 1900), 32–33
Organization of American States (OAS), 47

pacha (space and time in which we are located), 87, 119n5
Panama Canal, 56
pan-Mayanist movement. *See* Maya movement
Papa Ola Lokahi (Native Hawaiian Healthcare), 37
Pari, A., 121n21
Partido Revolucionario Institucional (PRI; Mexico), 154, 165–66
Partido Socialista de los Trabajadores (PST; Mexico), 154–55
Past, Ámbar, 173n8
Pate, Timoteo, 76n6
patriarchy, 196, 211, 215–16
Paz, Sarela, 86
PCÑ (*Conosur Ñawpagman*): articles for, 120n9; background on, 88–90, 120nn7–9; bimonthly publication of, 90; on communal organization, 112–13, 117; distribution and sale of, 10, 89–90; on education, 106–8; Garcés's collaboration with, 81, 118; meaning of *Ñawpagman*, 119n1; metaphors and similes in, 99–102; oral presence in, 94–97; on patents and technology that appropriate peasant knowledge, 112; on peasant mobilizations (1992), 121n20; on plagues, 111; politics of written orality and, 90–93, 95; Quechua in, 10–11, 85, 91–94; on

PCÑ (continued)
Quechua peasant vs. Western urban knowledge, 103–5; quotations in, 96–97; researching writing via, 115–16; Spanish in, 91–94; stories in, concluding, 94, 97; subjects addressed in, 90, 103; on weather prediction, 110–12. See also Quechua yachay
Peace Camps (Mexico), 174n14
peasant, meanings of, 85–86
peasant knowledge: anthropomorphization of, 101–2; modern technology vs., 88, 110–12, 117, 121n23; nature as teaching, 121n21
peasant organizations in Cochabamba, 10, 119n4, 120n8
PEBI (Bilingual and Intercultural Education Program; Colombia): history of, 124, 133–37, 141, 143n11, 143n15; influence and success of, 134; objectives of, 134; overview of, 82; political program of, 134–35, 137
Peres Tsu, Mariano, 153, 159, 164, 168–69
Pérez, Manuel, Salvador, and Pedro, 168
Pérez, Ricardo, *Historia de un pueblo evangelista*, 174n13
Peru in War of the Pacific, 55–56
petroglyphs, 128
Pewewardy, Cornel, 191
Pinochet, Augusto, 62
place, defense of, 102
plagues, 111
pluralism, 126–27, 134
política de estado, 70, 78n20
popular movements, 129
Pop Wuj (Popol Vuh), 200
Portales Center (Simón Patiño Foundation; Bolivia), 88
Portelli, Alessandro, 14
Pozas, Ricardo, *Juan, the Chamula*, 172n5
prescription, sovereignty via, 76–77n11
Presencia, 93

PRI (Partido Revolucionario Institucional; Mexico), 154, 165–66
Programa Nacional de Solidaridad (National Solidarity Program; PRONASOL; Mexico), 165–66
progress, 1–2, 211
Pro-Kanaka Maoli Independence Working Group, 28, 34
PRONASOL (Programa Nacional de Solidaridad; Mexico), 165–66
Protestants vs. traditionalists, 151–52, 155–57
Proyecto Fotográfico Maya, 173n8
PST (Partido Socialista de los Trabajadores; Mexico), 154–55

Quechua language and knowledge, 85, 87–90, 95–100, 118–19, 120n13; alphabet, 120n16; Bolivian linguistic policy toward, 115; colonial subalternization of, 86; discrimination against, 108–9; liberation via, 109; in Movimiento Al Socialismo, 82–83; neologisms in, 115–16; in newspapers, 93, 120n14; normalization of, 94, 114–15, 120n16; orality as basis of, 120n17; pan-Andean unification of, 115; on radio, 93; revitalization of, 11, 115; Spanish and, 10–11, 91–93, 109, 115; written, promotion of, 114–15, 121n25; *yachayniyku* (politics of Quechua knowledge), 101–14, 117. See also PCÑ; Quechua yachay
Quechua people (Peru, Ecuador, Bolivia, Chile, and Argentina), 55–56, 81, 86
Quechua yachay: community and cultural roots of, 103, 110–14, 117–18, 121n24; on development/modernization, 111–12; forms of local knowledge in, vs. Western categories, 83; knowledge and territoriality and, 116–18; language and, 103, 108–10; orality and meanings of, 86–87; in school

and community, 103, 105–8; subjects related with, 103; value of, 103–5
Quetzaltenango (Guatemala), 211

Racancoj, Víctor, 200
racial formation, 181, 192–93, 194n9, 195n22
racism: antimiscegenation laws, 181, 193n3; decolonization to combat, 192–93; one-drop rule, 11–12, 189; segregation and oppression of blacks, 187; "speaking secrets" about, 176–77; struggle against, 118; U.S. racial atmosphere and, 141–42n1; white privilege and, 2, 11–12; white supremacy and, 35, 49, 179, 186–87, 191–93, 194n8. *See also* Indians' antiblack racism
Radio Educación (Mexico), 159
Raibmon, Paige, 193n2
Ramos Pacho, Abelardo, 8, 10–11, 17, 82–83, 130, 141, 142n3, 143n10. *See also* collaboration and historical writing
Rapa Nui (Easter Island), 24; "Agreement of Wills," 56–57, 68, 73, 75n2, 76n11; airport in, 67; autonomy of, prospects for, 71–72, 74, 78n22; casino debate in, 65–66; Chilean annexation of, 6, 54, 56–57, 60, 66; Chilean consolidation of hold on, 59–60; Chilean evolution/imperialism and, 23; Chilean inscription of (1933), 60–61, 76–77nn10–12; Chilean naval presence in, 58–60, 66–67, 76n7, 76n9; clan system and leaders of, 56–59, 70–71, 74, 75n3, 76n9; collective landownership proposal in, 72, 78n23; colonialism to self-determination for, path of, 66–73; Commission on Historic Truth and New Relationship with Indigenous Peoples in, 68–69; *Compañía* in, 58–61, 67; Council of Elders in, 62, 64, 66, 69, 72, 77n14, 77n16, 78n24; Development Commission (CODEIPA) for, 64–66, 68; diseases introduced onto, 58–59; early Chilean colonization, 57–61, 66; foreign investments in, 65; history of, 55–57; identity/memory in, revitalization and recovery of, 23; immigration to, 78n23; independence for, 7–8; integrationism in, 57, 62–64, 73–74; kinship in, 7; land vs. territory in, 56–57, 59; Ley Indígena (1990) in, 63–66, 68, 74; Ley Pascua (1966) in, 61–63, 67–68, 74; Ley Pinochet (1979) in, 62–64, 74; millennium celebration on, 54; nonislanders, influx of, 67; partitioning of, 58; private property/land titles vs. communal/ancestral lands in, 57–65, 67–71, 73–74, 75n4, 75–76n6, 76n8, 77n14; Rapanui cultural identity, 54–55, 67–68, 74–75; Rapanui leaders and Chilean party politics, 64, 77nn16–17; Rapanui Parliament, 69, 73; Rapanui resistance to Chilean rule, 54–55, 69, 74, 76n8; Rapanui's Chilean citizenship, 61, 67; real estate market in, 65; sheep farming on, 58, 60, 66, 76n9; slave raids on, 58–59; Special Territory status of, 70–73, 78n24; stone statues (*moai*) on, 54; use-rights concessions by, 6
Rapanui National Park, 77n12
Rapanui University, 66
Rappaport, Joanne, 8–11, 82–83, 130, 141. *See also* collaboration and historical writing
Rapu, Mike, 65
Rapu Haoa, Alfonso, 78n19
Raqaypampa (Cochabamba, Bolivia), 88, 106, 110, 112, 118, 120n7
Reciprocity Treaty (1875), 30
research subjects, identification of, 163, 173n12
Retière, Alain, 159

Reuque, Isolde, 12, 19n7
revolutionary violence, 163
Rice v. Cayetano (U.S. Supreme Court), 36
rights-based discourse, 16–17
Riroroko, Simeon, 76n6
Rivera Cusicanqui, Silvia, 16–17
Rodríguez, Carlos, 171n1
Rodríguez, Demetrio, 197, 200
Romero, R., 121n24
Ross, Elizabeth, 173–74n13
Rountree, Helen, 181
Ruiz, Samuel, 171n1, 174n17
Rus, Diane L.: legitimacy in the Tzotzil community, 8–9; Taller Tzotzil, overview of, 8–10, 82–83; Tzotzil names of, 8–9, 153, 173n10; work of, on *Ta jlok'ta chobtik (Bordando Milpas)*, 12, 158–61, 164. *See also* Taller Tzotzil
Rus, Jan: legitimacy in the Tzotzil community, 8–9; Taller Tzotzil, overview of, 8–10, 82–83; Tzotzil names of, 8–9, 153, 173n10. *See also* Taller Tzotzil

Salinas de Gortari, Carlos, 164–66
Salomon, Frank, 9
San Andrés Peace Accords (1996), 174n17, 174n20
San Cristóbal de las Casas (Chiapas, Mexico), 10, 155–56
San José de Mizque Cooperative (Cochabamba, Bolivia), 88
saqra (cognitively intelligent children), 121n24
Saunt, Claudio, 187
Schele, Linda, 198–99
seeds, 95, 111–12
Settlers for Hawaiian Independence, 28
shamans, 128, 132; cosmovision and, 137–39, 199
Sieder, Rachel, 207
Silva, Noenoe, 12–13, 15, 32, 219

SIL/WBT (Summer Institute of Linguistics/Wycliffe Bible Translators), 152, 172n2, 172–73n7, 173n9
Simón Patiño Foundation (Bolivia), 88
sistematización, 143n15
Smith, Linda Tuhiwai, 2, 14–15, 18n2, 176; *Decolonizing Methodologies*, 192–93, 193n1
Sna Jtz'ibajom, 172n2
Sojom, Jacinto Arias, 152–53, 172n2
solidarity, 170
sovereignty: autonomy and, 142n5; Hawaiian, 28–29, 34, 38–39; indigenous rights and, 46–47; over territories, 76–77n11; territory and, 128
Spanish: in PCÑ, 91–94; Quechua and, 10–11, 91–93, 109, 115
Spanish-American War (1898), 6–7
Special Committee of 24 on Decolonization (UN), 51n5
spiral motif, 128, 136
Spiritual Nation of Kā—Hui Ea Council of Sovereigns, 28
State of Hawaii v. Office of Hawaiian Affairs (U.S. Supreme Court), 38, 51–52n8, 52n13
Stevens, John L., 31–32
storytelling traditions' importance, 4
Street, B., 95
struggle, 13, 22–23, 119n3
Suazo, Siles, 120n16
Subercaseaux, Bernardo, 75n5
Summer Institute of Linguistics/Wycliffe Bible Translators. *See* SIL/WBT
sunqu (heart), 98–100

Tademy, Lalita, 194n7
Tahiti, 56
Ta jlok'ta chobtik (Bordando Milpas; D. L. Rus), 158–61, 164
Taller Leñateros, 172n2, 173n8
Taller Tzotzil (Chiapas, Mexico): author-

ship of, 145, 153, 156–57, 160, 163–64, 169; bilingual editions of, 151–52, 154, 157, 160; Chiapas in mid-1980s, 147–49; community collaborations, 157–64; dialect choice for, 152–53; distribution and sale of publications, 150, 155–56, 159–60, 172–73n7; documenting narratives, 149–53; economic crisis and, 10, 144, 147, 155, 157–58; editing of, 161–63; editors' introductions, 152; funding for, 171n1; goals of, 10; monolingual vs. bilingual publication, 151–52; orthography of, 152, 173n9; overview and background of, 8–10, 82–83, 144–47, 171–72nn1–2; photographs in, 153, 155; political and cultural factions and, 153–57, 173n11; reflections on, 170–71; tape cassettes considered for, 172n6; transitions and, 164–66; translation of, 160–61; voices, 150; women's participation in, 150–51; Zapatista uprising's effects on, 10, 83, 167–69

Taller Tzotzil, publications of: *Abtel ta Pinka*, 149–57, 160, 173n7; *Buch'u Lasmeltzan Jobel?* 155–58; "Conversaciones ininterrumpidas," 168; *Historia de un pueblo evangelista*, 174n13; *Ja' k'u x'elan ta jpojbatik ta ilbajinel yu'un jkaxlanetik*, 148; *Jchi'iltak ta Slumal Kalifornya*, 168–69; *K'alal ich'ay mosoal*, 148; *Kipaltik: K'u cha'al lajmankutik jpinkakutik*, 159–64; *Lo'il yu'un Kuskat*, 151–52, 156; "Los primeros meses de los zapatistas," 168–69, 174n19; San Cristóbal shantytowns' history (in progress), 169; *Slo'il ch'vo' kumpareil*, 166, 173–74n13; *Ta jlok'ta chobtik ta ku'il* (*Bordando Milpas*), 12, 158–62, 164, 166; "A Tzotzil Chronicle of the Zapatista Uprising," 168

Task Force on Native Hawaiian Issues, 36

Teave, Daniel María, 75–76n6

technology, modern: biotechnology, 116; from green revolution, 112; peasant knowledge vs., 88, 110–12, 117, 121n23

Tepano, Juan, 76n9

territory: integrity of, and indigenous rights, 46–47; land vs., 56–57, 59, 128; sovereignty and, 128; space and, 128

testimonio, 160, 172n5. *See also* Taller Tzotzil

theorization. *See under* collaboration and historical writing

Thiong'o, Ngugi wa, 192

Tiawuanaku manifesto (Bolivia, 1973), 86

Ties that Bind: The Story of an Afro-Cherokee Family in Slavery and Freedom (Miles), 192

Titicachi (Peru), 121n24

Toro, Pedro Pablo, 57–58, 73

Toro Hurtado, Policarpo, 56–57

Totora (Cochabamba, Bolivia), 88–89

trade agreements, 116–17, 127, 164–65, 214

traditional authority, 142n9

transformist hegemony, 206

translation, 4

translation vs. writing/inscription, 8–9. *See also* Taller Tzotzil

trees, communal ownership of, 114

Tribal Nations policy (U.S.), 27

tribal vs. foreign nations, 39–40

truth, rules of evidence for, 14

Tuki, Rafael ("Rinko"), 73

Tunica-Biloxi Tribe (Mississippi and Louisiana), 182, 189

Tyler, John, 30

Tzotzil Maya people (Chiapas, Mexico): coffee work by, 149–51, 165; critical historical narrative among, 170; migration of, 10; Protestant, 151, 155; as undocumented workers in California, 168–69; writing by, 145, 170, 172n2. *See also* Taller Tzotzil

INDEX 261

UDU (Unión de Uniones; Mexico), 159–60, 164–65
uma (head), 98–99
undocumented migration, 168–69, 174n19
Unión de Uniones (UDU; Mexico), 159–60, 164–65
Unión Revolucionaria Nacional Guatemalteca (URNG), 205, 218n14
United Confederation of Bolivian Workers and Peasants (CSUTCB), 89, 114
United Nations: Charter (1945), 29, 34, 43; Commission on Human Rights, 44–45, 47–48; Economic and Social Council, 44; Hawai'i's inclusion on list of non-self-governing territories, 33–34, 51n3; Human Rights Council, 45, 53n19, 69; on indigenous rights, 2, 22–23. *See also* Declaration on the Rights of Indigenous Peoples
United States: Constitution of, 32, 39; Hawai'i on indigenous rights, 45; polarized racial atmosphere of, 141–42n1; victory in Spanish-American War, 6–7. *See also* Hawai'i
United States Department of Defense, 40, 42
United States Department of Justice, 42
United States Department of State, 40
United States Department of the Interior, 39–40
United States National Security Council, 47–48
United States Office of Native Hawaiian Relations, 39–40, 42
United States Senate Committee on Indian Affairs, 42
Universidad de los Andes (Bogotá, Colombia), 124
URNG (Unión Revolucionaria Nacional Guatemalteca), 205, 218n14
use rights vs. property rights, 6

Valparaíso, Chile, 56–58, 66–67, 70
Varese, Stéfano, 12–13, 15, 17, 219
Virginia antimiscegenation laws, 181, 193n3

Waitangi, Treaty of, 75n2
War of the Pacific (1879–84), 6–7, 55–56
Warren, Kay, 198–99
Watanabe, J., 218n21
weather prediction, 110–12
white privilege, 2, 11–12
white supremacy, 35, 49, 179, 186–87, 191–93, 194n8
Williams, Brackette, 206
Williamson Balfour and Company (*Compañía*; Scotland), 58–61, 67
Wilson, Angela Cavender, 2, 15, 17
Winant, H., 195n22
women, indigenous: Komes's weaving and embroidering cooperative, 12, 158, 161–62, 165–66; marginalization of, 19n7; Maya, 211; writing by, 150–51, 173n8
Women's Organization of Kuyupaya, 95
Working Group on Indigenous Populations (WGIP; UN), 44–46
Workshop for the Handling of Potato and Corn Varieties, 95–96
writing vs. orality, 95

yachayniyku (politics of Quechua knowledge), 101–14, 117
Yapita, Juan de Dios, 121n25

Zapatistas (Mexico): EZLN, 84, 167, 174n17; government repression of, 167, 174nn14–15; "Los primeros meses de los zapatistas," 168–69, 174n19; protecting leaders' identities, 164; rebellion by (1994), 10, 83, 144, 150, 154, 166–69, 174n19; Taller Tzotzil and, 10, 83, 167–69. *See also* EZLN
Zavala, Virginia, 119n1, 121n19

FLORENCIA E. MALLON is the Julieta Kirkwood Professor of History and Latin American Studies and chair of the History Department at the University of Wisconsin. She is the author of *Courage Tastes of Blood: The Mapuche Indigenous Community of Nicolás Ailío and the Chilean State, 1906–2000* (Duke, 2005); *Peasant and Nation: The Making of Postcolonial Mexico and Peru* (1995); and *The Defense of Community in Peru's Central Highlands: Peasant Struggle and Capitalist Transition, 1860–1940* (1983) and the editor and translator of Rosa Isolde Reuque Paillalef, *When a Flower Is Reborn: The Life and Times of a Mapuche Feminist* (Duke, 2002).

Library of Congress Cataloging-in-Publication Data
Decolonizing native histories : collaboration, knowledge, and language in the Americas / edited by Florencia E. Mallon ; selected essays translated by Gladys McCormick.
p. cm. — (Narrating native histories)
Includes bibliographical references and index.
ISBN 978-0-8223-5137-5 (cloth : alk. paper) — ISBN 978-0-8223-5152-8 (pbk. : alk. paper)
1. Language and languages—Political aspects. 2. Language and culture—America.
3. Indigenous peoples and mass media—America. I. Mallon, Florencia E., 1951–
II. Series: Narrating native histories.
P119.3.D43 2012
306.44′6097—dc23   2011027459

www.ingramcontent.com/pod-product-compliance
Lightning Source LLC
Chambersburg PA
CBHW070757230426
43665CB00017B/2398